AMAZING AGE

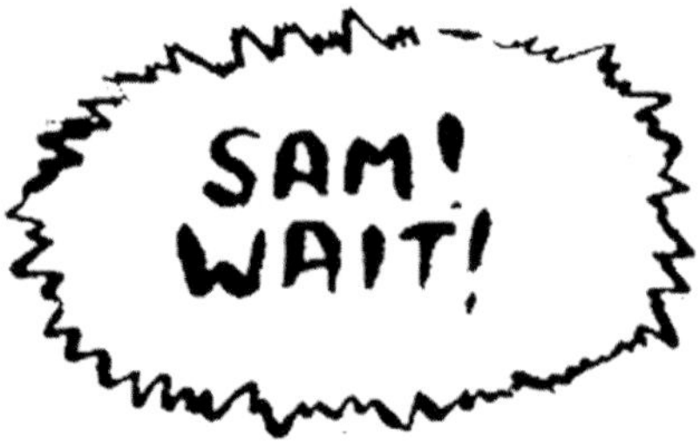
SAM! WAIT!

AMAZING AGE
9781945762208
2018 FIRST PRINTING
Published by Alterna Comics, Inc.

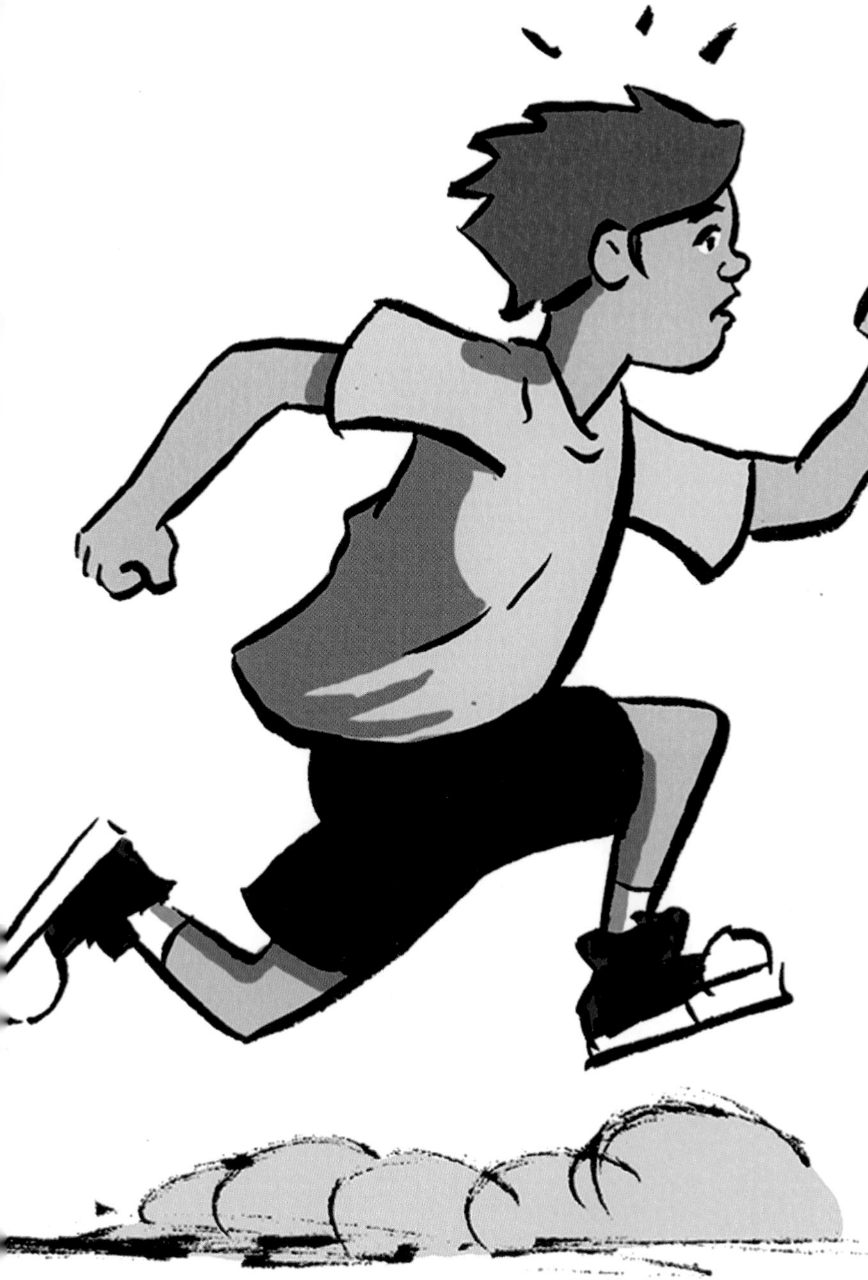

WRITER & CO-CREATOR
MATTHEW DAVID SMITH

ARTIST & CO-CREATOR
JEREMY MASSIE

COLORIST
CHRISTINE BRUNSON

WORLDS COLLIDE!

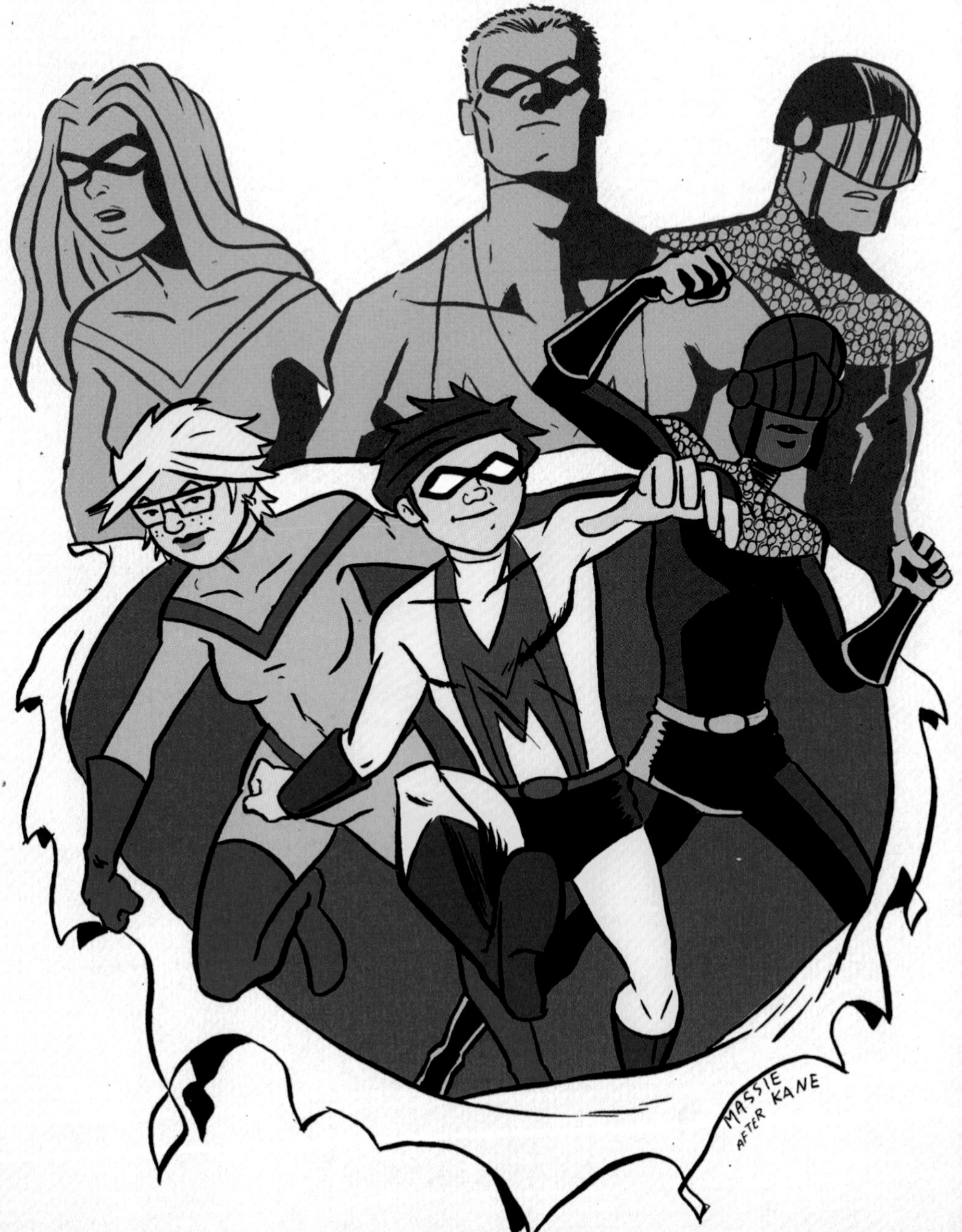
MASSIE AFTER KANE

AMAZING AGE

PART ONE OF FIVE

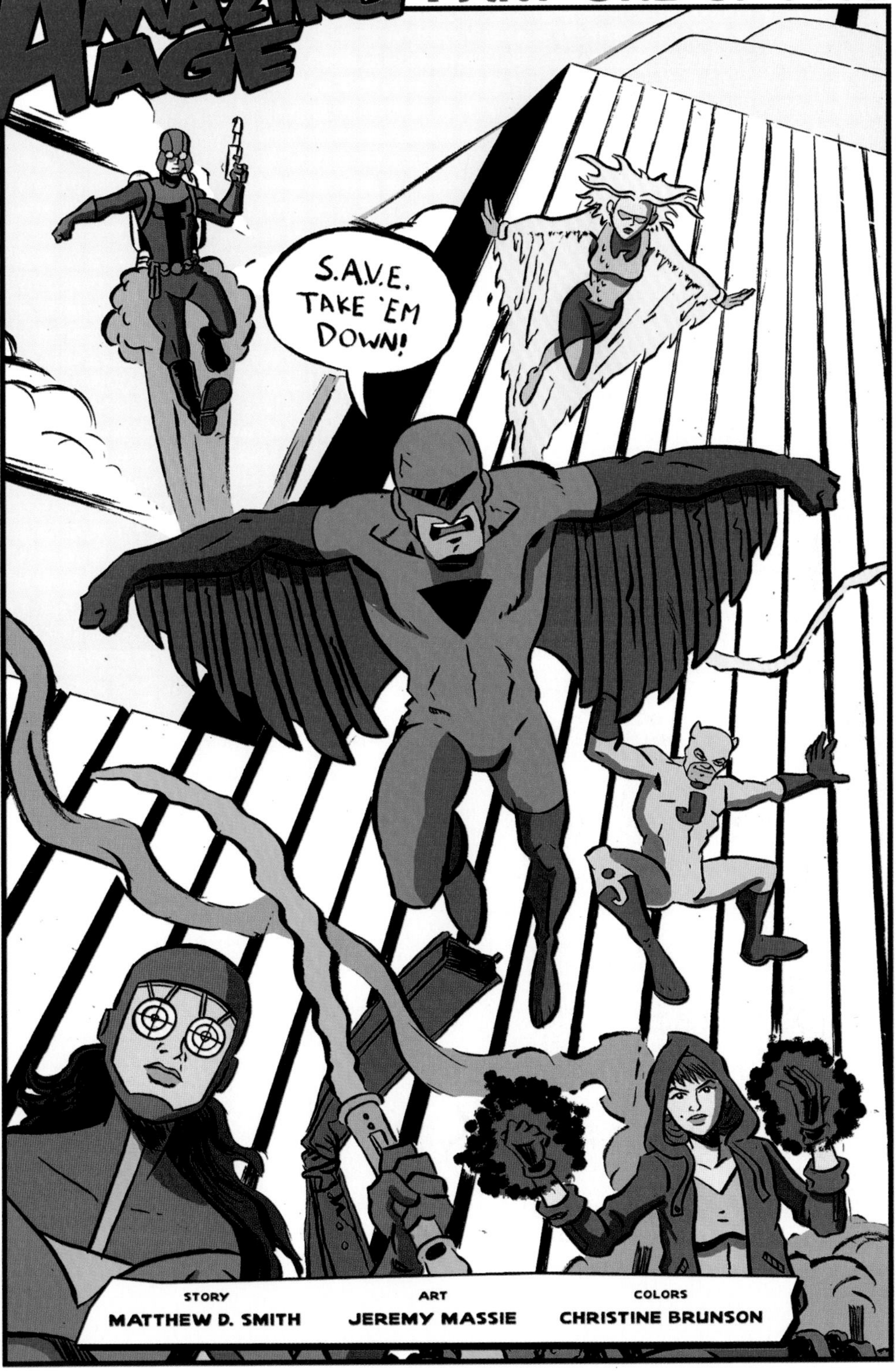
S.A.V.E. TAKE 'EM DOWN!

STORY
MATTHEW D. SMITH

ART
JEREMY MASSIE

COLORS
CHRISTINE BRUNSON

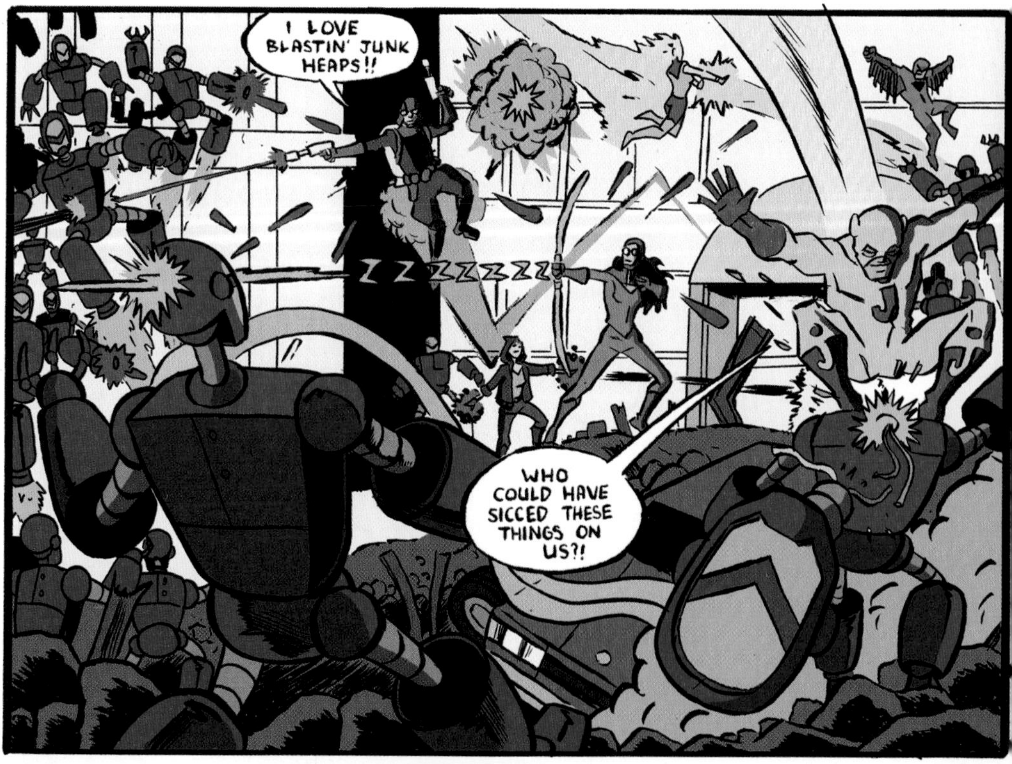
I LOVE BLASTIN' JUNK HEAPS!!
Z Z ZZZZZZZ
WHO COULD HAVE SICCED THESE THINGS ON US?!

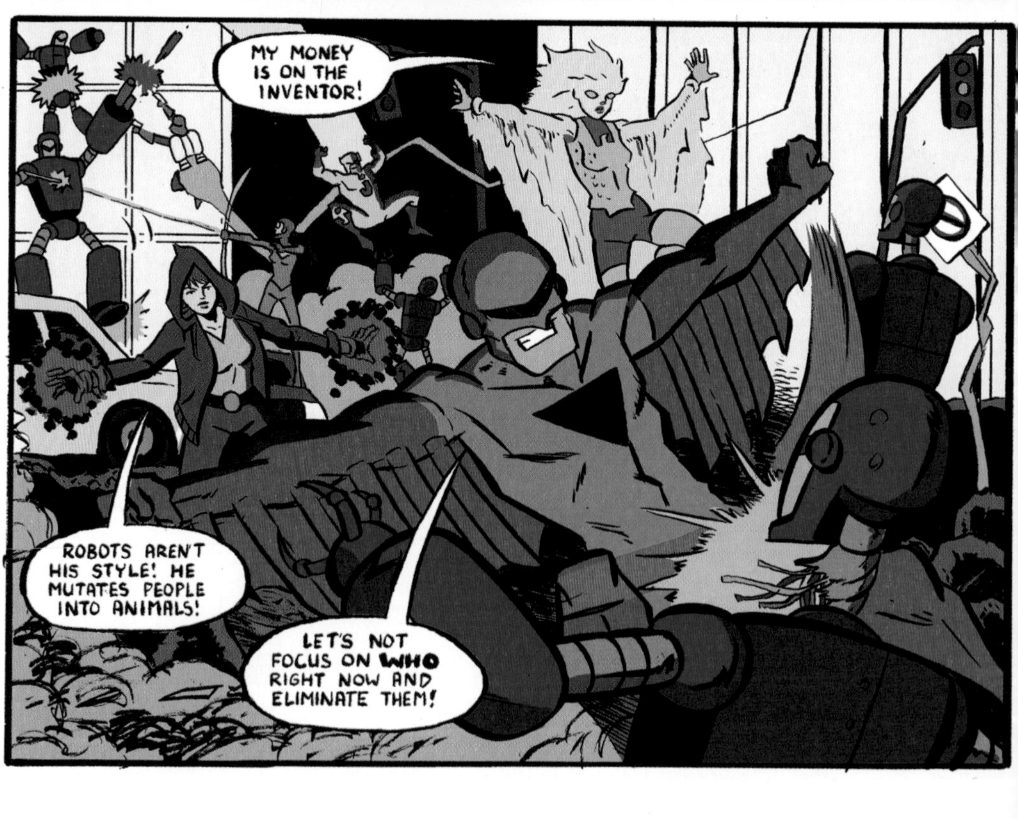
MY MONEY IS ON THE INVENTOR!
ROBOTS AREN'T HIS STYLE! HE MUTATES PEOPLE INTO ANIMALS!
LET'S NOT FOCUS ON **WHO** RIGHT NOW AND ELIMINATE THEM!

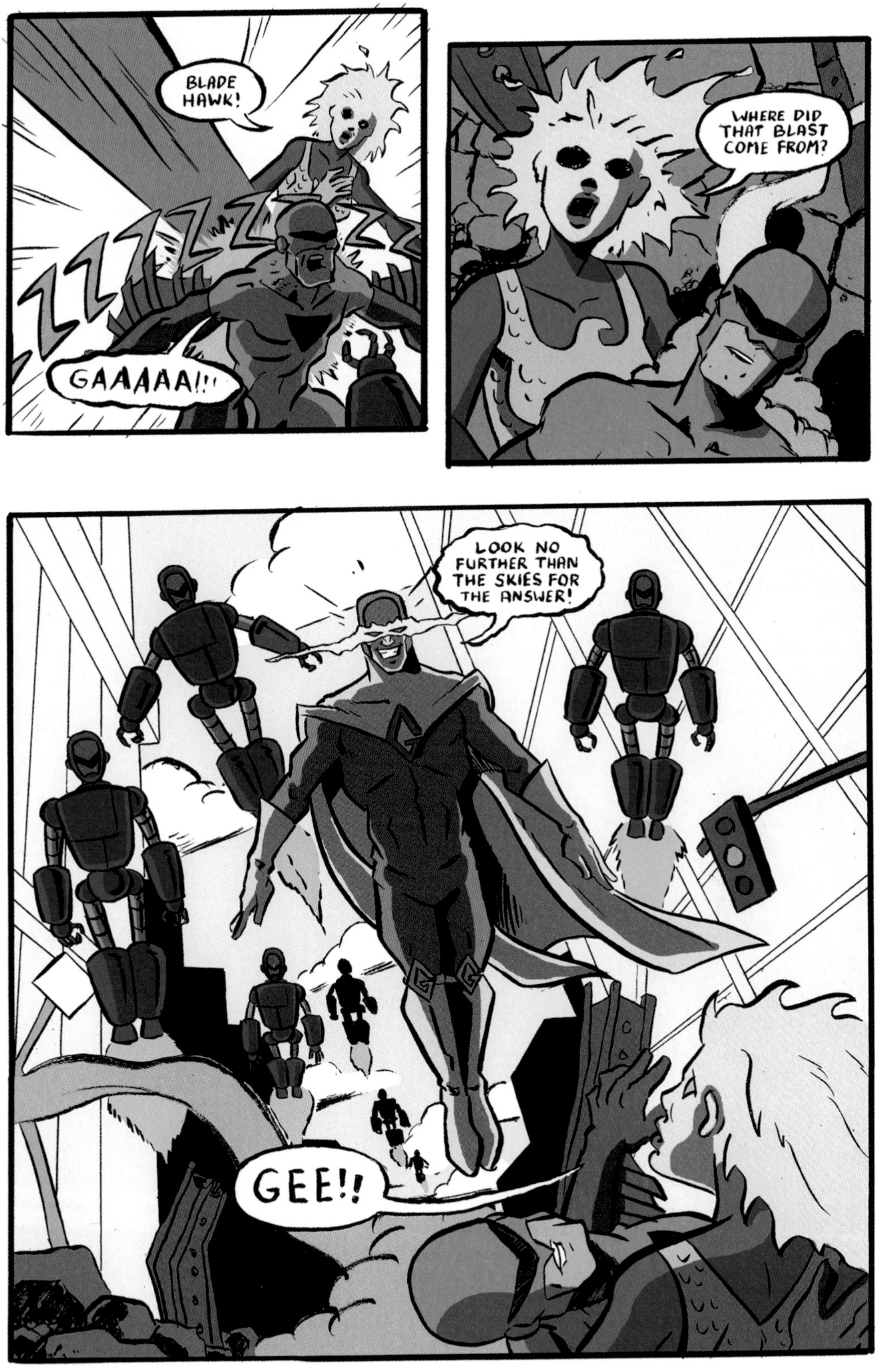
BLADE HAWK!
ZZZZZZZZ
GAAAAA!!!
WHERE DID THAT BLAST COME FROM?
LOOK NO FURTHER THAN THE SKIES FOR THE ANSWER!
GEE!!

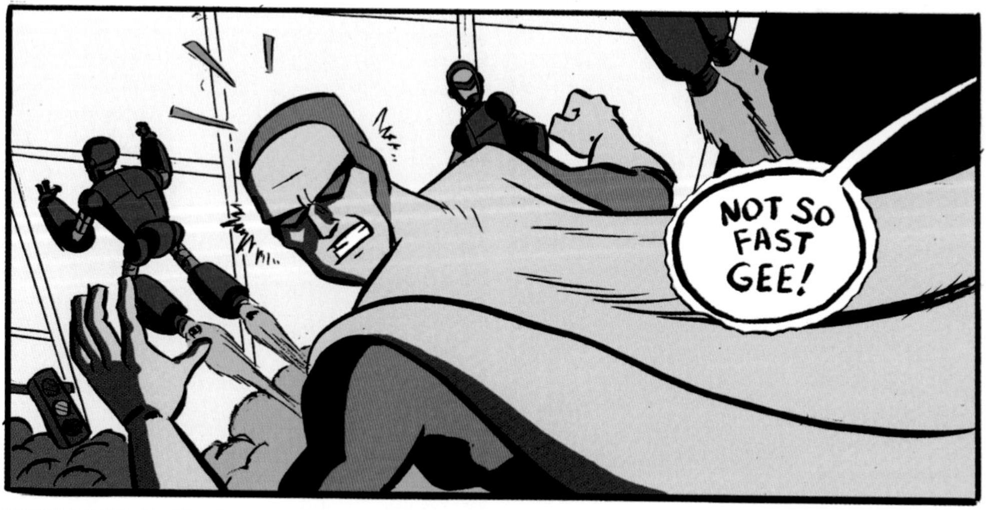
NOT SO FAST GEE!

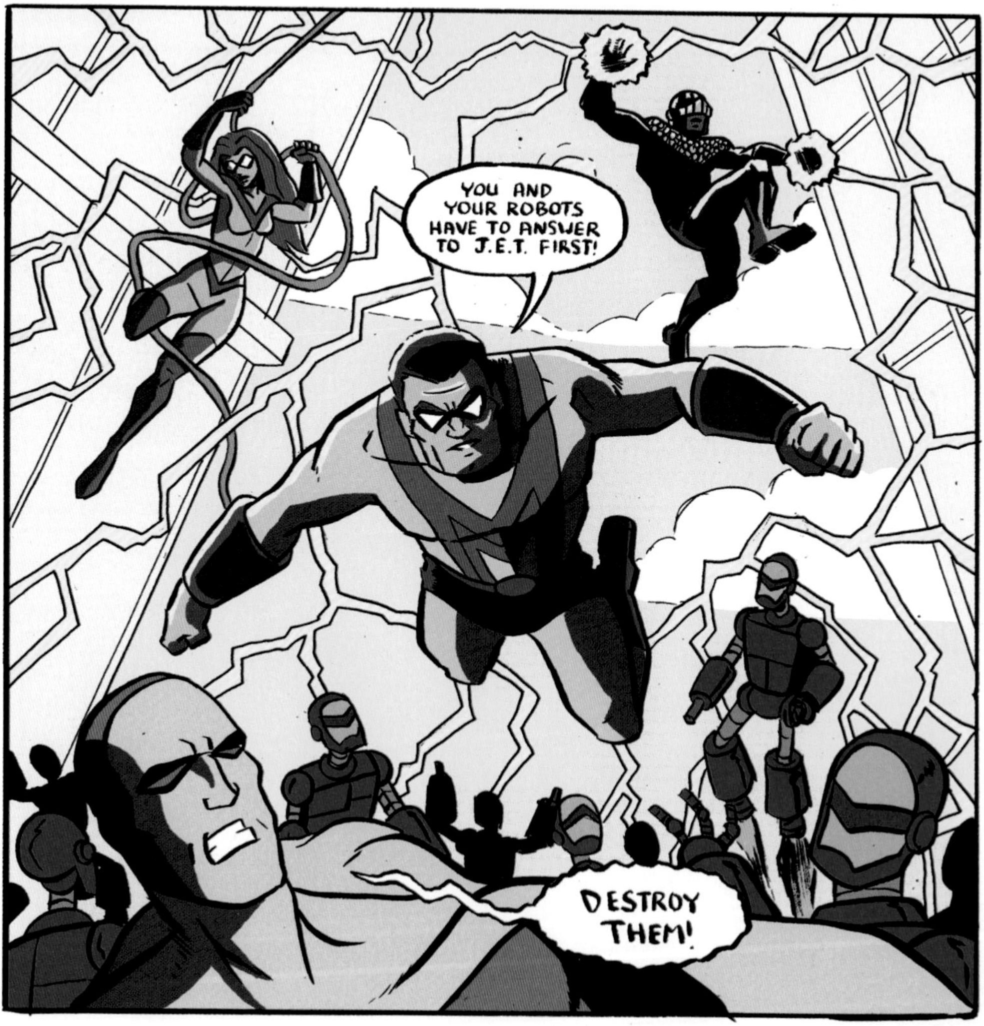
YOU AND YOUR ROBOTS HAVE TO ANSWER TO J.E.T. FIRST!
DESTROY THEM!

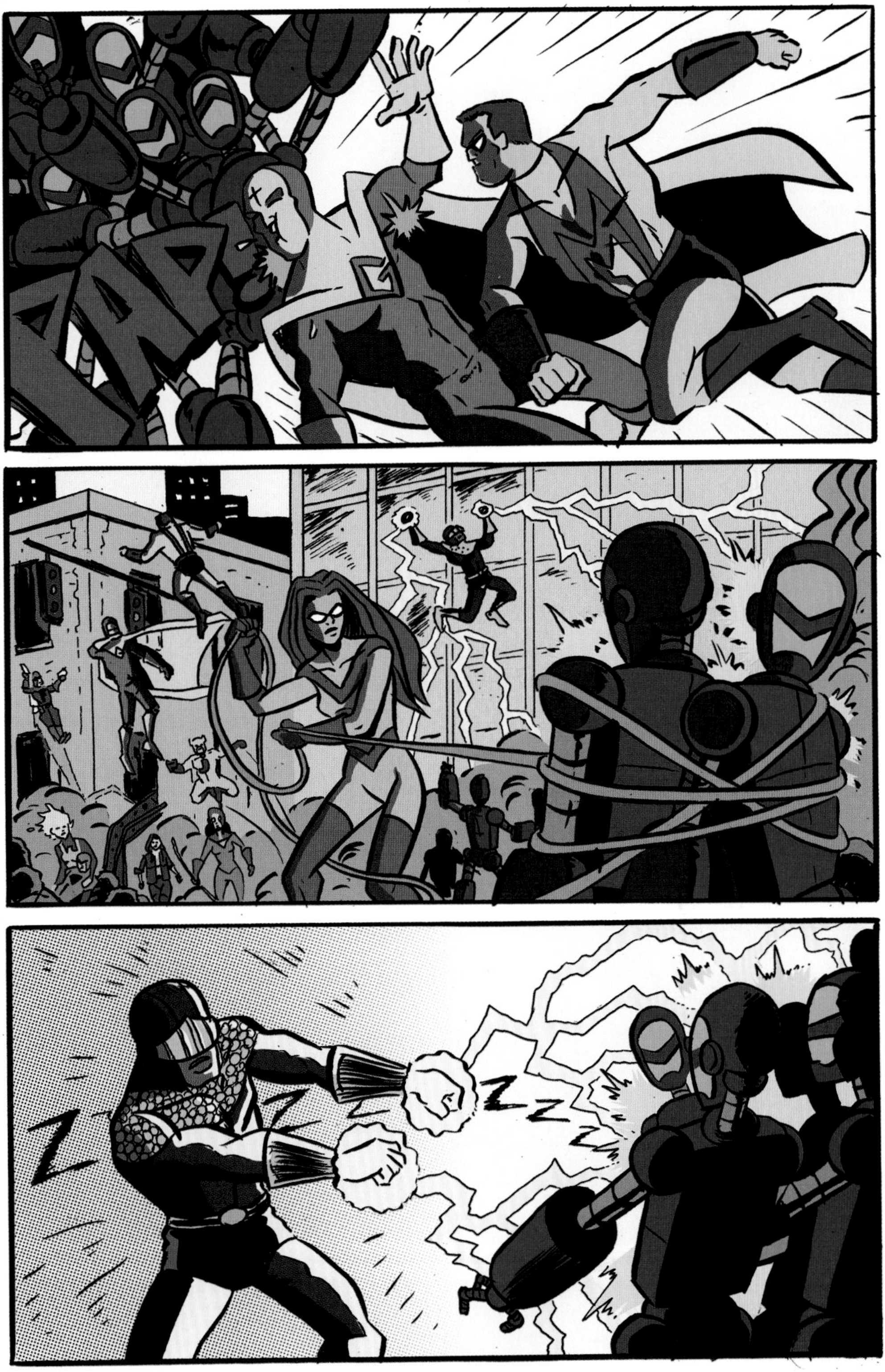
Z Z
Z Z Z

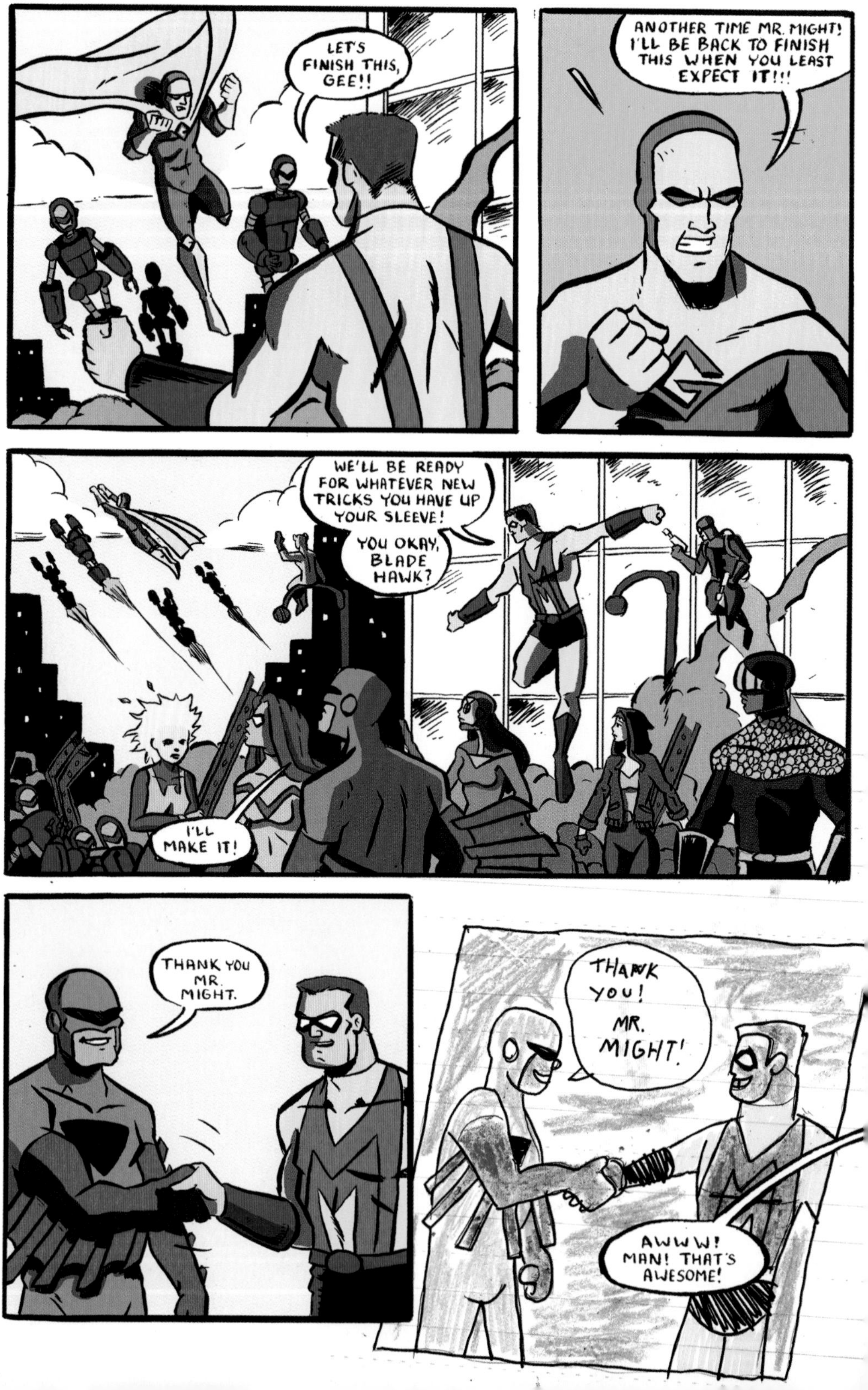
LET'S FINISH THIS, GEE!!
ANOTHER TIME MR. MIGHT! I'LL BE BACK TO FINISH THIS WHEN YOU LEAST EXPECT IT!!!
WE'LL BE READY FOR WHATEVER NEW TRICKS YOU HAVE UP YOUR SLEEVE!
YOU OKAY, BLADE HAWK?
I'LL MAKE IT!
THANK YOU MR. MIGHT.
THANK YOU! MR. MIGHT!
AWWW! MAN! THAT'S AWESOME!

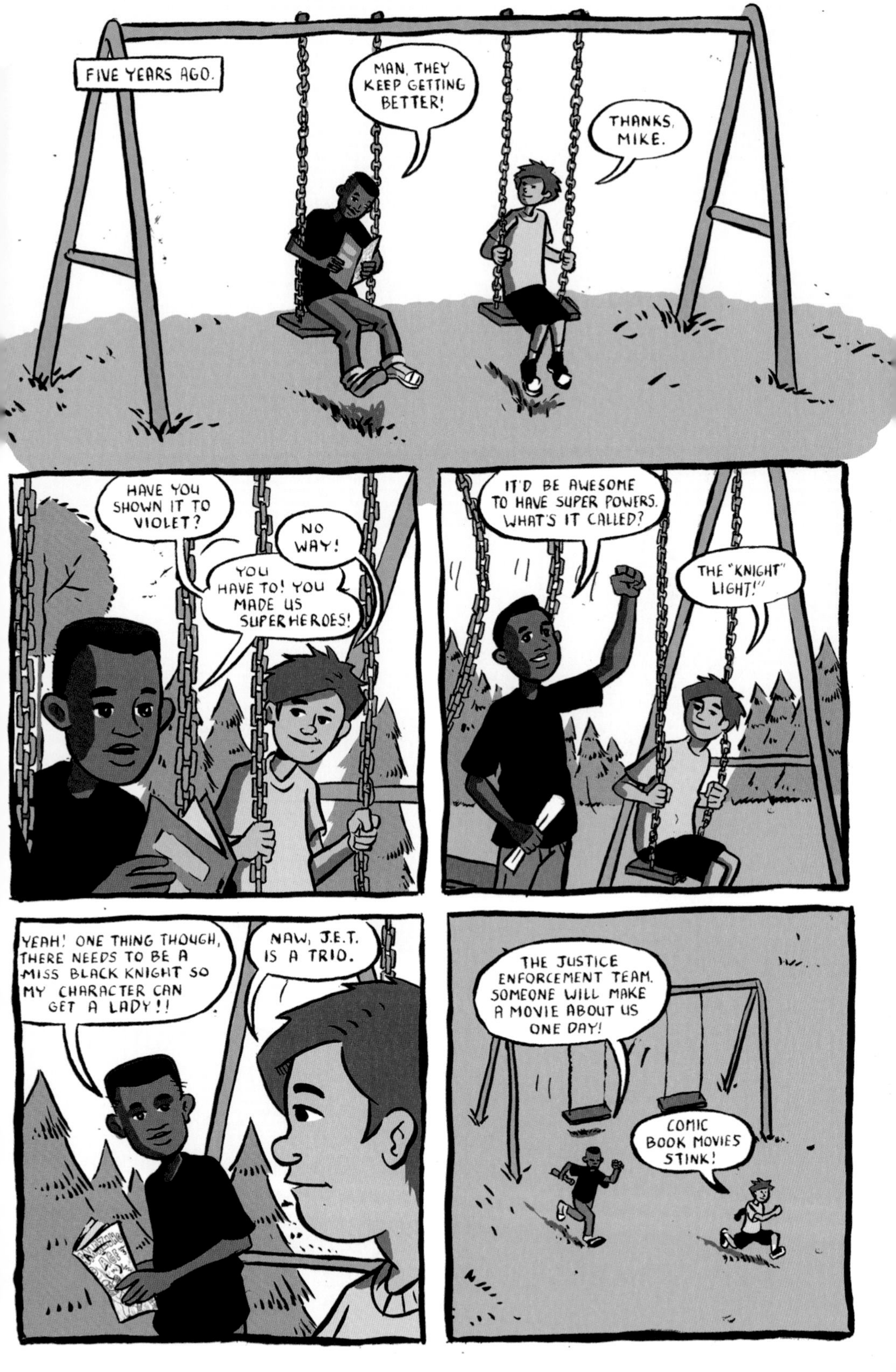
FIVE YEARS AGO.
MAN, THEY KEEP GETTING BETTER!
THANKS, MIKE.
HAVE YOU SHOWN IT TO VIOLET?
NO WAY!
YOU HAVE TO! YOU MADE US SUPERHEROES!
IT'D BE AWESOME TO HAVE SUPER POWERS. WHAT'S IT CALLED?
THE "KNIGHT" LIGHT!"
YEAH! ONE THING THOUGH, THERE NEEDS TO BE A MISS BLACK KNIGHT SO MY CHARACTER CAN GET A LADY!!
NAW, J.E.T. IS A TRIO.
THE JUSTICE ENFORCEMENT TEAM. SOMEONE WILL MAKE A MOVIE ABOUT US ONE DAY!
COMIC BOOK MOVIES STINK!

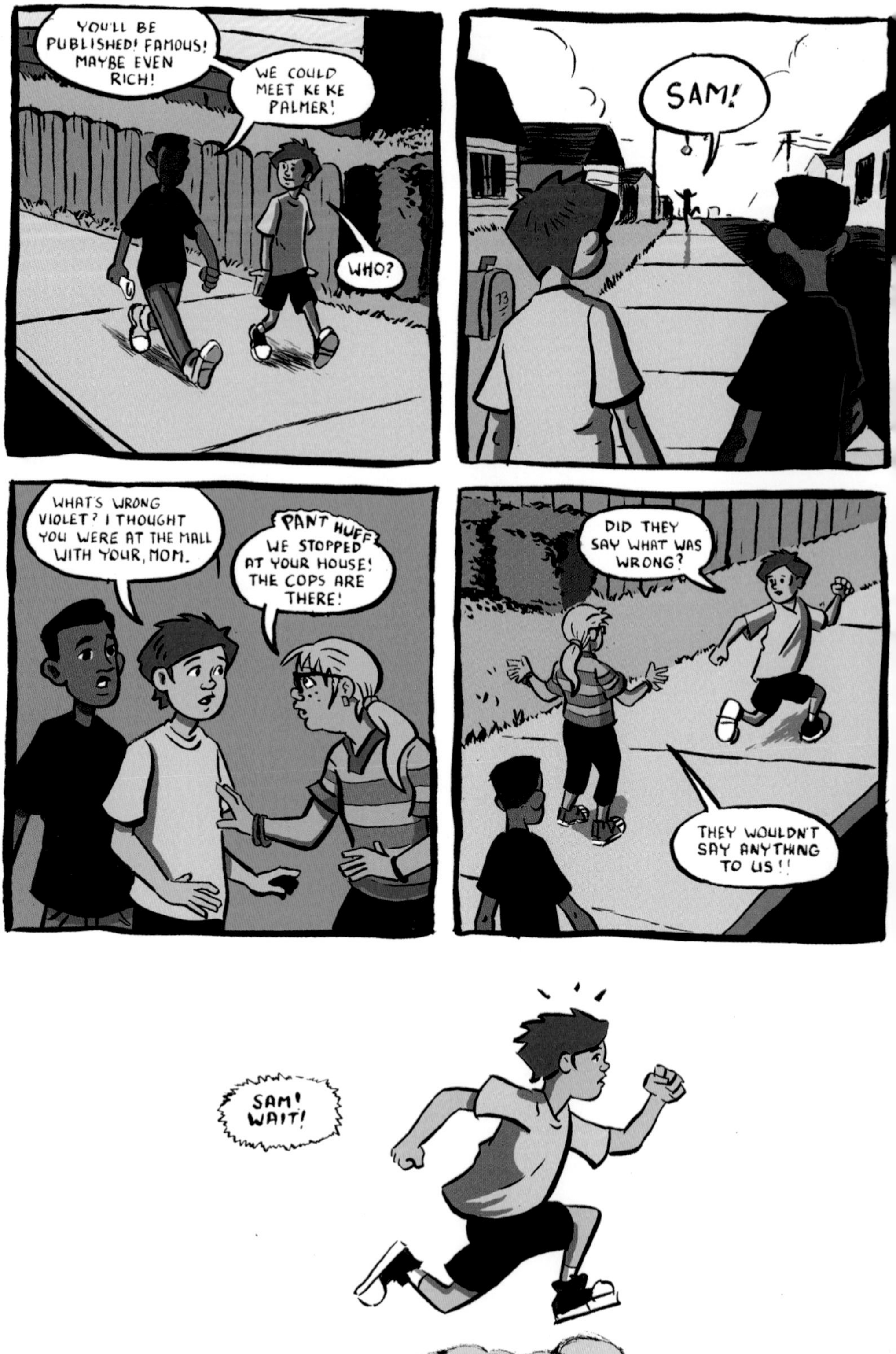
YOU'LL BE PUBLISHED! FAMOUS! MAYBE EVEN RICH!
WE COULD MEET KE KE PALMER!
WHO?
SAM!
WHAT'S WRONG VIOLET? I THOUGHT YOU WERE AT THE MALL WITH YOUR, MOM.
PANT HUFF
WE STOPPED AT YOUR HOUSE! THE COPS ARE THERE!
DID THEY SAY WHAT WAS WRONG?
THEY WOULDN'T SAY ANYTHING TO US!!
SAM! WAIT!

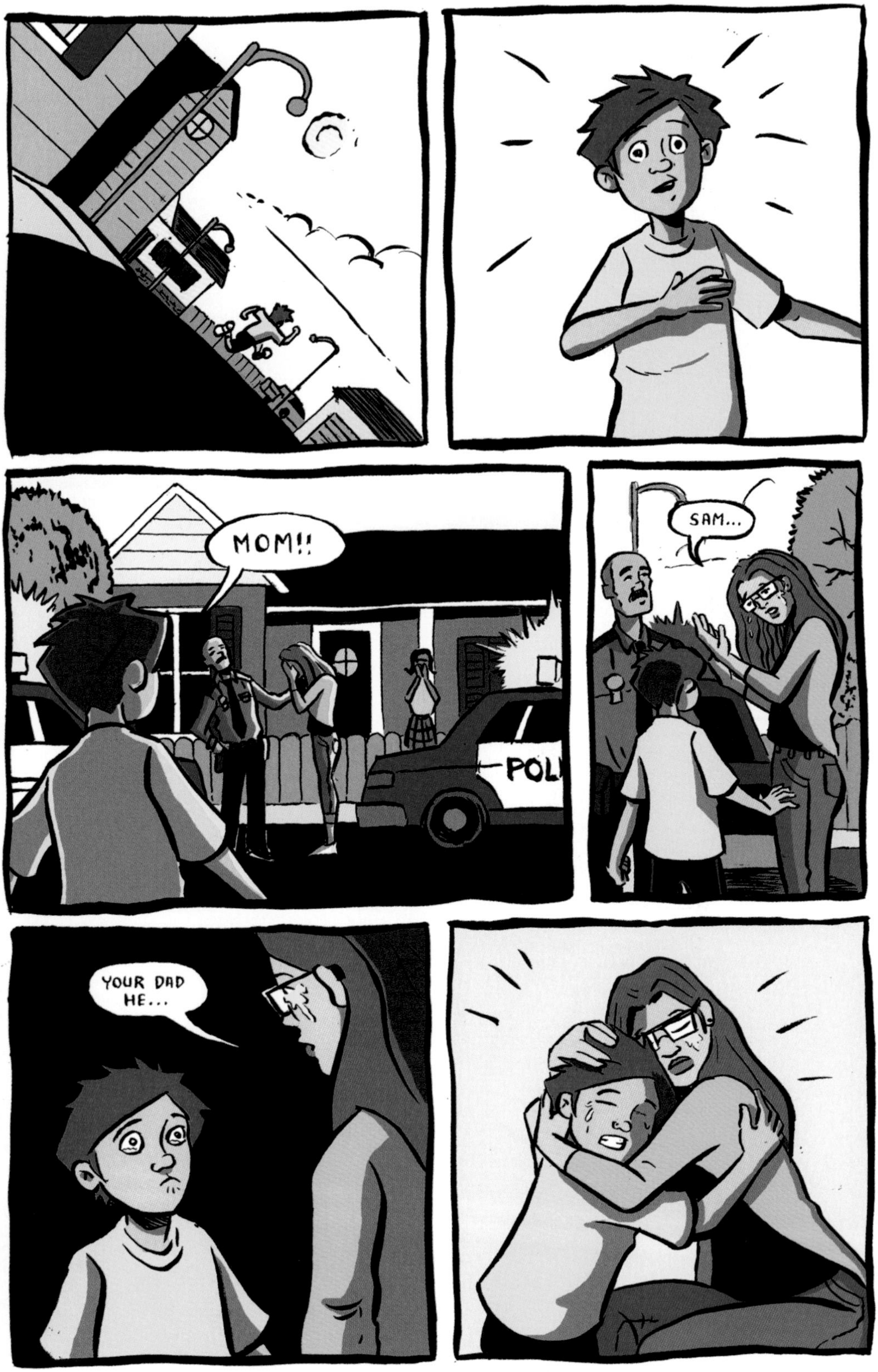
MOM!!
SAM...
POLI
YOUR DAD
HE...

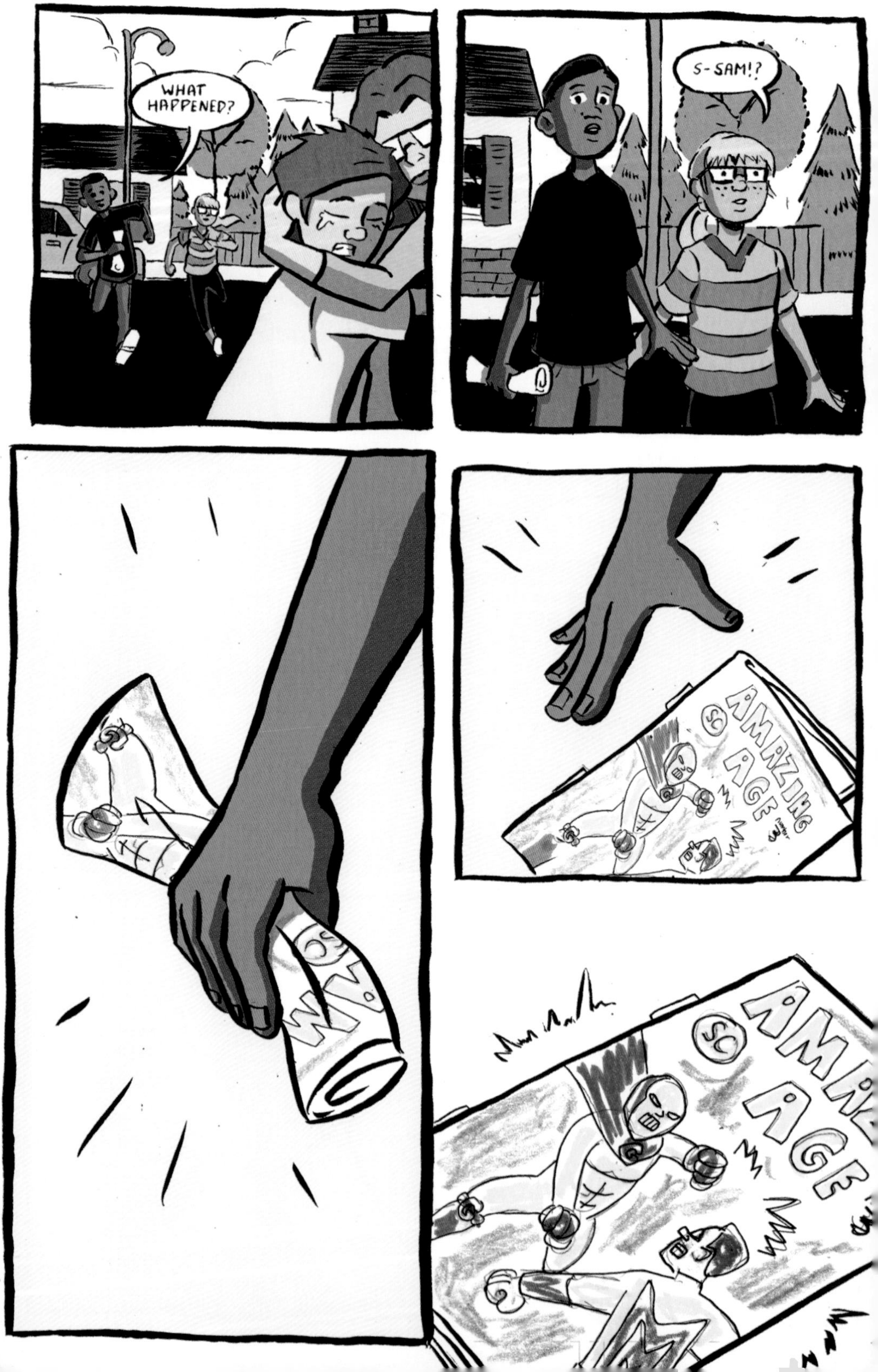
WHAT HAPPENED?
S-SAM!?
AMAZING AGE

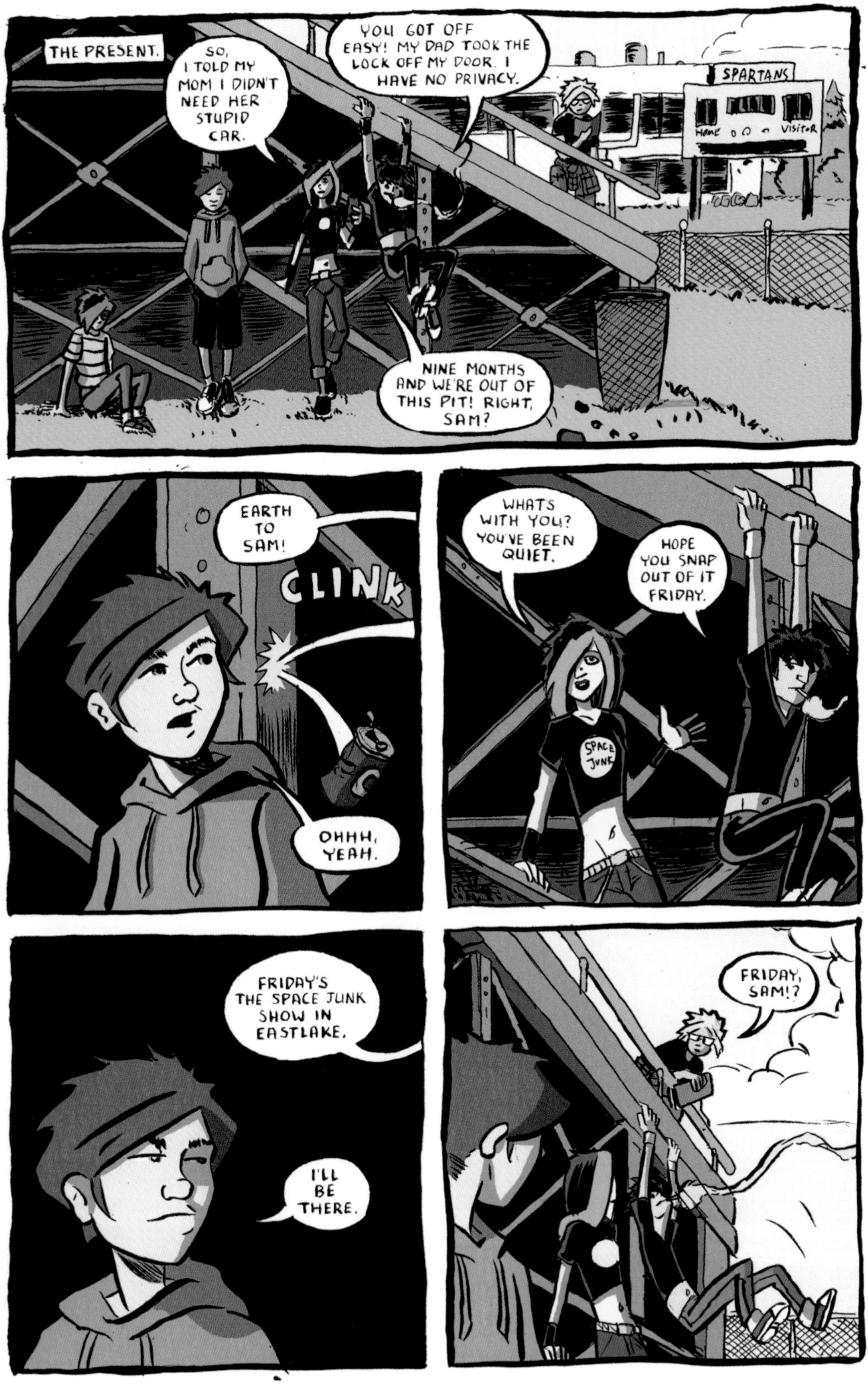
THE PRESENT.
SO, I TOLD MY MOM I DIDN'T NEED HER STUPID CAR.
YOU GOT OFF EASY! MY DAD TOOK THE LOCK OFF MY DOOR. I HAVE NO PRIVACY.
SPARTANS
HOME VISITOR
NINE MONTHS AND WE'RE OUT OF THIS PIT! RIGHT, SAM?
EARTH TO SAM!
CLINK
OHHH, YEAH.
WHATS WITH YOU? YOU'VE BEEN QUIET.
HOPE YOU SNAP OUT OF IT FRIDAY.
SPACE JUNK
FRIDAY'S THE SPACE JUNK SHOW IN EASTLAKE.
I'LL BE THERE.
FRIDAY, SAM!?

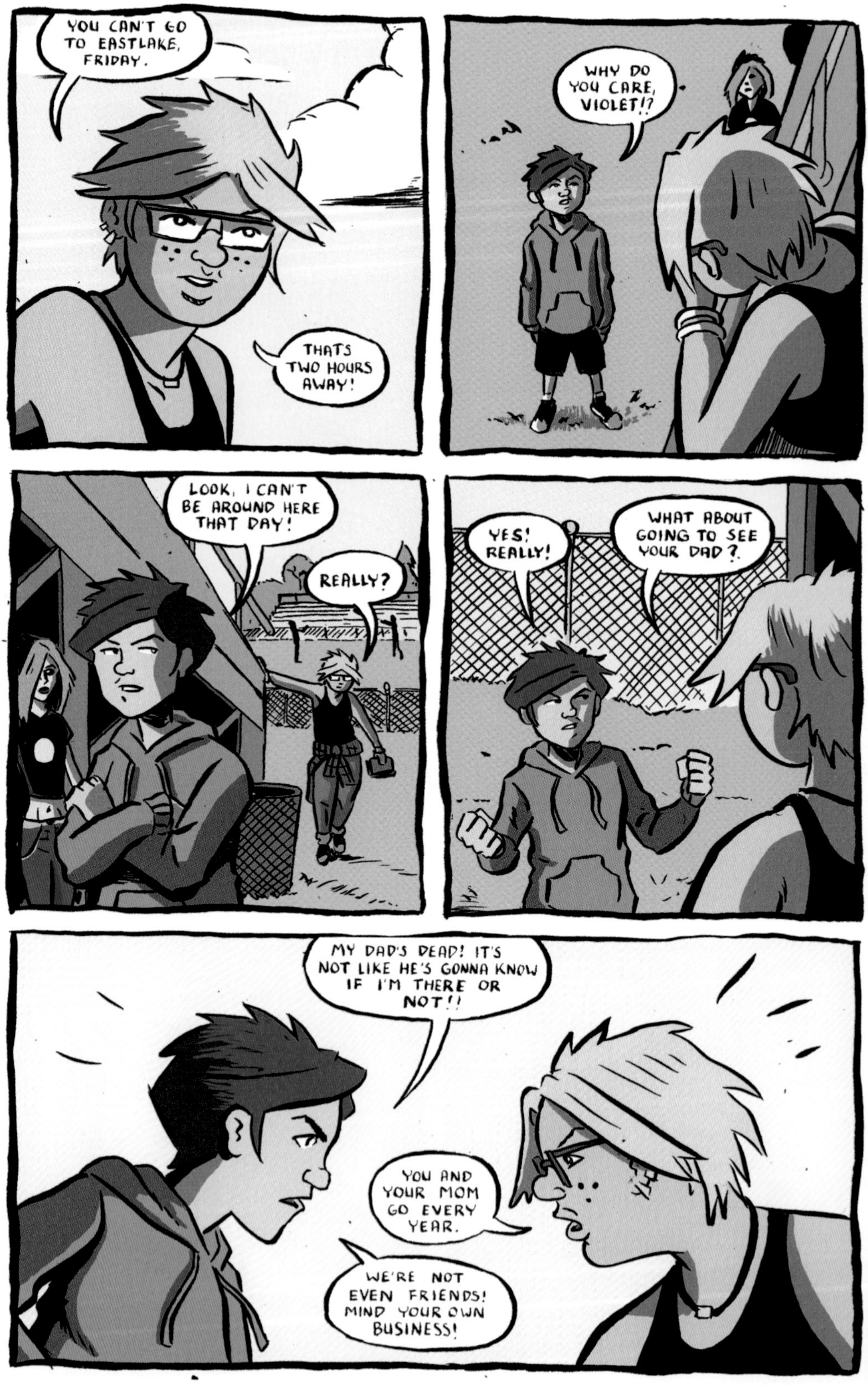
YOU CAN'T GO TO EASTLAKE, FRIDAY.
THATS TWO HOURS AWAY!
WHY DO YOU CARE, VIOLET!?
LOOK, I CAN'T BE AROUND HERE THAT DAY!
REALLY?
YES! REALLY!
WHAT ABOUT GOING TO SEE YOUR DAD?
MY DAD'S DEAD! IT'S NOT LIKE HE'S GONNA KNOW IF I'M THERE OR NOT!!
YOU AND YOUR MOM GO EVERY YEAR.
WE'RE NOT EVEN FRIENDS! MIND YOUR OWN BUSINESS!

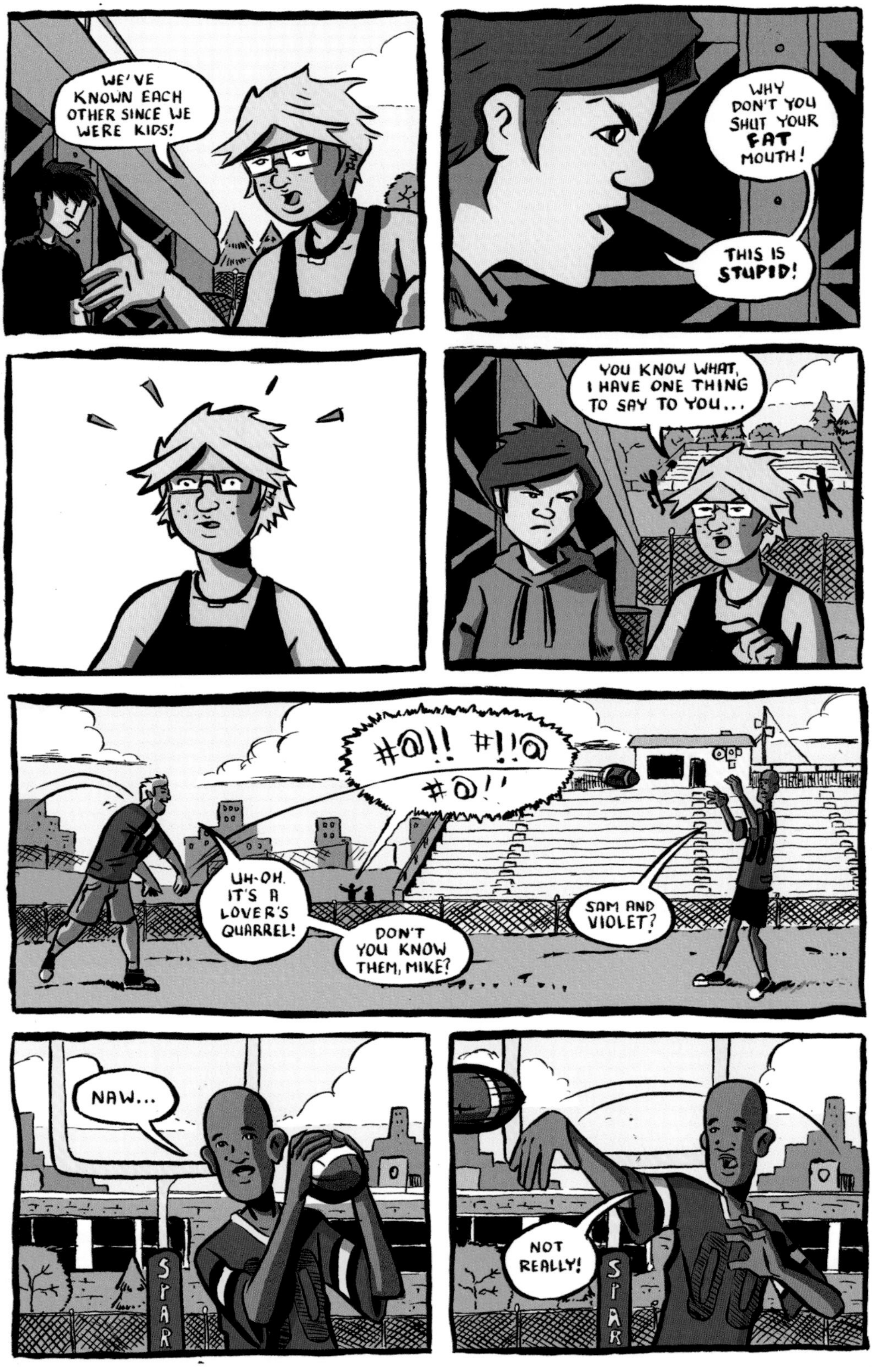
WE'VE KNOWN EACH OTHER SINCE WE WERE KIDS!
WHY DON'T YOU SHUT YOUR FAT MOUTH!
THIS IS STUPID!
YOU KNOW WHAT, I HAVE ONE THING TO SAY TO YOU...
#@!! #!!@ #@!!
UH-OH. IT'S A LOVER'S QUARREL!
DON'T YOU KNOW THEM, MIKE?
SAM AND VIOLET?
NAW...
NOT REALLY!

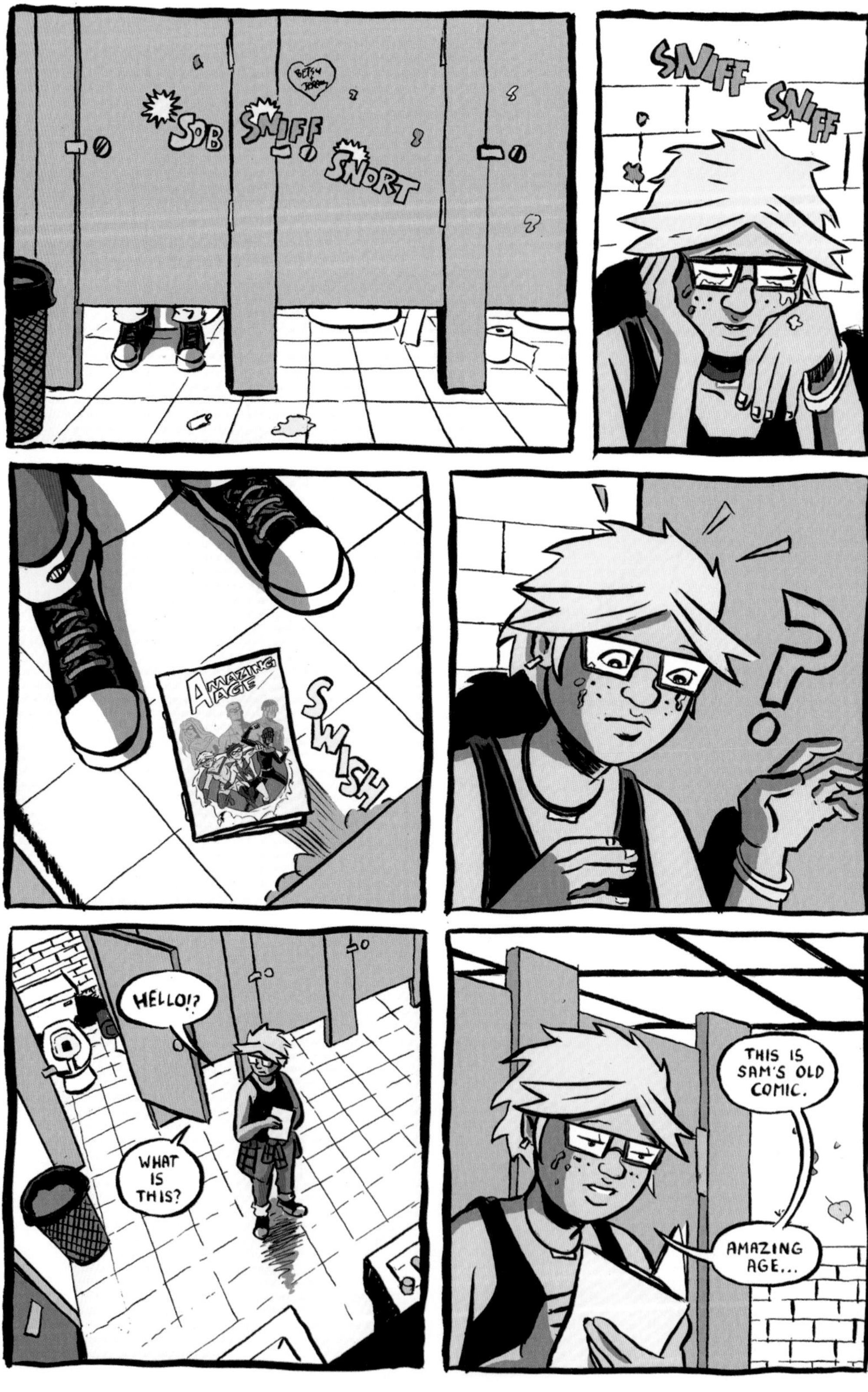
SOB
SNIFF
SNORT
SNIFF
SNIFF
AMAZING AGE
SWISH
HELLO!?
WHAT IS THIS?
THIS IS SAM'S OLD COMIC.
AMAZING AGE...

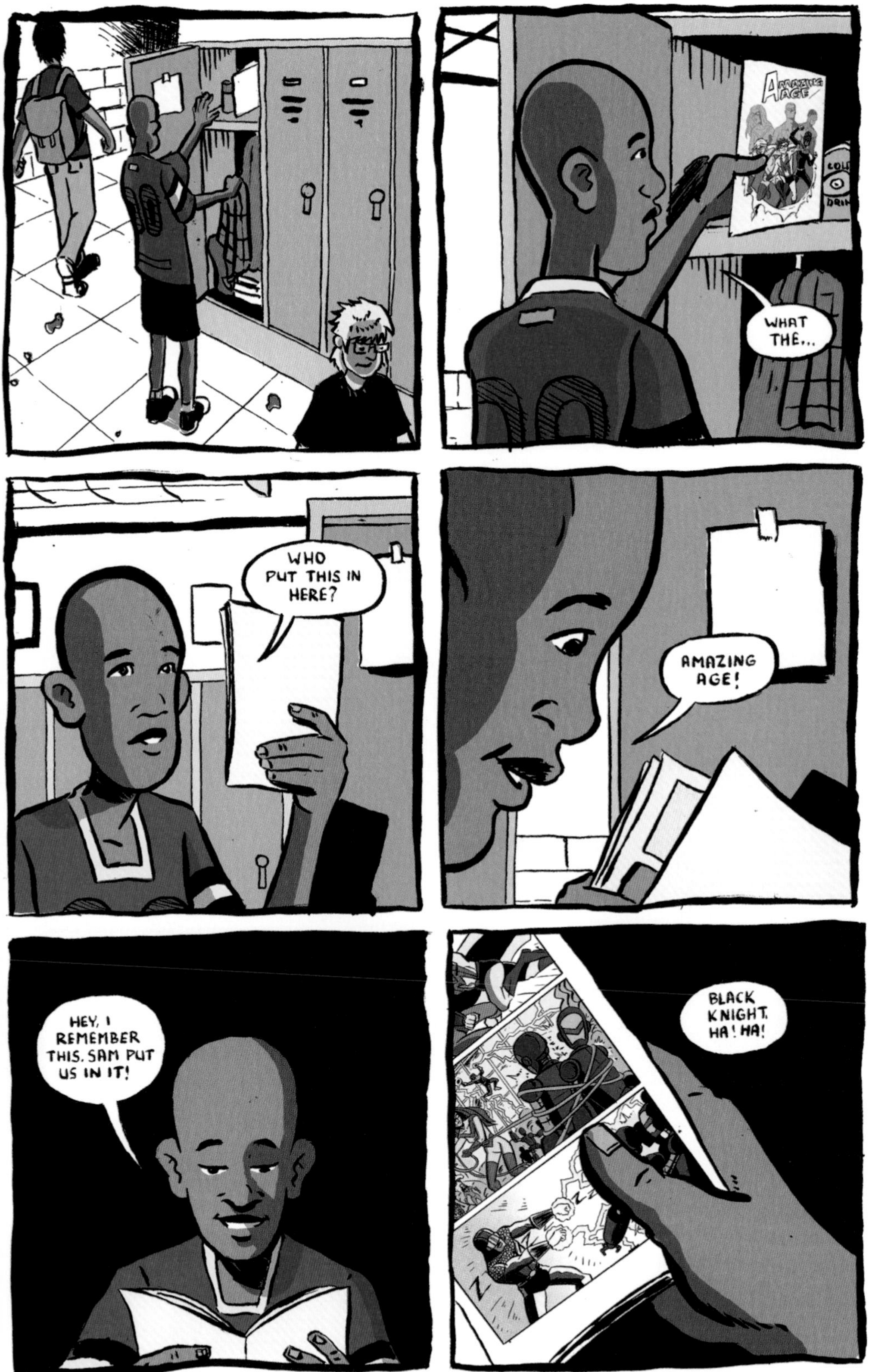
WHAT THE...
WHO PUT THIS IN HERE?
AMAZING AGE!
HEY, I REMEMBER THIS. SAM PUT US IN IT!
BLACK KNIGHT. HA! HA!

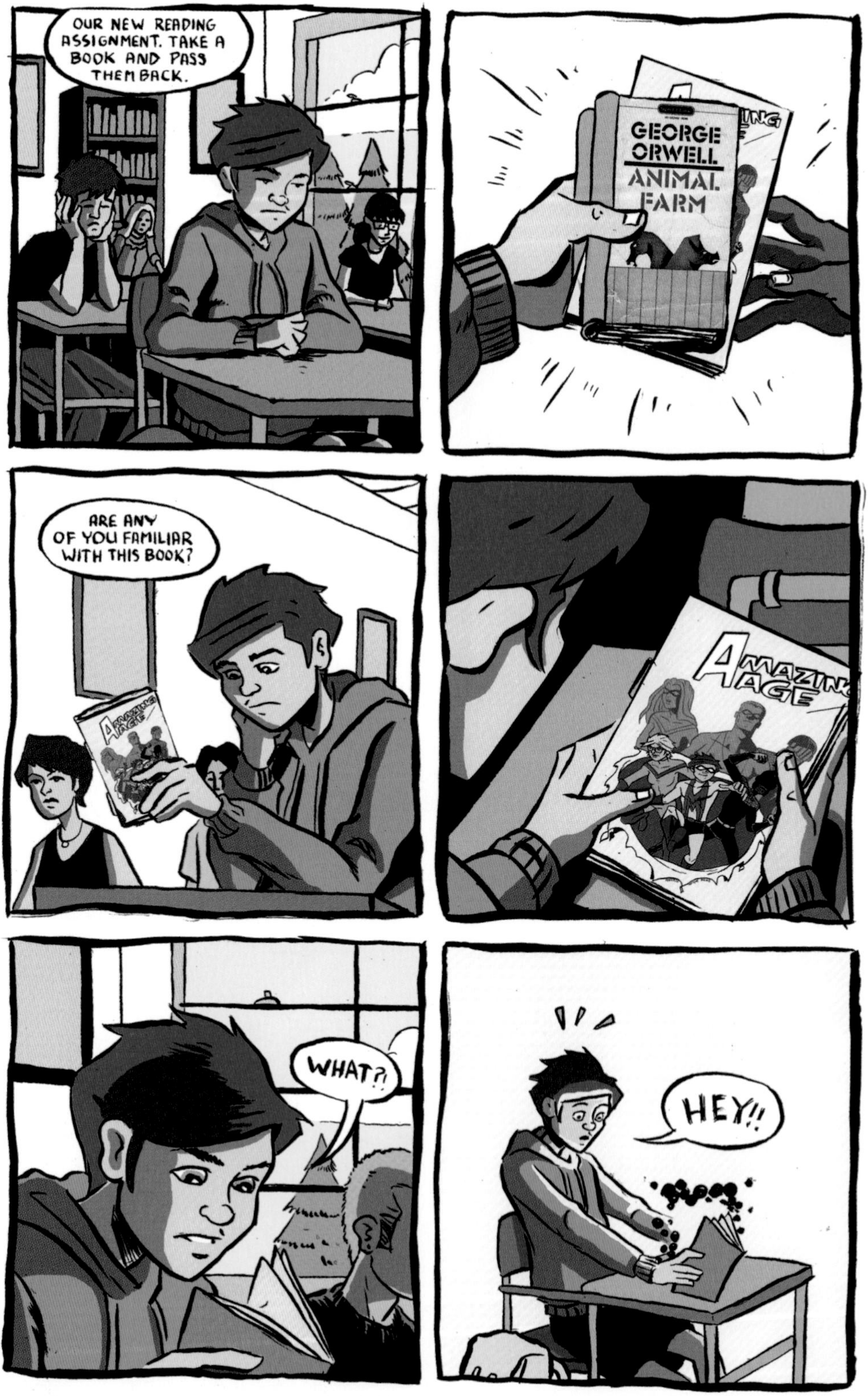
OUR NEW READING ASSIGNMENT. TAKE A BOOK AND PASS THEM BACK.
GEORGE ORWELL
ANIMAL FARM
ARE ANY OF YOU FAMILIAR WITH THIS BOOK?
AMAZING AGE
WHAT?!
HEY!!

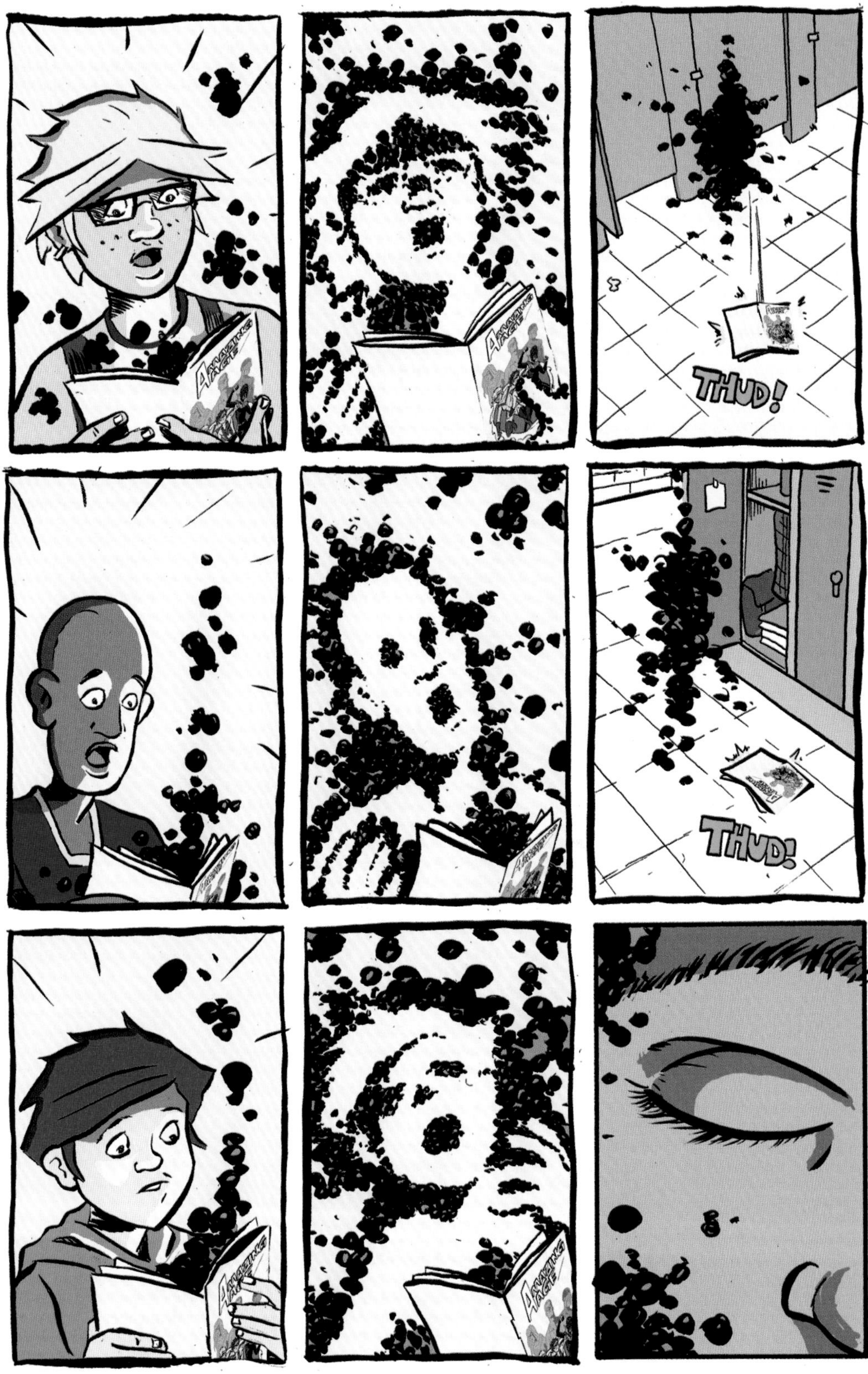
THUD!
THUD!

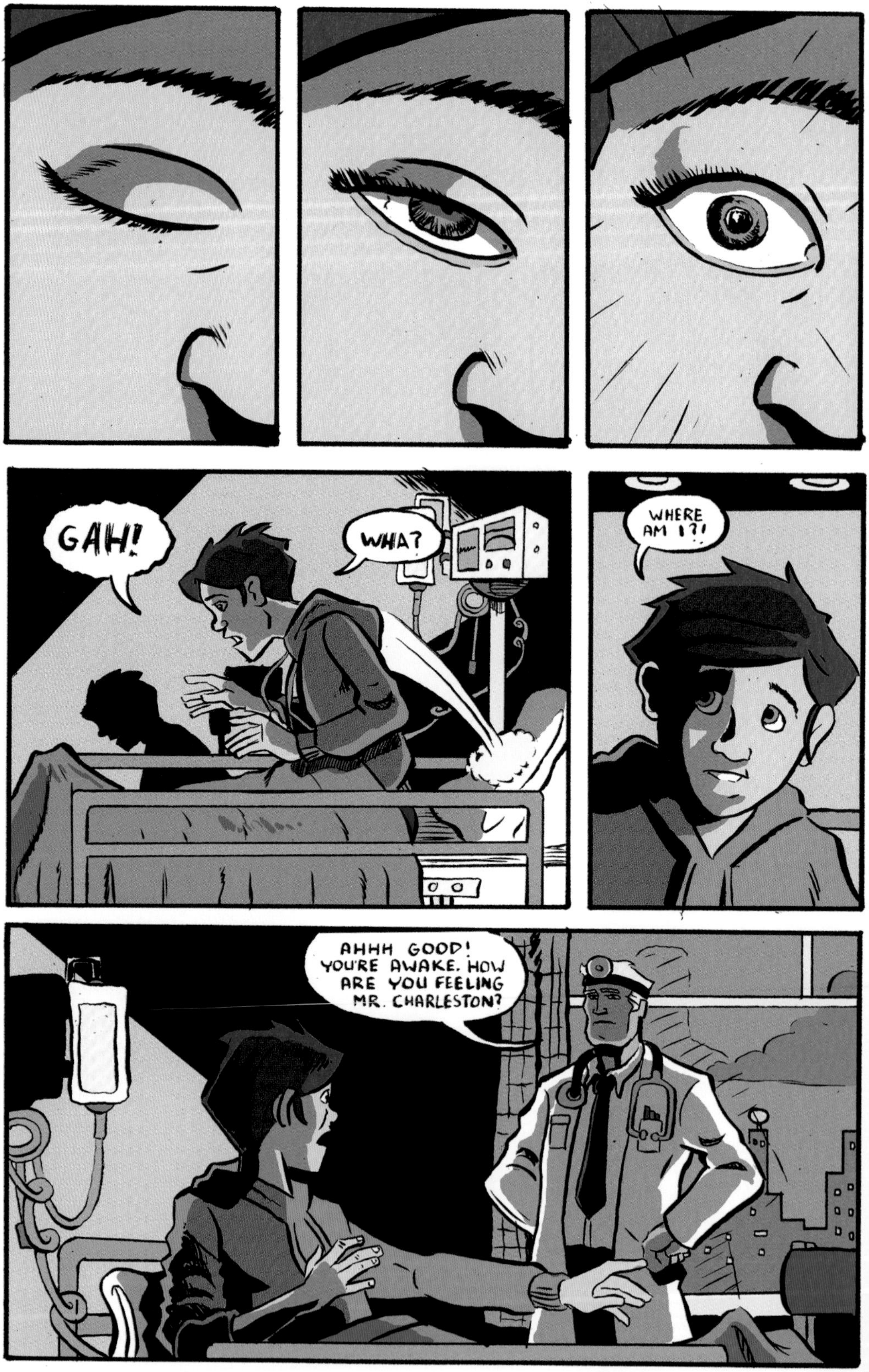
GAH!
WHA?
WHERE AM I?!
AHHH GOOD! YOU'RE AWAKE. HOW ARE YOU FEELING MR. CHARLESTON?

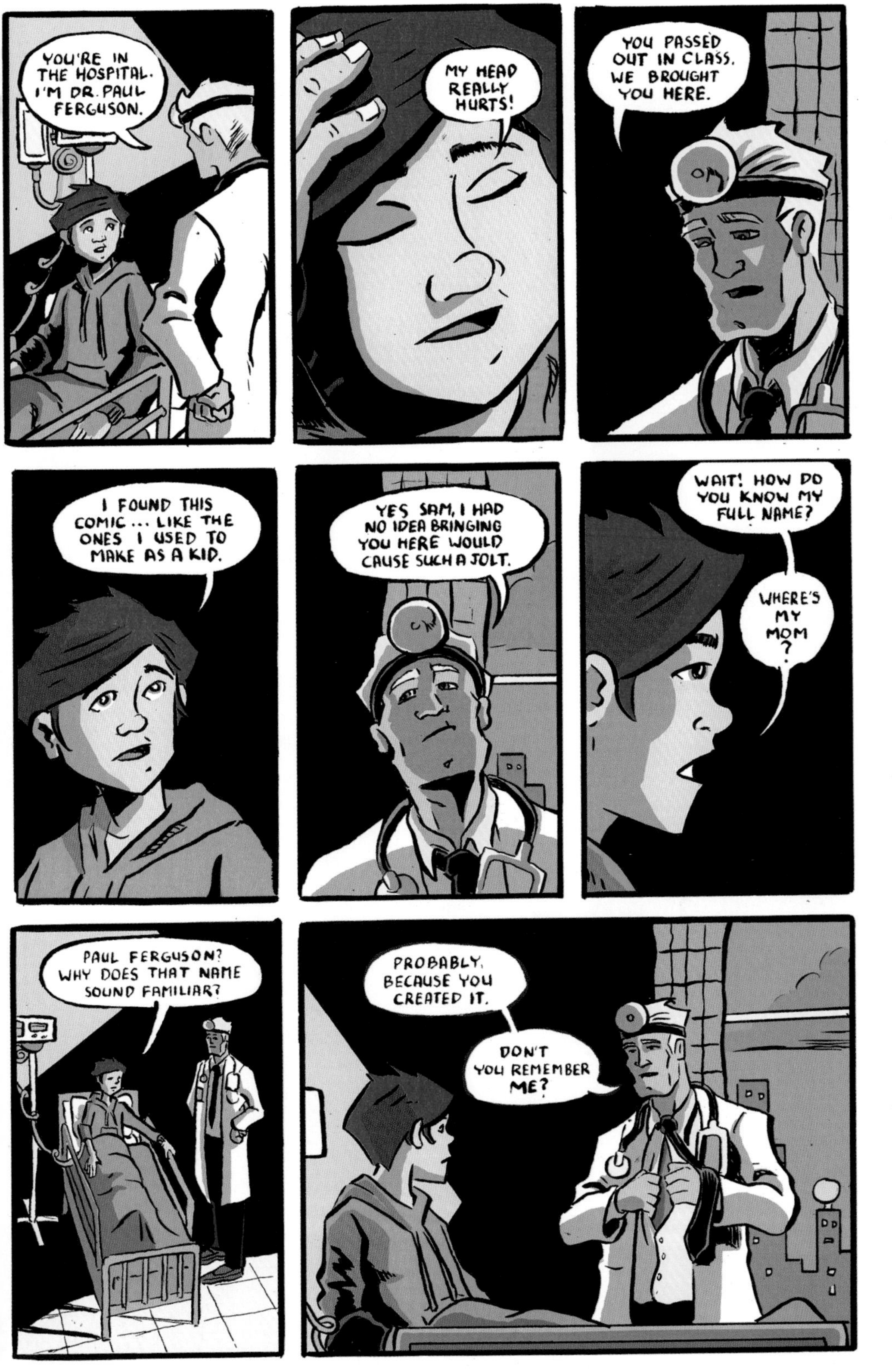
YOU'RE IN THE HOSPITAL. I'M DR. PAUL FERGUSON.
MY HEAD REALLY HURTS!
YOU PASSED OUT IN CLASS. WE BROUGHT YOU HERE.
I FOUND THIS COMIC ... LIKE THE ONES I USED TO MAKE AS A KID.
YES SAM, I HAD NO IDEA BRINGING YOU HERE WOULD CAUSE SUCH A JOLT.
WAIT! HOW DO YOU KNOW MY FULL NAME?
WHERE'S MY MOM ?
PAUL FERGUSON? WHY DOES THAT NAME SOUND FAMILIAR?
PROBABLY, BECAUSE YOU CREATED IT.
DON'T YOU REMEMBER ME?

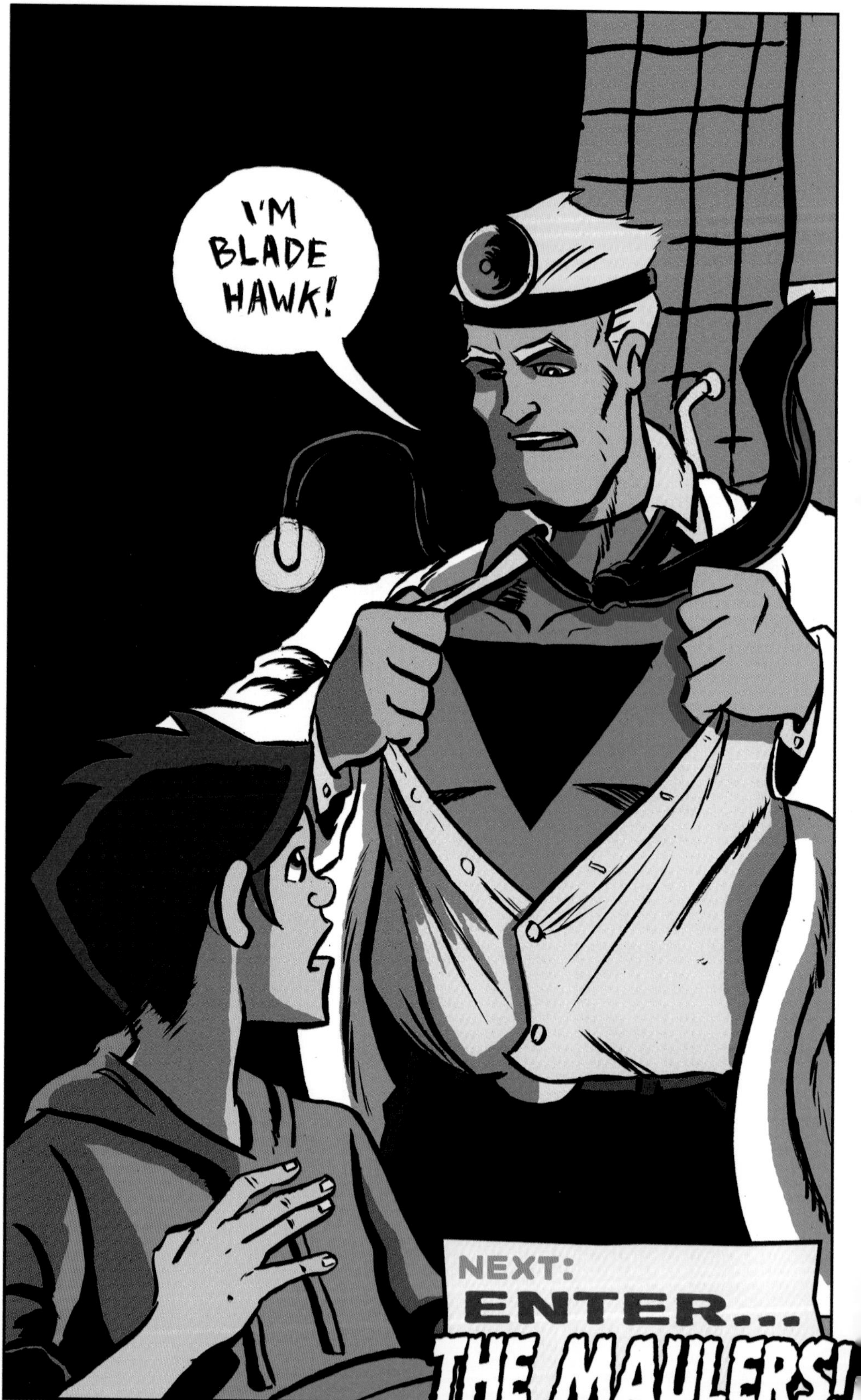
I'M BLADE HAWK!
NEXT:
ENTER...
THE MAULERS!

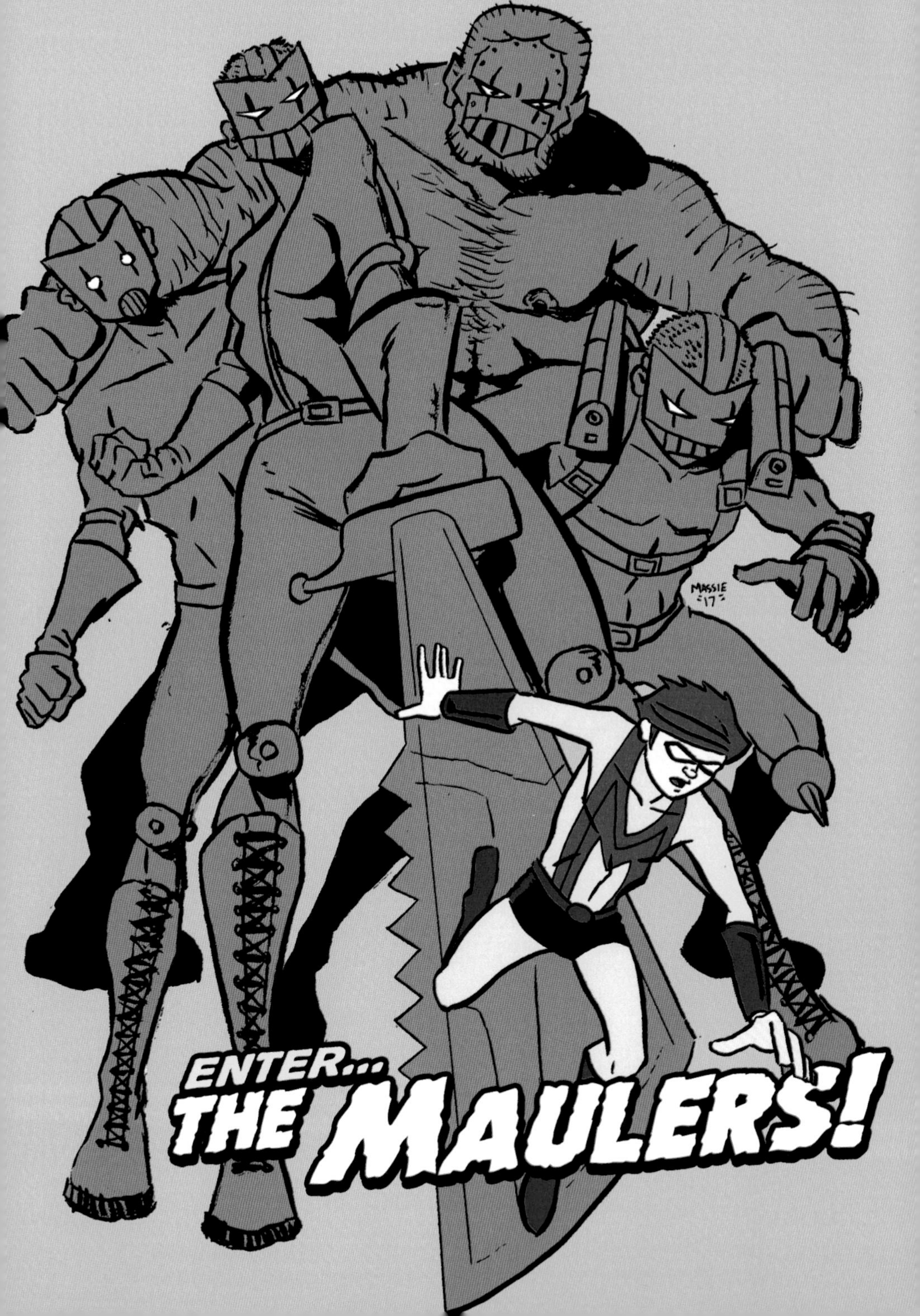
MASSIE '17
ENTER...
THE MAULERS!

AMAZING AGE PART TWO OF FIVE

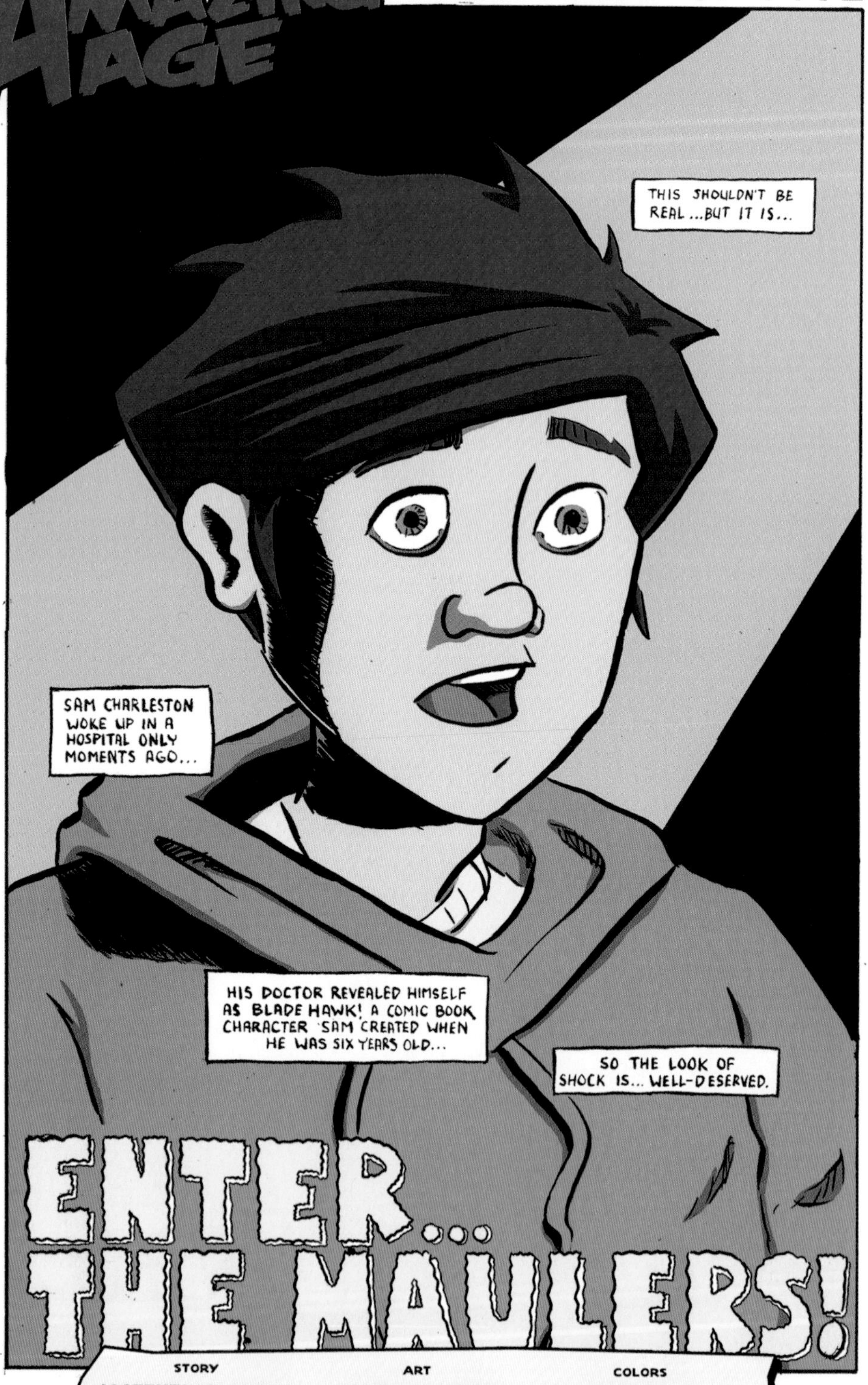
THIS SHOULDN'T BE REAL ...BUT IT IS...
SAM CHARLESTON WOKE UP IN A HOSPITAL ONLY MOMENTS AGO...
HIS DOCTOR REVEALED HIMSELF AS BLADE HAWK! A COMIC BOOK CHARACTER SAM CREATED WHEN HE WAS SIX YEARS OLD...
SO THE LOOK OF SHOCK IS... WELL-DESERVED.
ENTER... THE MÄULERS!

STORY MATTHEW D. SMITH · ART JEREMY MASSIE · COLORS CHRISTINE BRUNSON

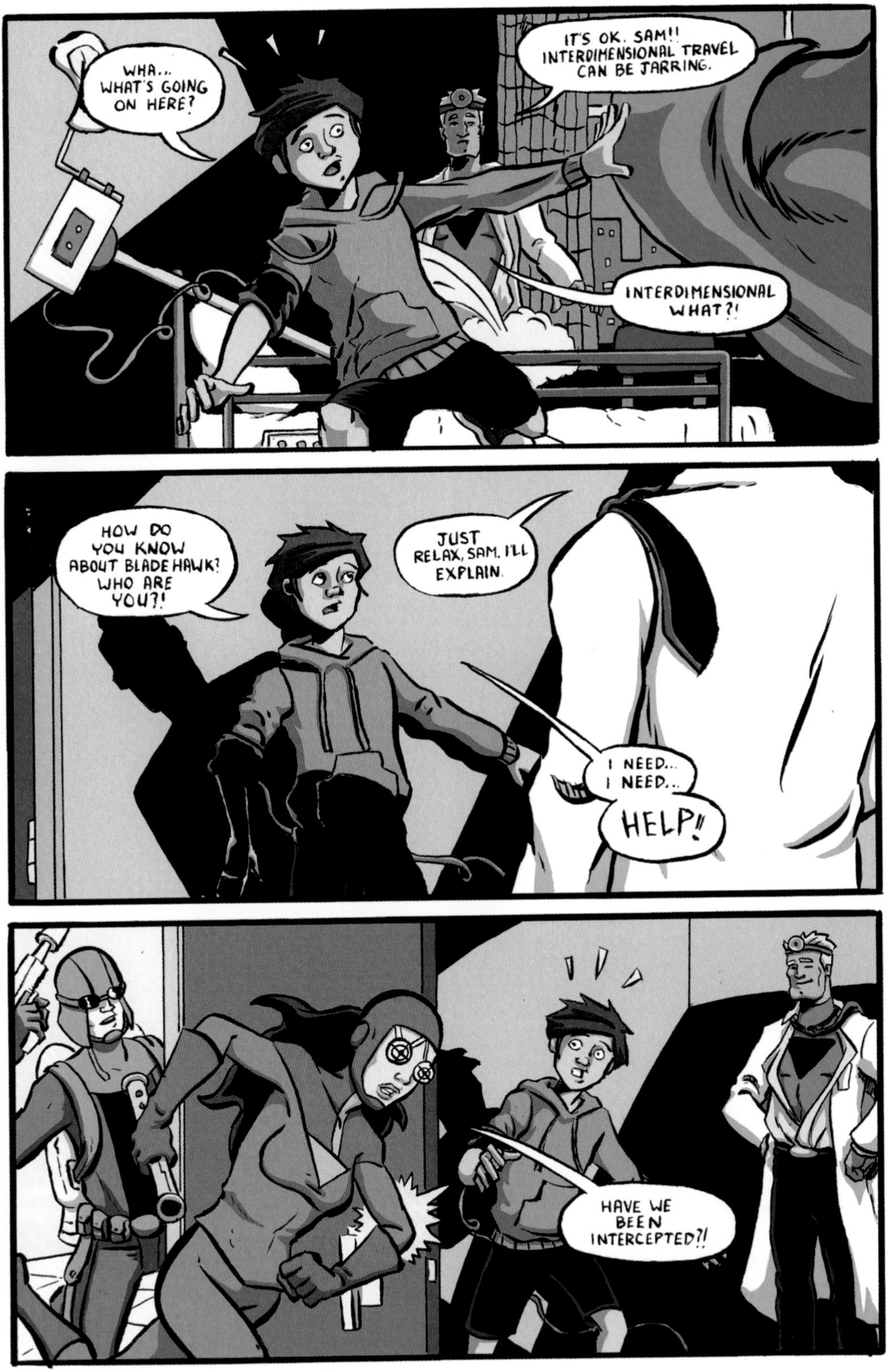
WHA... WHAT'S GOING ON HERE?
IT'S OK, SAM!! INTERDIMENSIONAL TRAVEL CAN BE JARRING.
INTERDIMENSIONAL WHAT?!
HOW DO YOU KNOW ABOUT BLADEHAWK? WHO ARE YOU?!
JUST RELAX, SAM. I'LL EXPLAIN.
I NEED... I NEED...
HELP!
HAVE WE BEEN INTERCEPTED?!

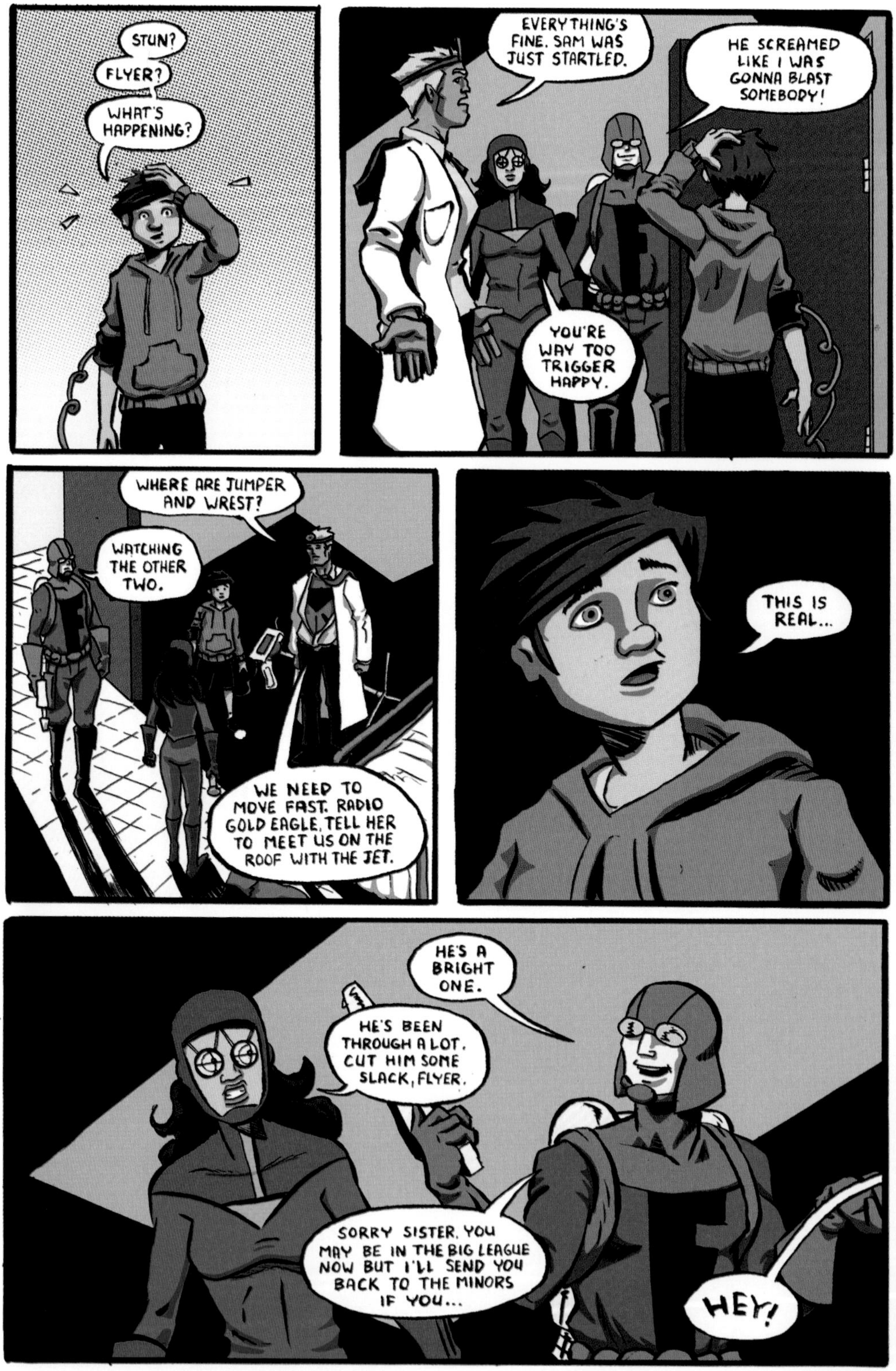
STUN?
FLYER?
WHAT'S HAPPENING?
EVERYTHING'S FINE. SAM WAS JUST STARTLED.
HE SCREAMED LIKE I WAS GONNA BLAST SOMEBODY!
YOU'RE WAY TOO TRIGGER HAPPY.
WHERE ARE JUMPER AND WREST?
WATCHING THE OTHER TWO.
WE NEED TO MOVE FAST. RADIO GOLD EAGLE. TELL HER TO MEET US ON THE ROOF WITH THE JET.
THIS IS REAL...
HE'S A BRIGHT ONE.
HE'S BEEN THROUGH A LOT. CUT HIM SOME SLACK, FLYER.
SORRY SISTER. YOU MAY BE IN THE BIG LEAGUE NOW BUT I'LL SEND YOU BACK TO THE MINORS IF YOU...
HEY!

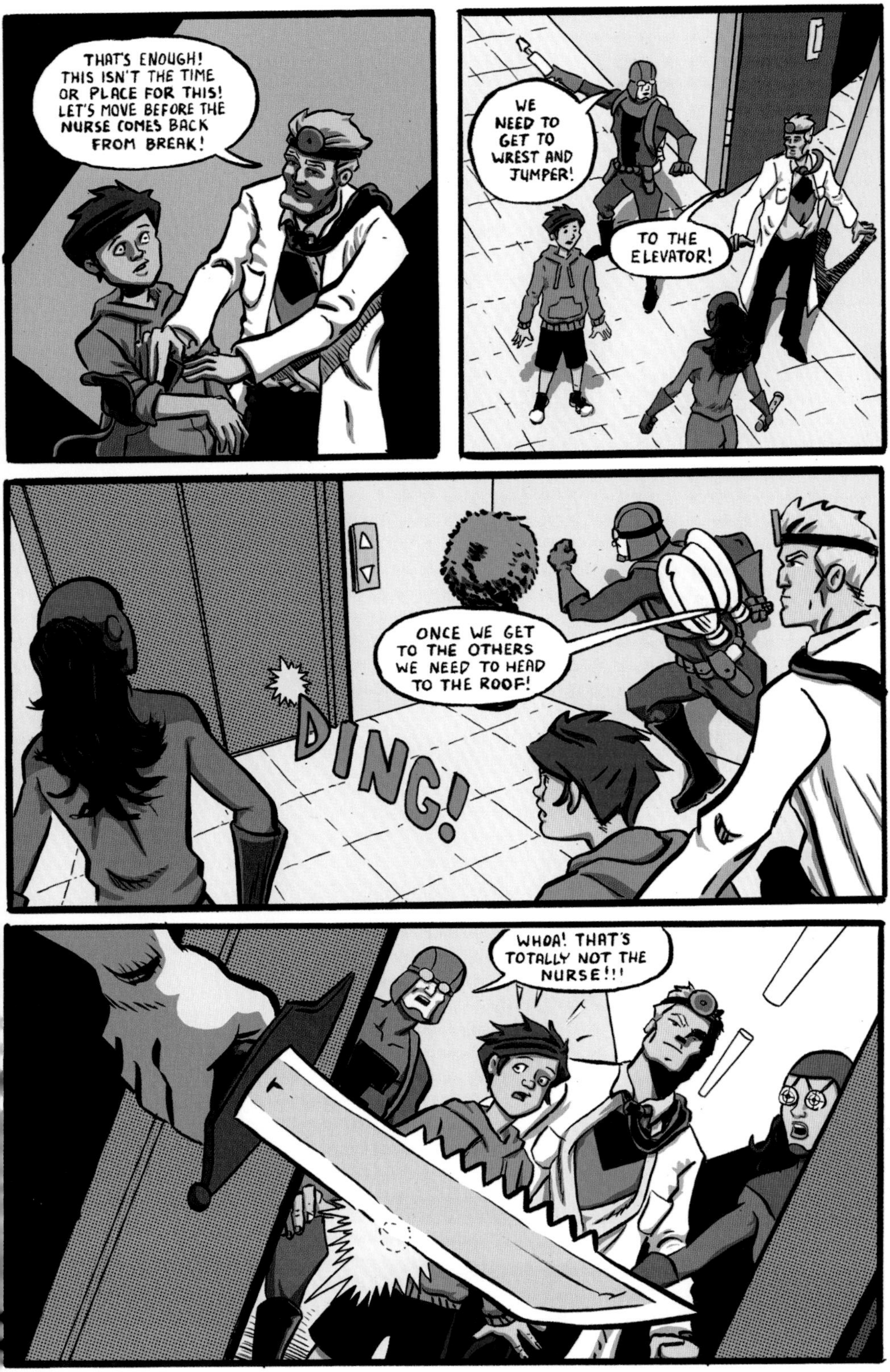
THAT'S ENOUGH! THIS ISN'T THE TIME OR PLACE FOR THIS! LET'S MOVE BEFORE THE NURSE COMES BACK FROM BREAK!
WE NEED TO GET TO WREST AND JUMPER!
TO THE ELEVATOR!
ONCE WE GET TO THE OTHERS WE NEED TO HEAD TO THE ROOF!
DING!
WHOA! THAT'S TOTALLY NOT THE NURSE!!!

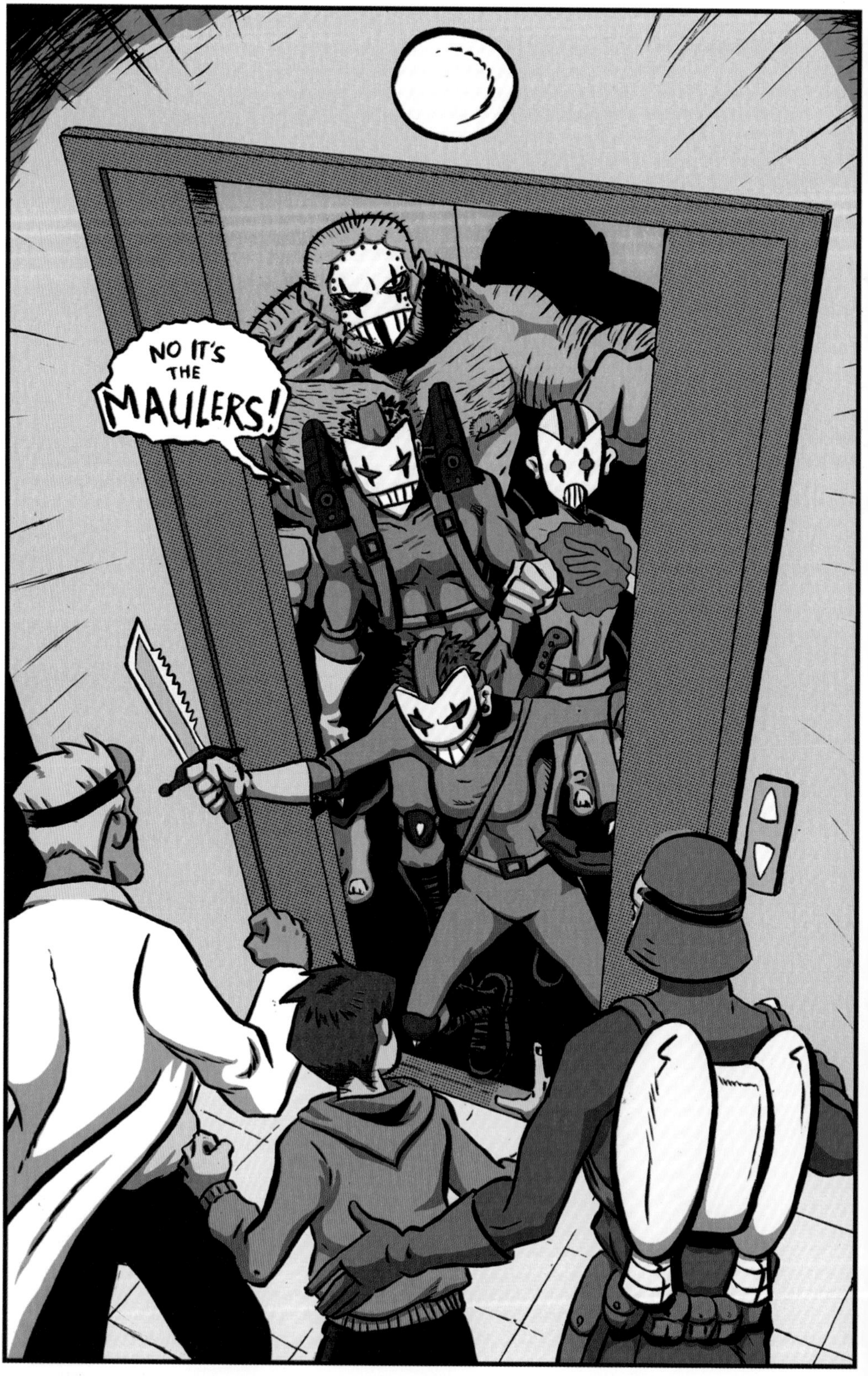
NO IT'S THE MAULERS!

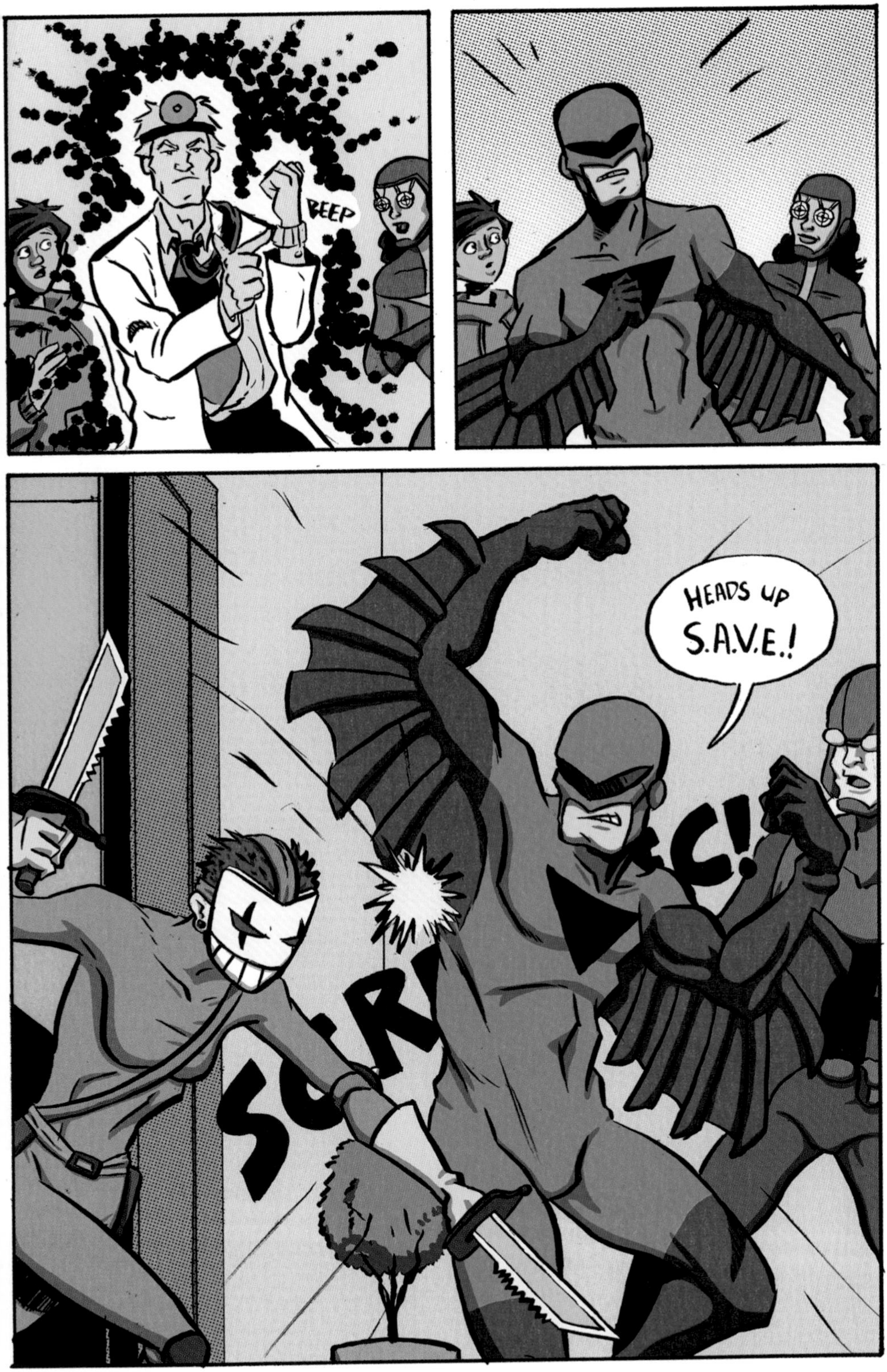
BEEP
HEADS UP S.A.V.E.!
SCR
EC!

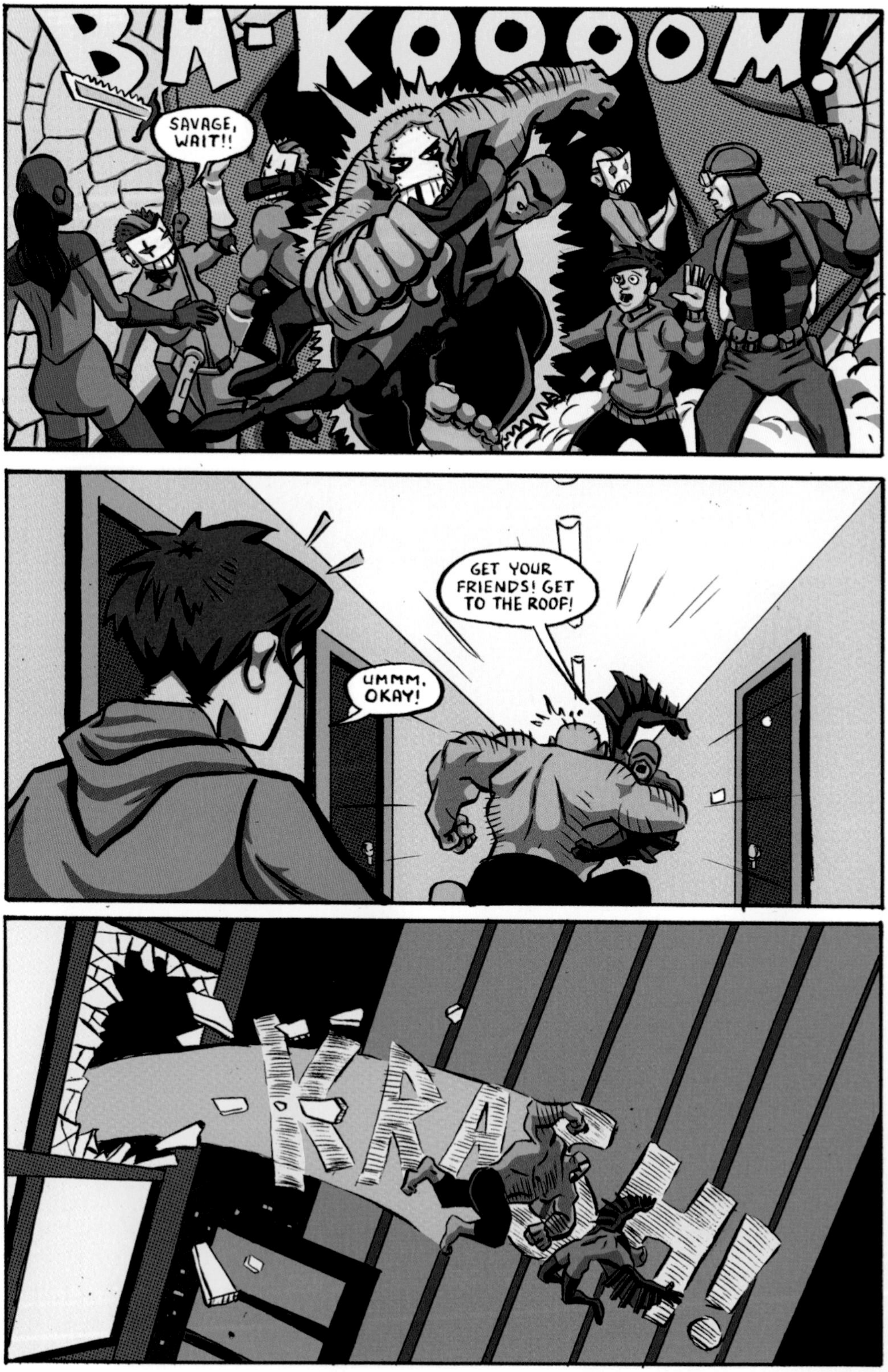
BA-KOOOOM!
SAVAGE, WAIT!!
GET YOUR FRIENDS! GET TO THE ROOF!
UMMM, OKAY!
-KRASH!

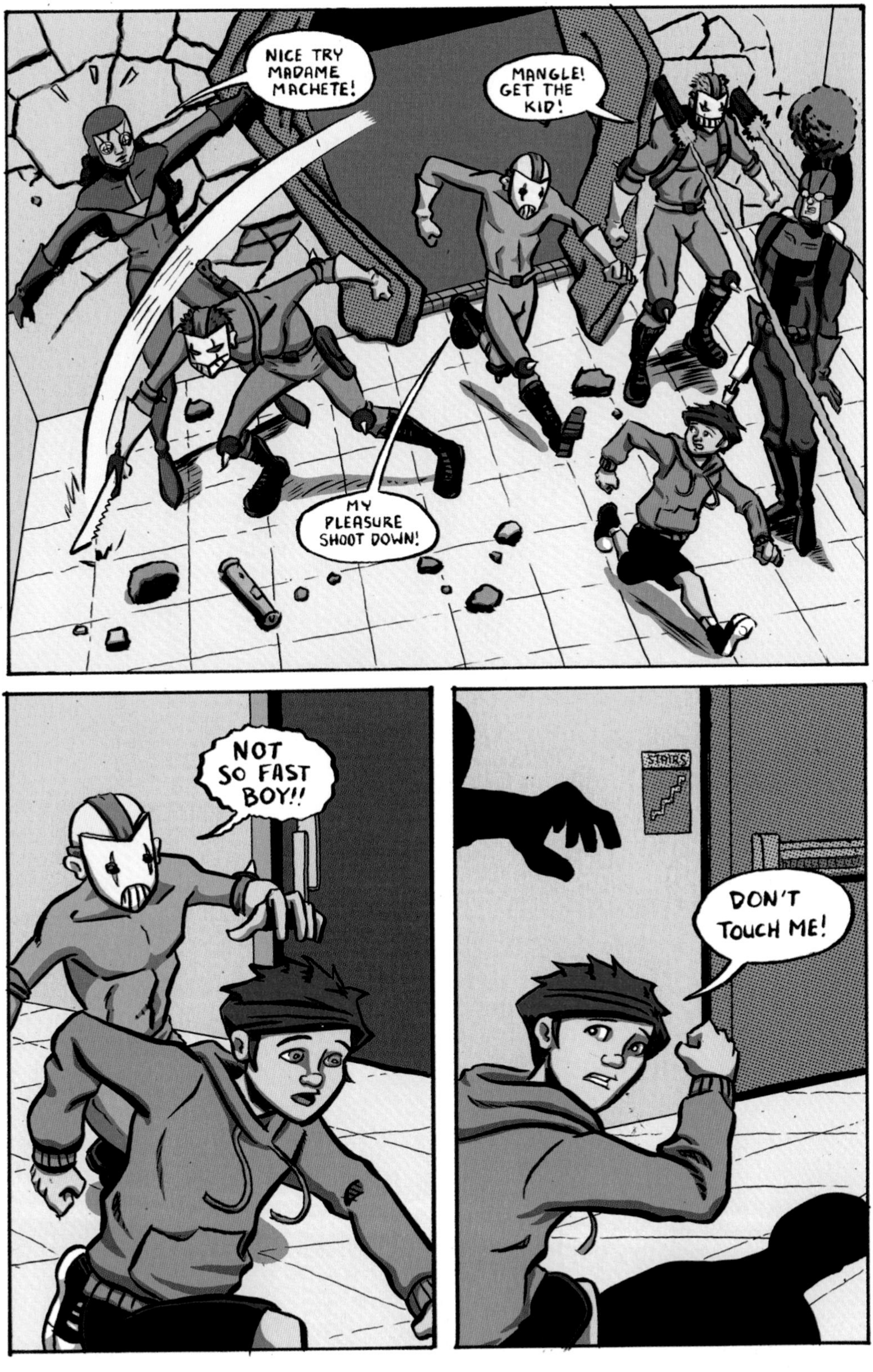
NICE TRY MADAME MACHETE!
MANGLE! GET THE KID!
MY PLEASURE SHOOT DOWN!
NOT SO FAST BOY!!
STAIRS
DON'T TOUCH ME!

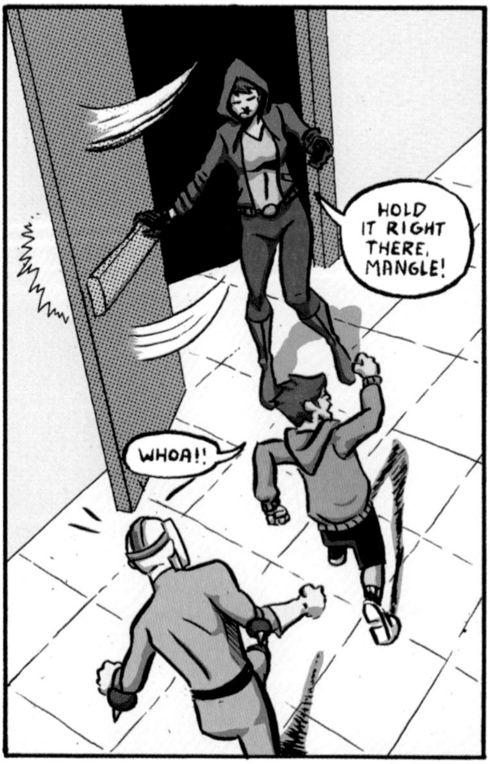
HOLD IT RIGHT THERE, MANGLE!
WHOA!!

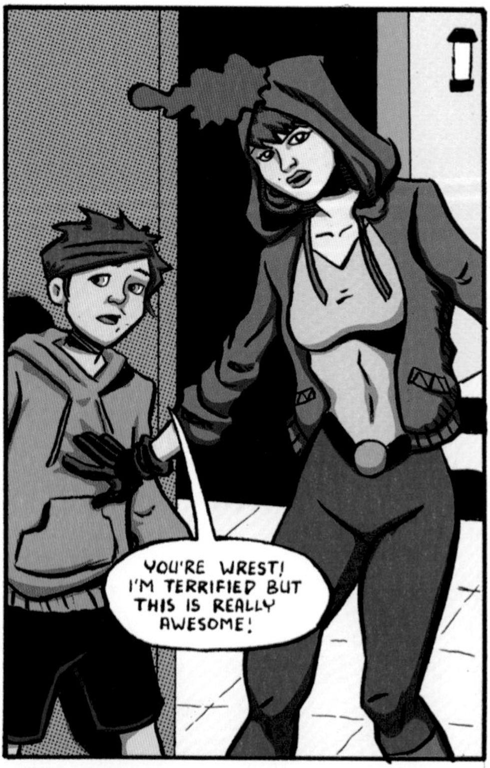
YOU'RE WREST! I'M TERRIFIED BUT THIS IS REALLY AWESOME!

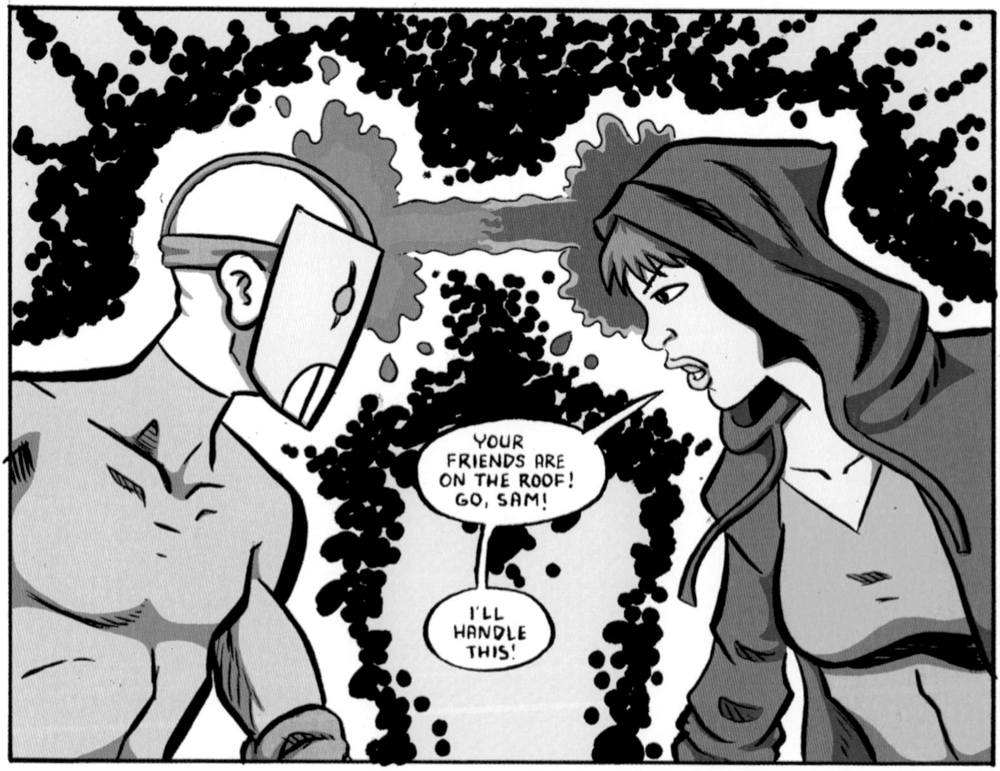
YOUR FRIENDS ARE ON THE ROOF! GO, SAM!
I'LL HANDLE THIS!

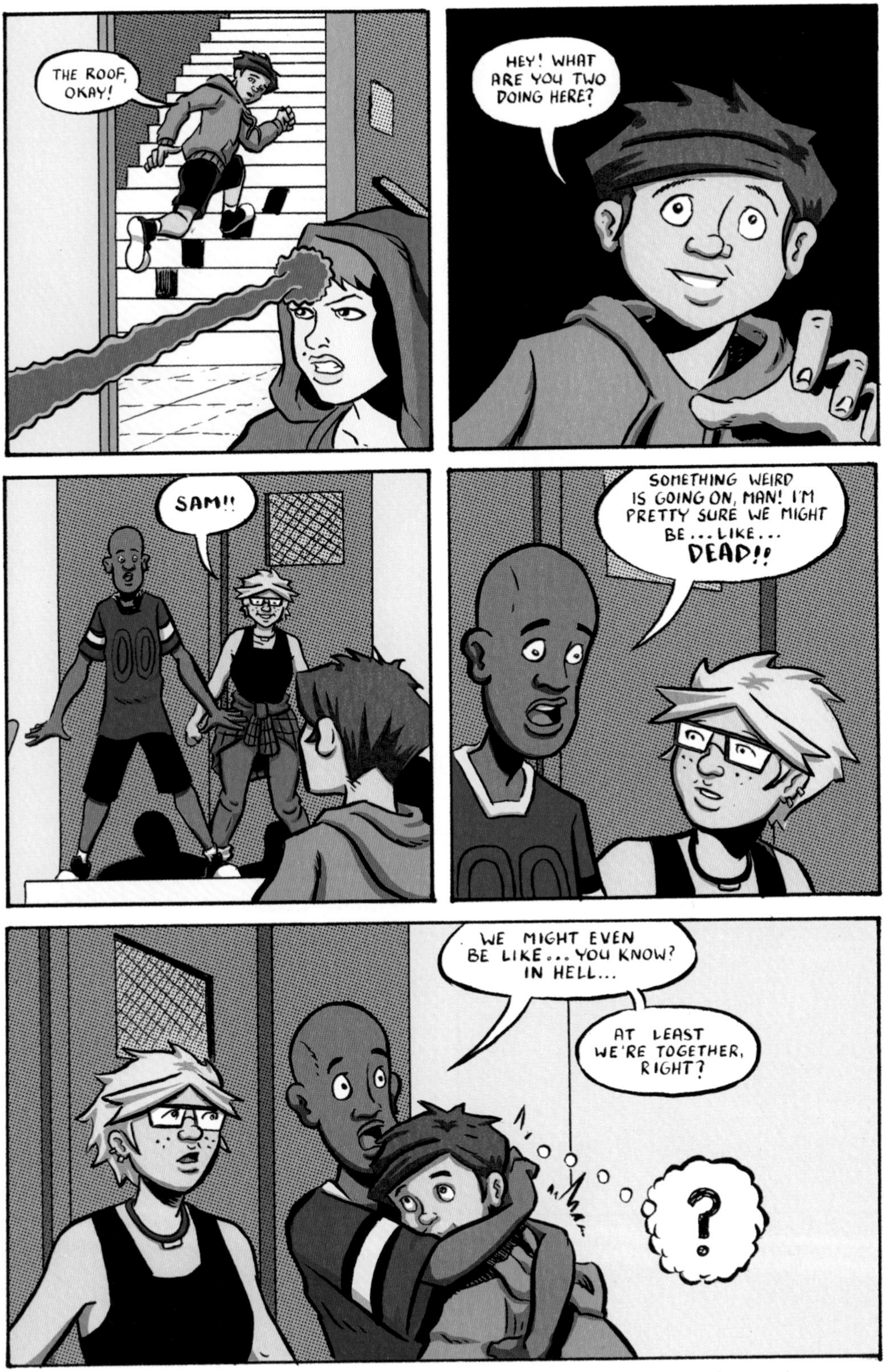
THE ROOF, OKAY!
HEY! WHAT ARE YOU TWO DOING HERE?
SAM!!
SOMETHING WEIRD IS GOING ON, MAN! I'M PRETTY SURE WE MIGHT BE... LIKE... DEAD!!
WE MIGHT EVEN BE LIKE... YOU KNOW? IN HELL...
AT LEAST WE'RE TOGETHER, RIGHT?
?

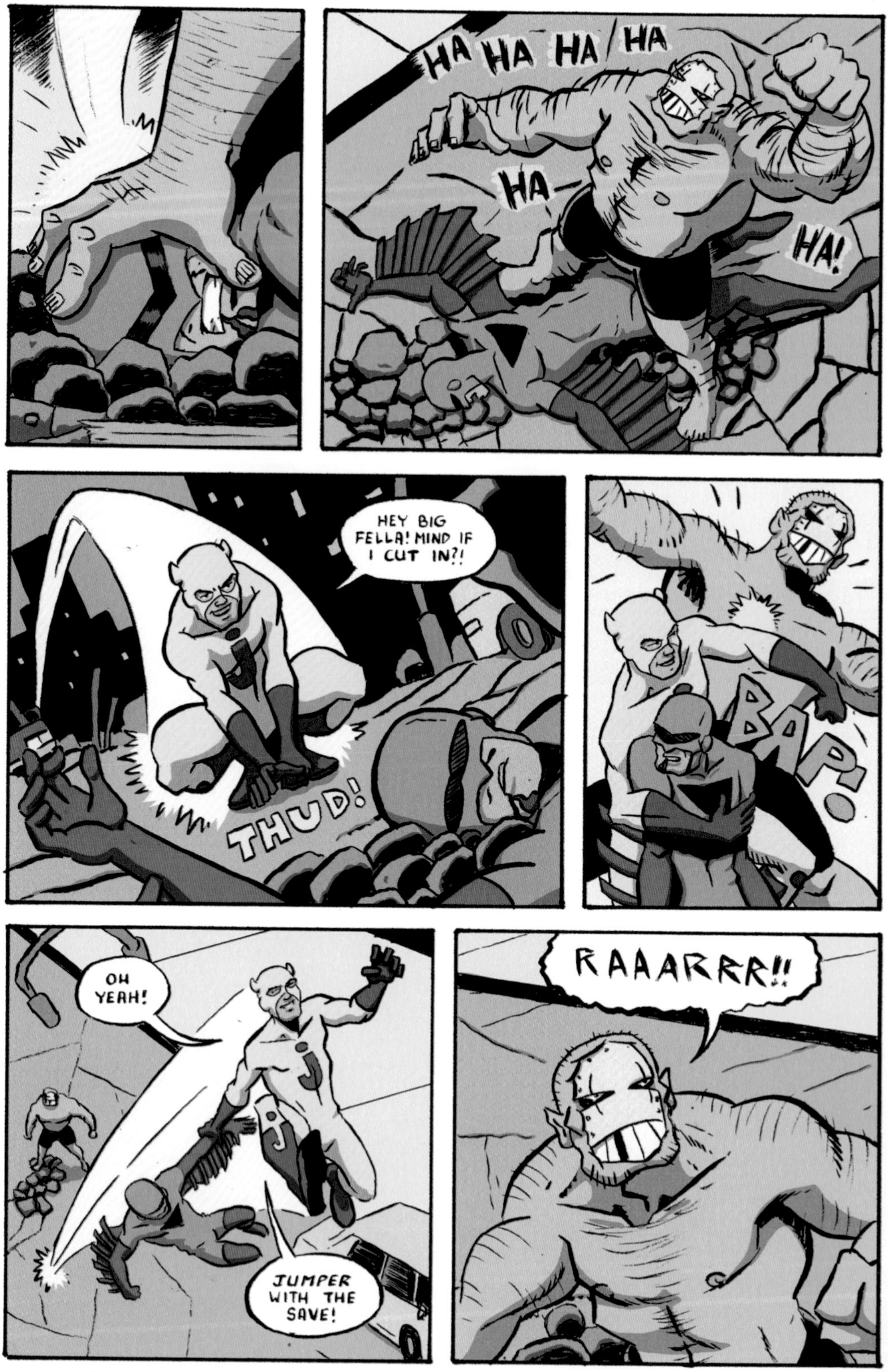
HA HA HA HA
HA
HA!
HEY BIG FELLA! MIND IF I CUT IN?!
THUD!
BAP!
OH YEAH!
JUMPER WITH THE SAVE!
RAAARRR!!

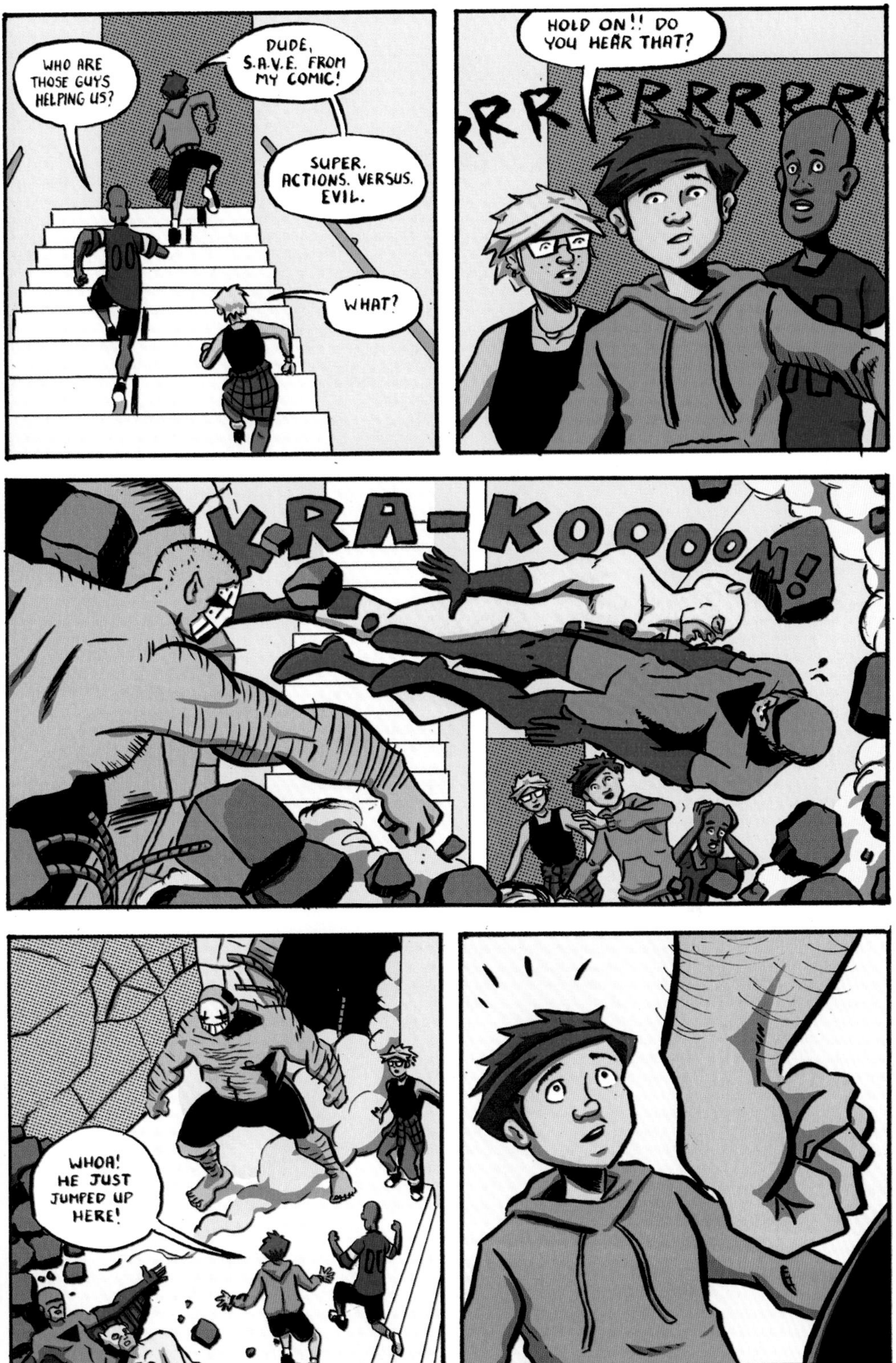
WHO ARE THOSE GUYS HELPING US?
DUDE, S.A.V.E. FROM MY COMIC!
SUPER. ACTIONS. VERSUS. EVIL.
WHAT?
HOLD ON!! DO YOU HEAR THAT?
RRRRRRRRRRR
K-RA-KOOOOM!
WHOA! HE JUST JUMPED UP HERE!

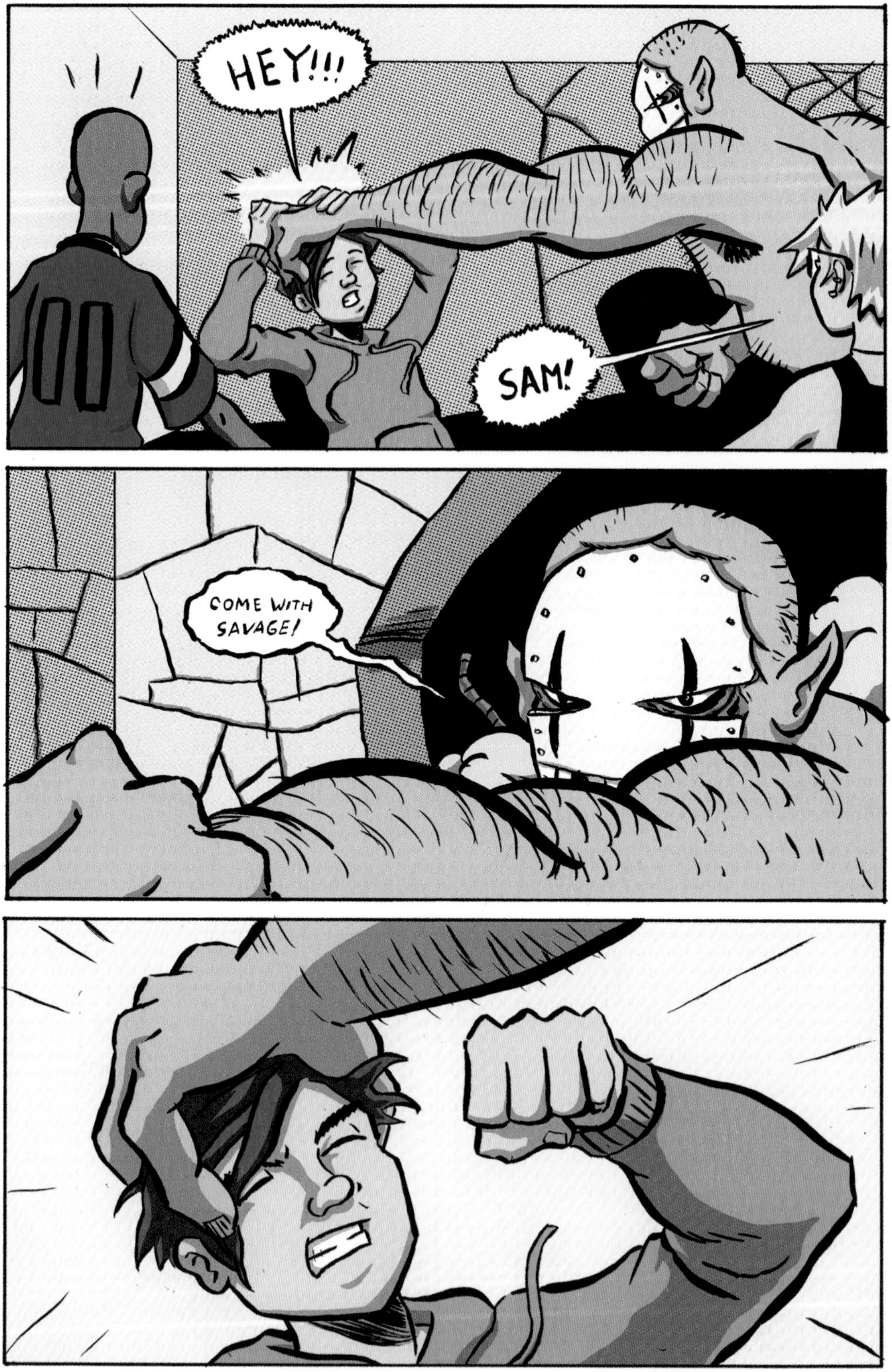
HEY!!!
SAM!
COME WITH SAVAGE!

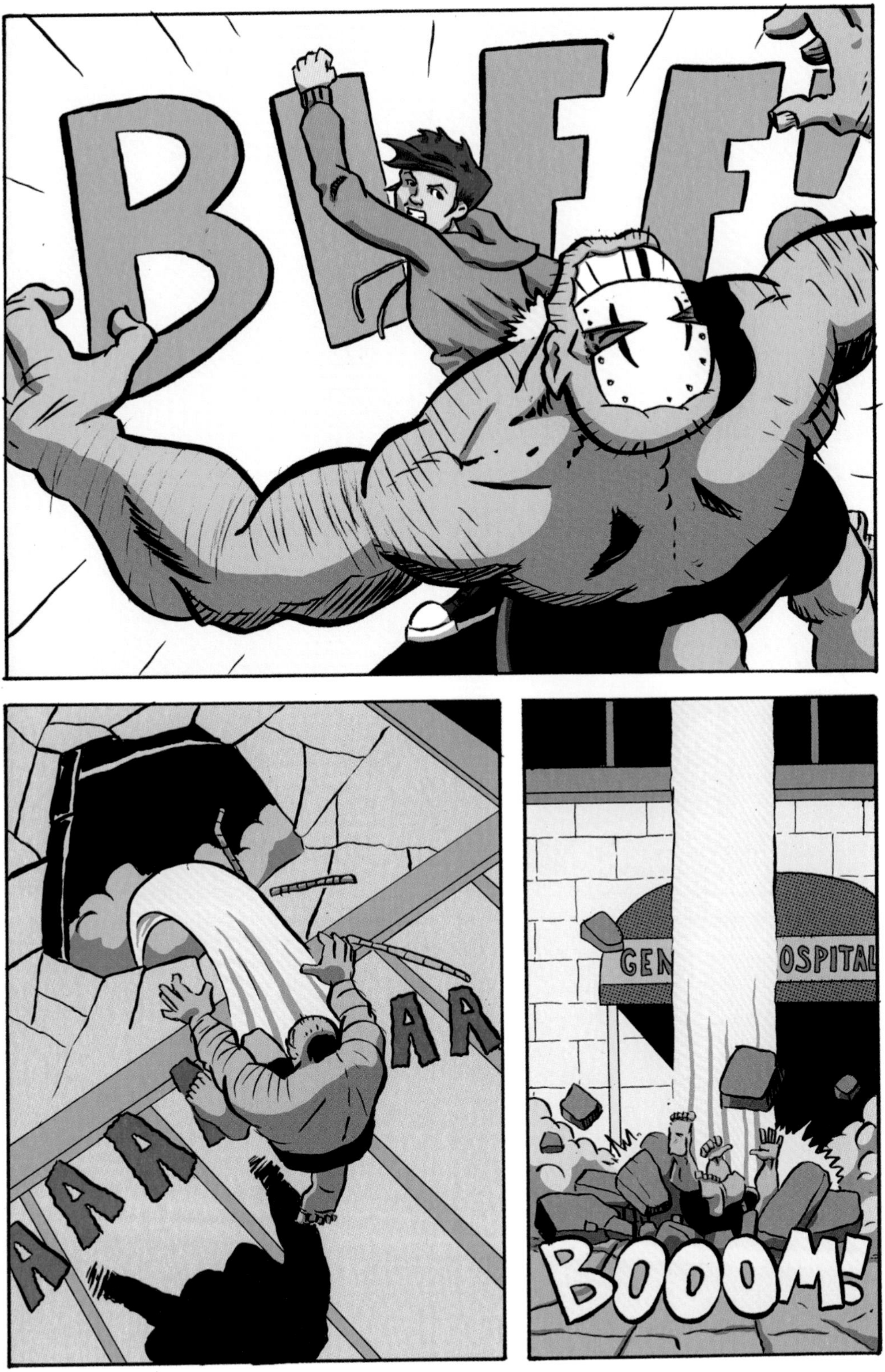
BIFF!
AAAAAR
GEN
OSPITAL
BOOOM!

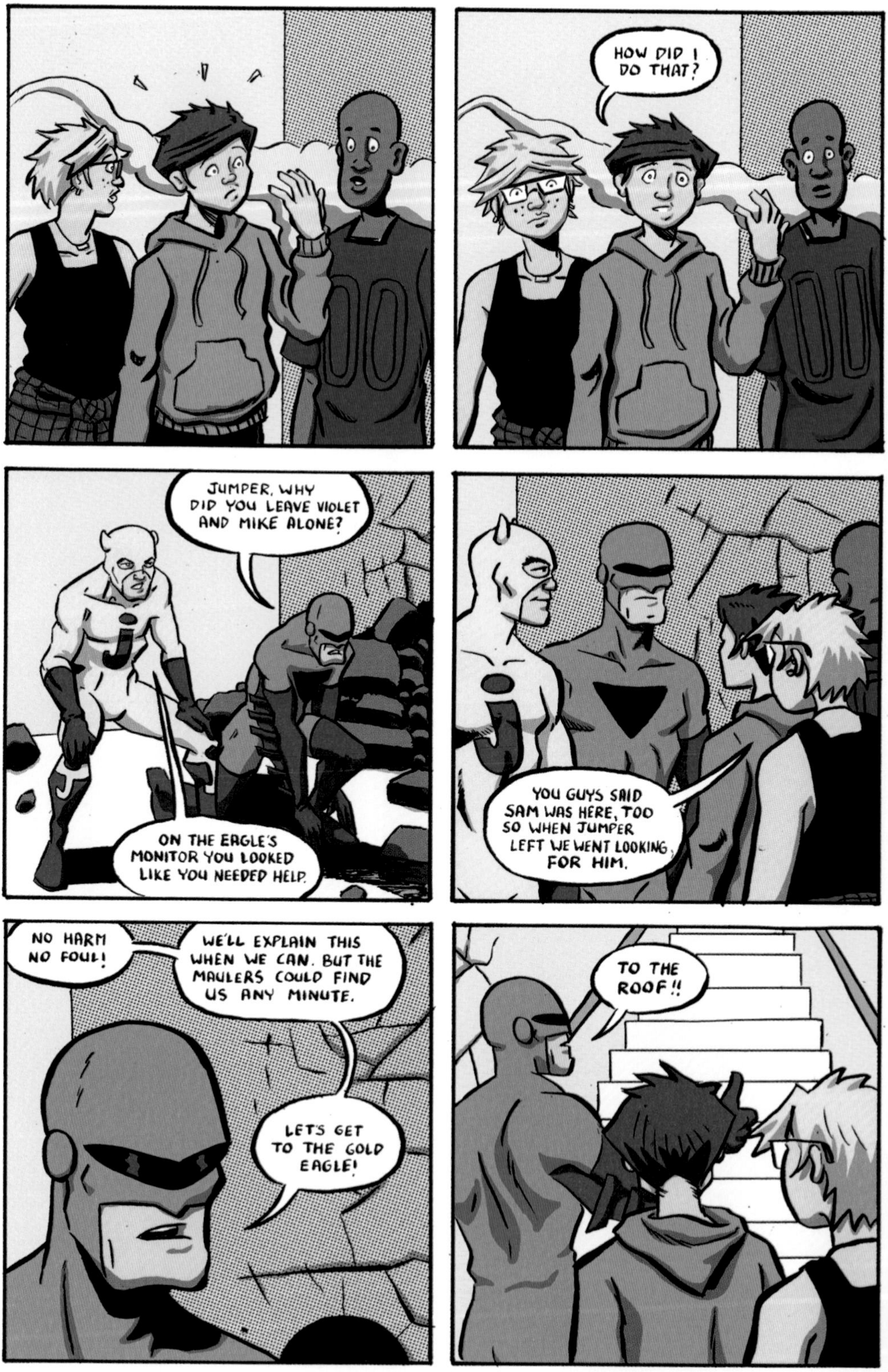
HOW DID I DO THAT?
JUMPER, WHY DID YOU LEAVE VIOLET AND MIKE ALONE?
ON THE EAGLE'S MONITOR YOU LOOKED LIKE YOU NEEDED HELP.
YOU GUYS SAID SAM WAS HERE, TOO SO WHEN JUMPER LEFT WE WENT LOOKING FOR HIM.
NO HARM NO FOUL!
WE'LL EXPLAIN THIS WHEN WE CAN. BUT THE MAULERS COULD FIND US ANY MINUTE.
LET'S GET TO THE GOLD EAGLE!
TO THE ROOF!!

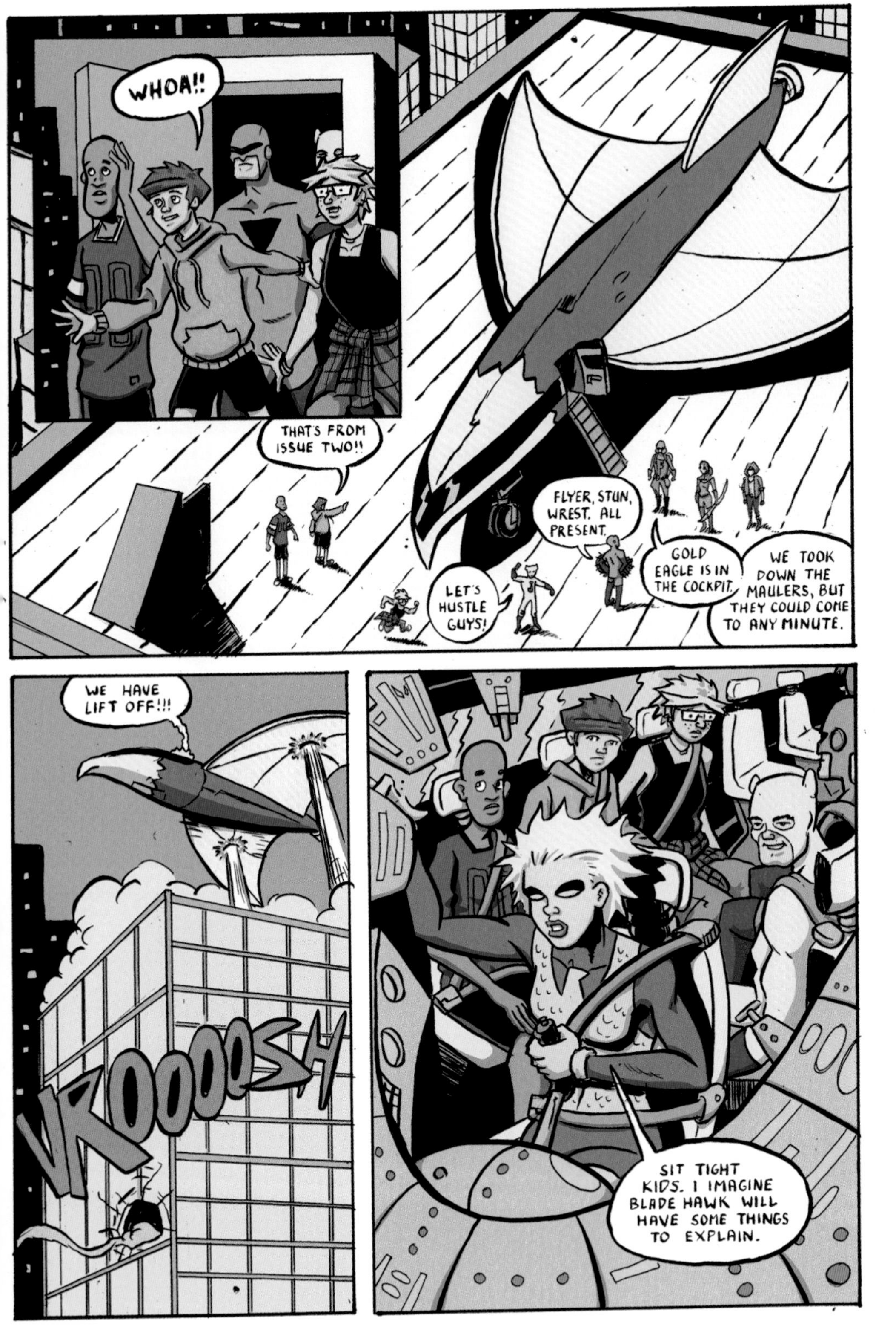
WHOA!!
THAT'S FROM ISSUE TWO!!
LET'S HUSTLE GUYS!
FLYER, STUN, WREST. ALL PRESENT.
GOLD EAGLE IS IN THE COCKPIT.
WE TOOK DOWN THE MAULERS, BUT THEY COULD COME TO ANY MINUTE.
WE HAVE LIFT OFF!!!
VROOOOSH
SIT TIGHT KIDS. I IMAGINE BLADE HAWK WILL HAVE SOME THINGS TO EXPLAIN.

LATER...

J.E.T.

THE JUSTICE ENFORCEMENT TEAM. YOU AND THOSE ACRONYMS.

HA HA YEAH!

WAIT! I'VE NEVER BEEN HERE...LIKE EVER! HOW ARE WE J.E.T.?

I SUPPOSE WE DO NEED TO CLEAR THAT ALL UP.

MR. MIGHT!

VIOLET!

BLACK KNIGHT!

BEEP! BOP! BEEP!

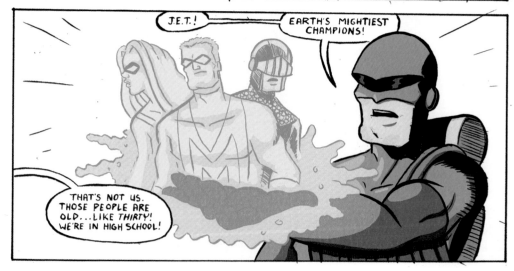

J.E.T.!

EARTH'S MIGHTIEST CHAMPIONS!

THAT'S NOT US. THOSE PEOPLE ARE OLD...LIKE THIRTY! WE'RE IN HIGH SCHOOL!

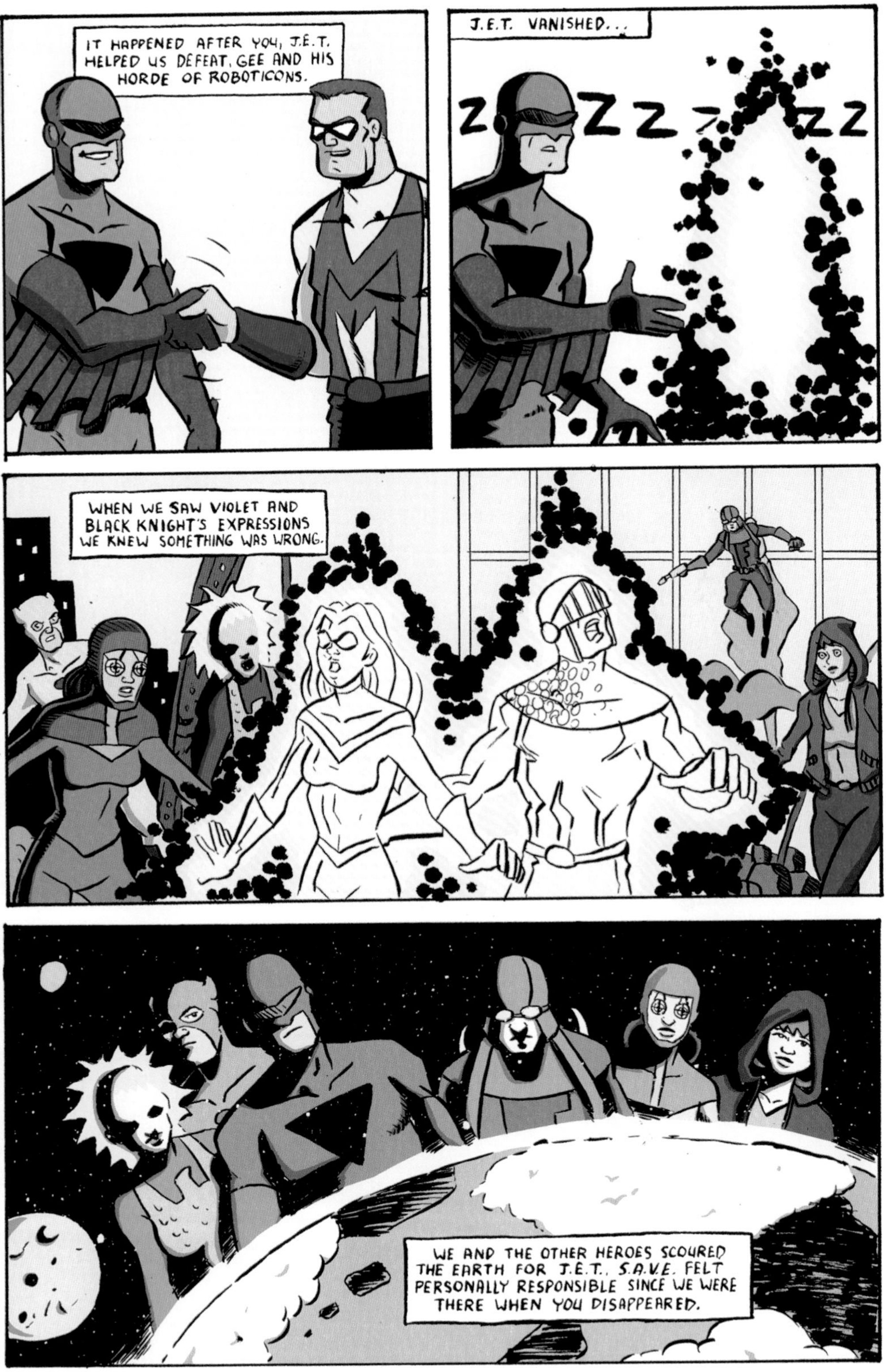
IT HAPPENED AFTER YOU, J.E.T. HELPED US DEFEAT GEE AND HIS HORDE OF ROBOTICONS.
J.E.T. VANISHED...
ZZZZZZ
WHEN WE SAW VIOLET AND BLACK KNIGHT'S EXPRESSIONS WE KNEW SOMETHING WAS WRONG.
WE AND THE OTHER HEROES SCOURED THE EARTH FOR J.E.T., S.A.V.E. FELT PERSONALLY RESPONSIBLE SINCE WE WERE THERE WHEN YOU DISAPPEARED.

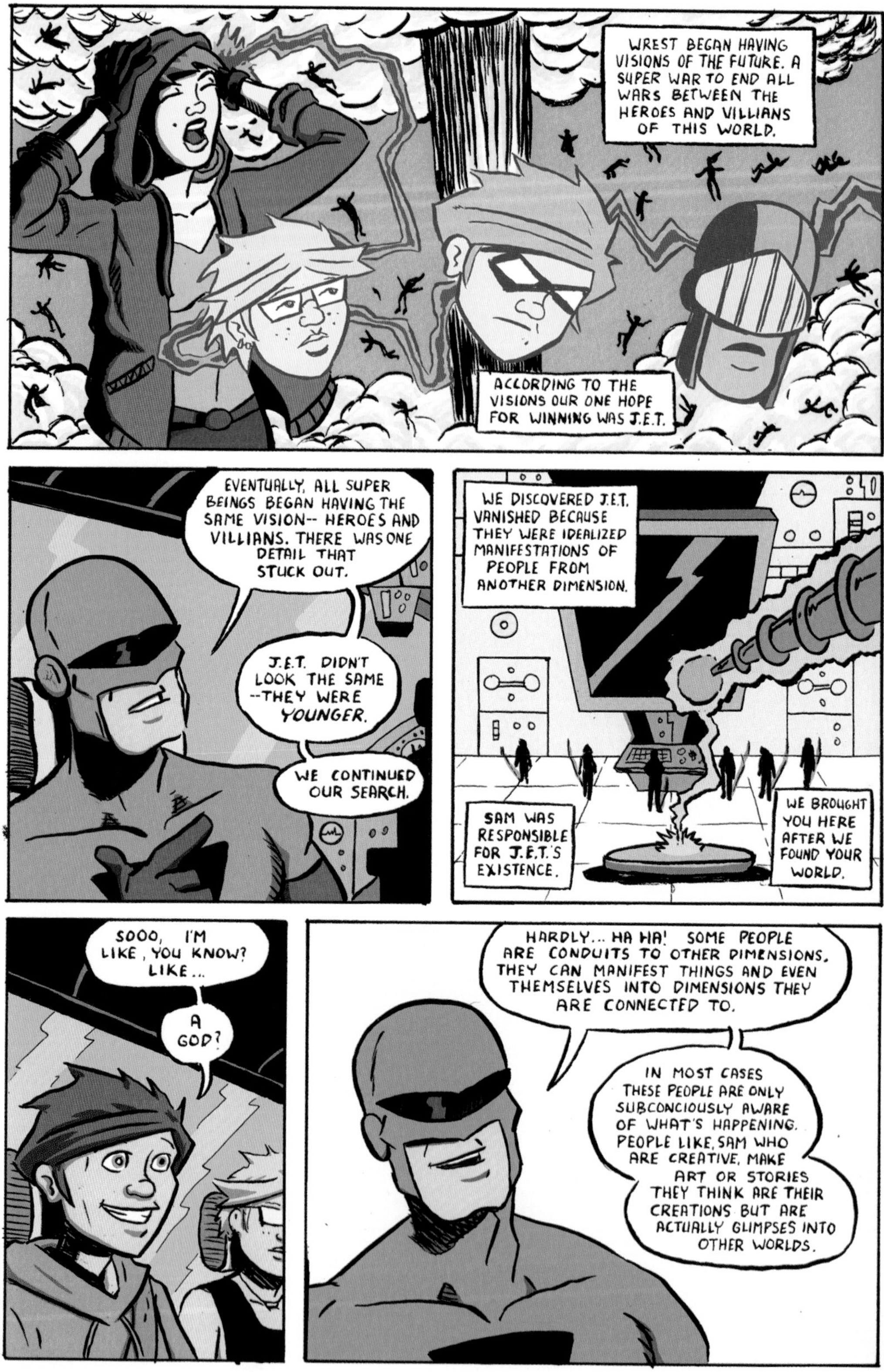
WREST BEGAN HAVING VISIONS OF THE FUTURE. A SUPER WAR TO END ALL WARS BETWEEN THE HEROES AND VILLIANS OF THIS WORLD.
ACCORDING TO THE VISIONS OUR ONE HOPE FOR WINNING WAS J.E.T.
EVENTUALLY, ALL SUPER BEINGS BEGAN HAVING THE SAME VISION-- HEROES AND VILLIANS. THERE WAS ONE DETAIL THAT STUCK OUT.
J.E.T. DIDN'T LOOK THE SAME --THEY WERE YOUNGER.
WE CONTINUED OUR SEARCH.
WE DISCOVERED J.E.T. VANISHED BECAUSE THEY WERE IDEALIZED MANIFESTATIONS OF PEOPLE FROM ANOTHER DIMENSION.
SAM WAS RESPONSIBLE FOR J.E.T.'S EXISTENCE.
WE BROUGHT YOU HERE AFTER WE FOUND YOUR WORLD.
SOOO, I'M LIKE, YOU KNOW? LIKE...
A GOD?
HARDLY... HA HA! SOME PEOPLE ARE CONDUITS TO OTHER DIMENSIONS. THEY CAN MANIFEST THINGS AND EVEN THEMSELVES INTO DIMENSIONS THEY ARE CONNECTED TO.
IN MOST CASES THESE PEOPLE ARE ONLY SUBCONCIOUSLY AWARE OF WHAT'S HAPPENING. PEOPLE LIKE, SAM WHO ARE CREATIVE, MAKE ART OR STORIES THEY THINK ARE THEIR CREATIONS BUT ARE ACTUALLY GLIMPSES INTO OTHER WORLDS.

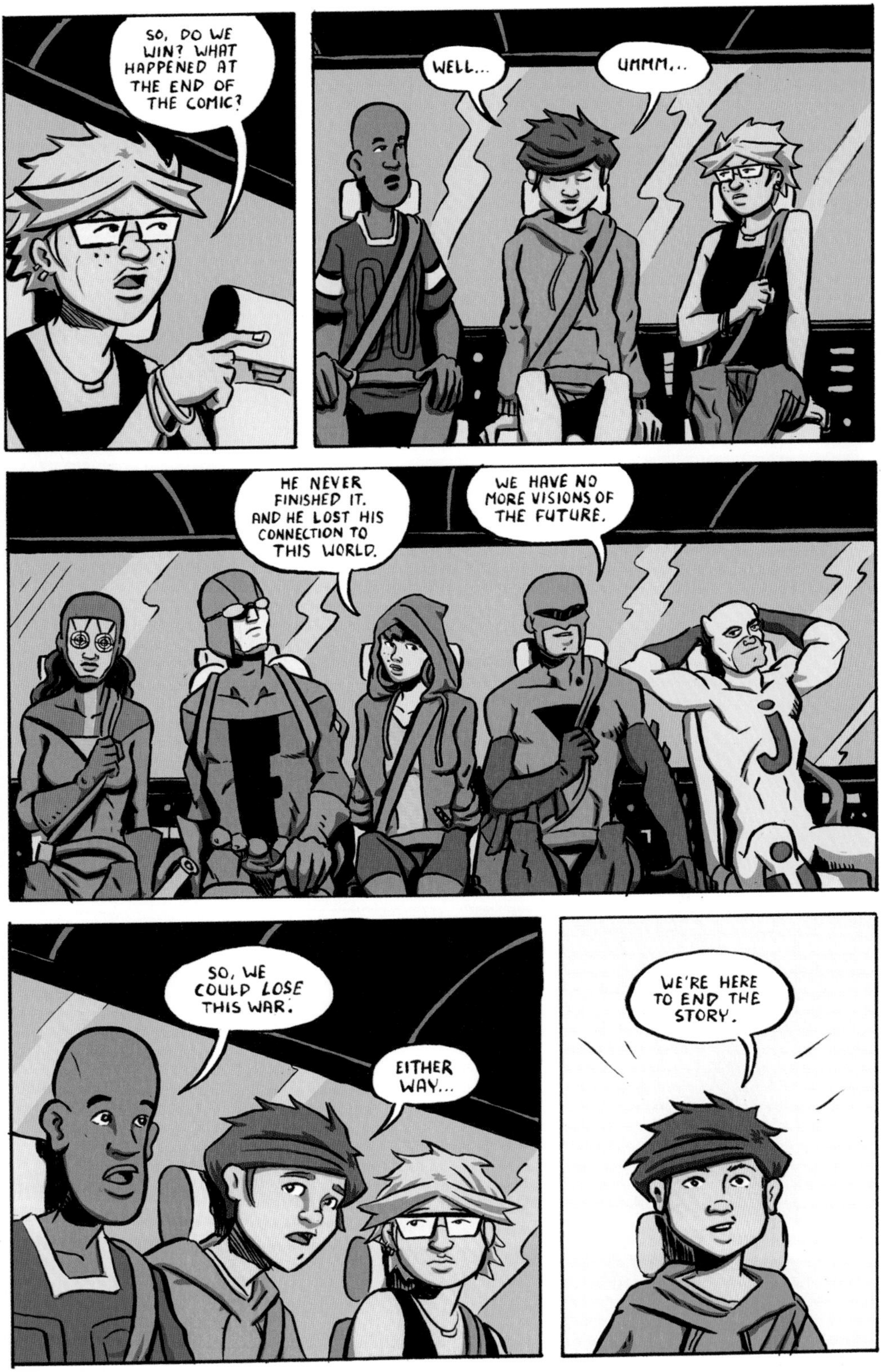
SO, DO WE WIN? WHAT HAPPENED AT THE END OF THE COMIC?
WELL...
UMMM...
HE NEVER FINISHED IT. AND HE LOST HIS CONNECTION TO THIS WORLD.
WE HAVE NO MORE VISIONS OF THE FUTURE.
SO, WE COULD LOSE THIS WAR.
EITHER WAY...
WE'RE HERE TO END THE STORY.

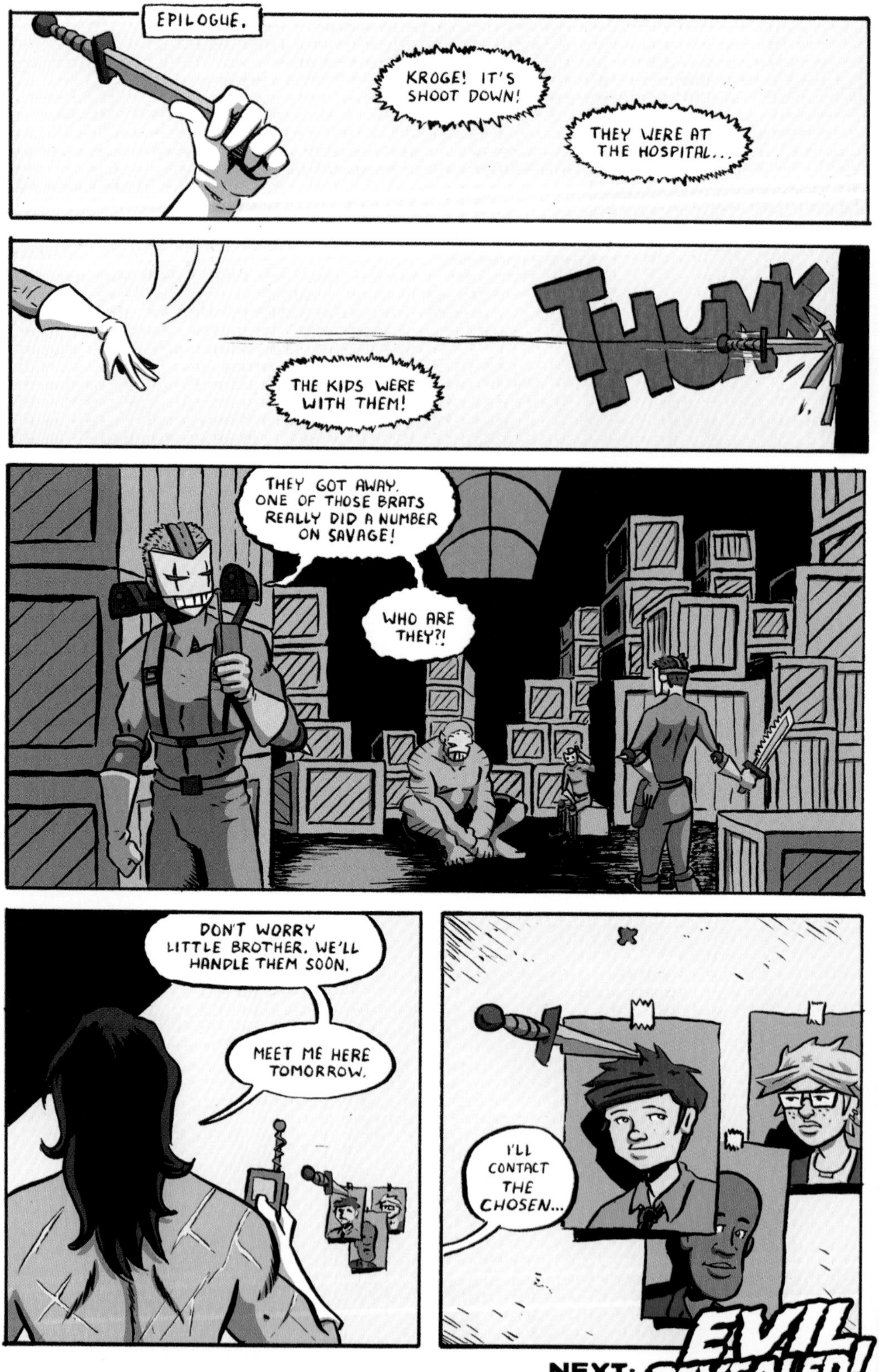
EPILOGUE.
KROGE! IT'S SHOOT DOWN!
THEY WERE AT THE HOSPITAL...
THE KIDS WERE WITH THEM!
THUNK
THEY GOT AWAY. ONE OF THOSE BRATS REALLY DID A NUMBER ON SAVAGE!
WHO ARE THEY?!
DON'T WORRY LITTLE BROTHER. WE'LL HANDLE THEM SOON.
MEET ME HERE TOMORROW.
I'LL CONTACT THE CHOSEN...
NEXT: EVIL REVEALED!

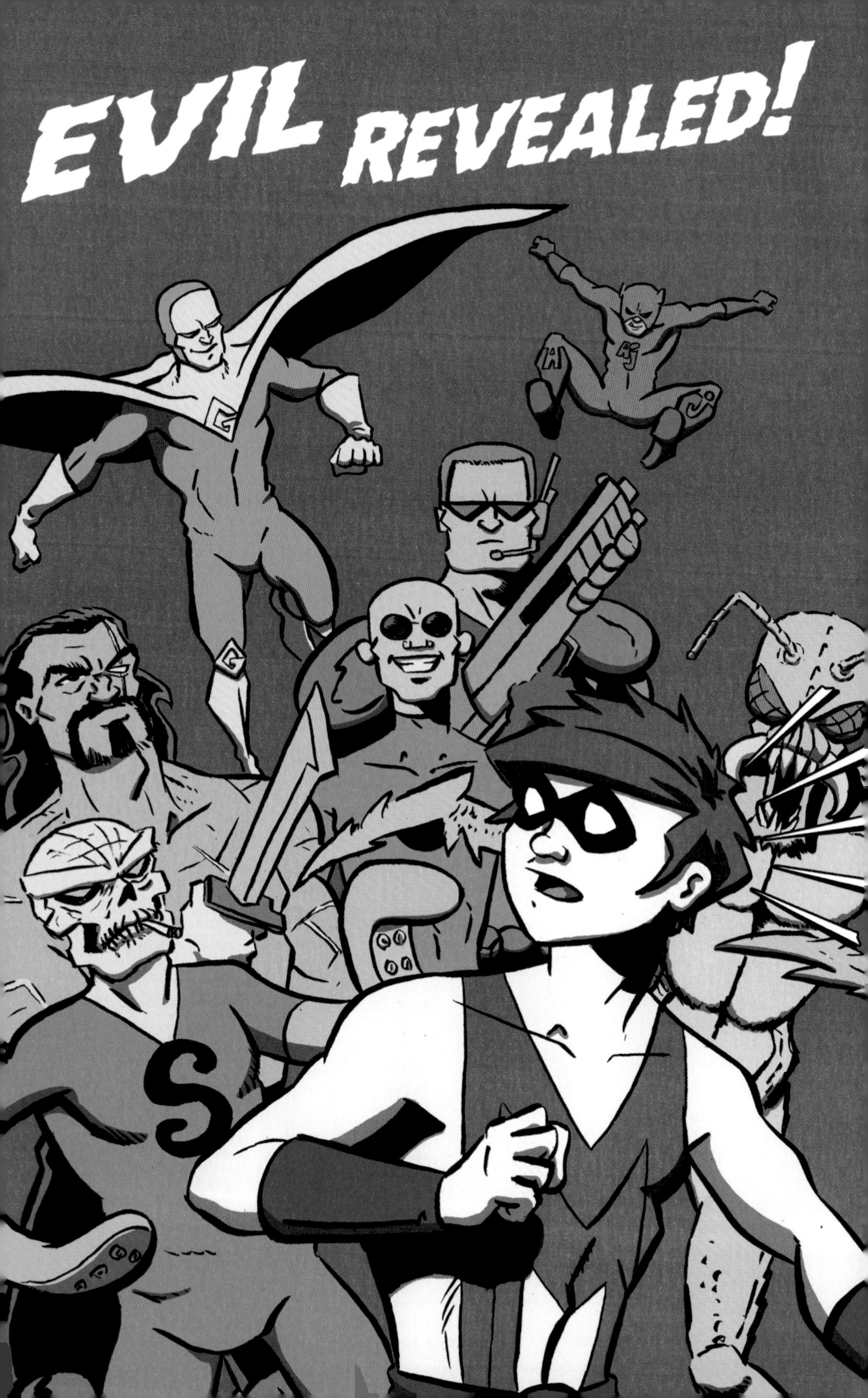
EVIL REVEALED!

PART THREE OF FIVE

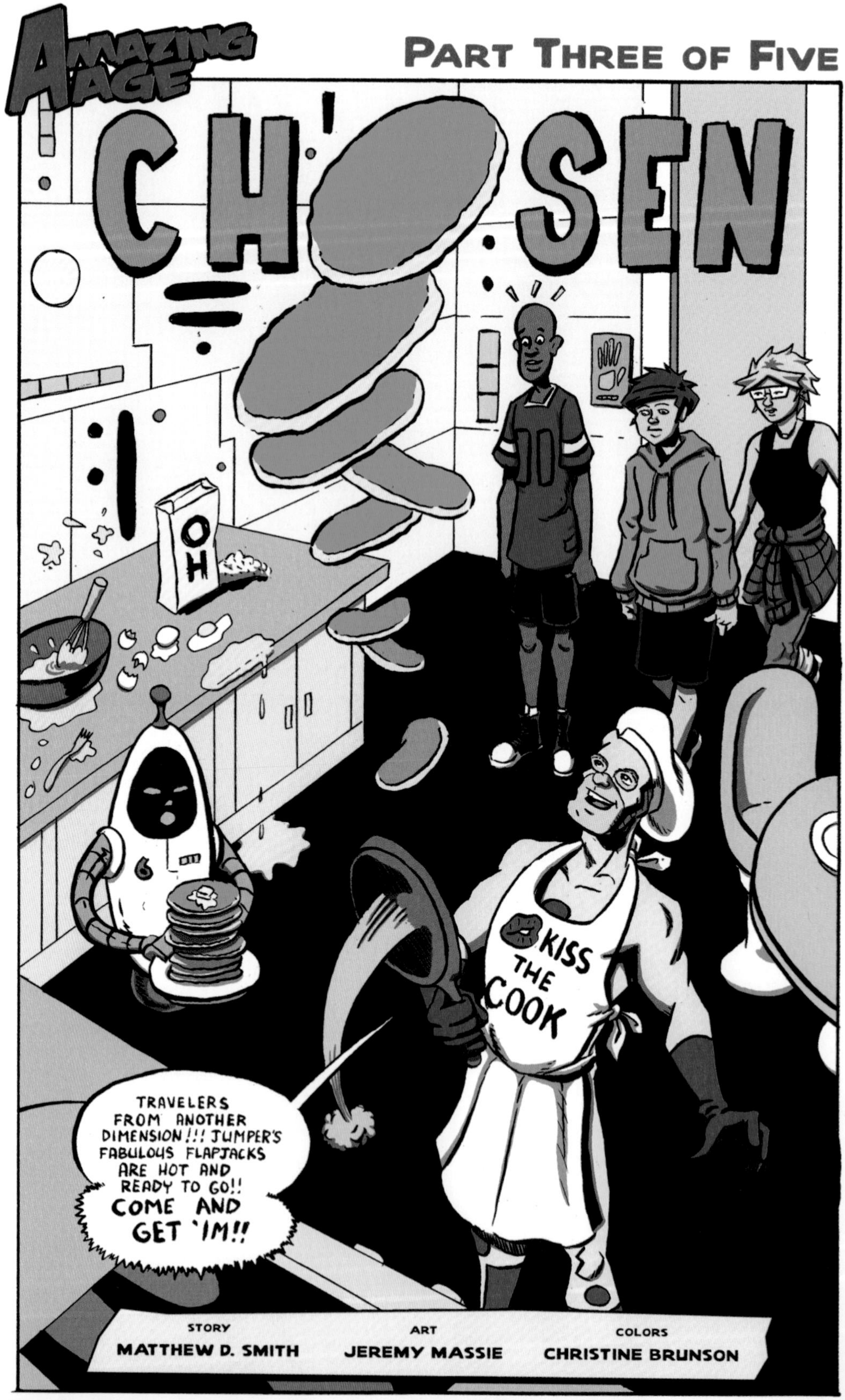
CHOSEN
OH
KISS THE COOK
TRAVELERS FROM ANOTHER DIMENSION!!! JUMPER'S FABULOUS FLAPJACKS ARE HOT AND READY TO GO!!
COME AND GET 'IM!!
STORY MATTHEW D. SMITH
ART JEREMY MASSIE
COLORS CHRISTINE BRUNSON

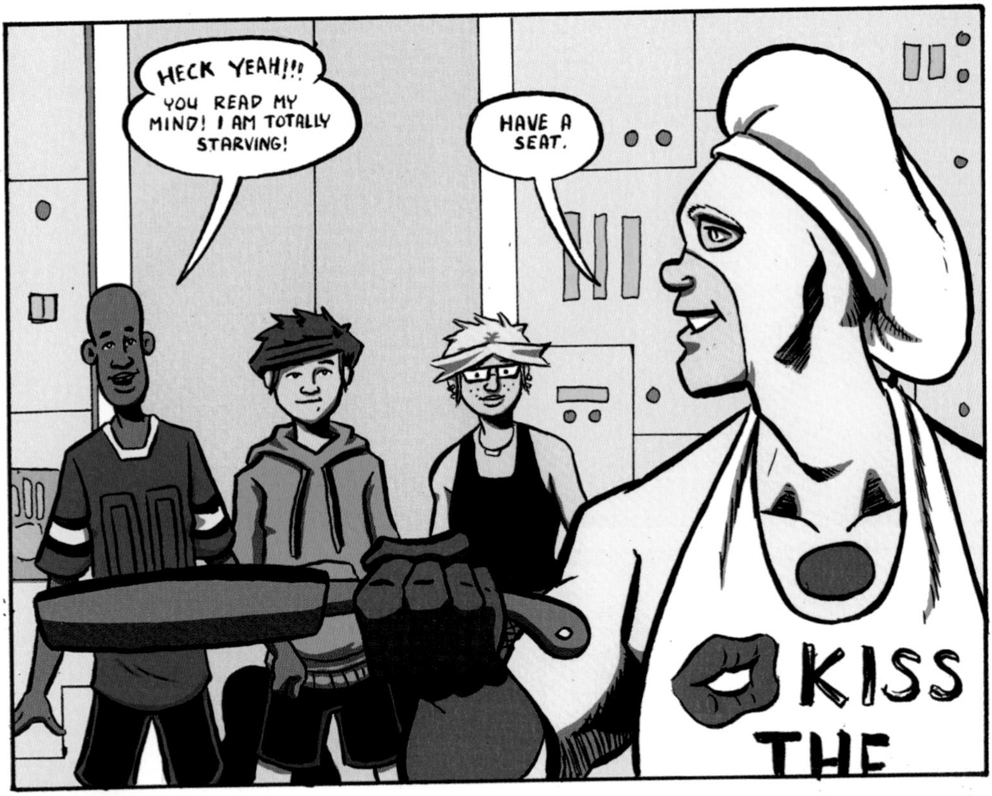
HECK YEAH!!! YOU READ MY MIND! I AM TOTALLY STARVING!
HAVE A SEAT.
KISS THE

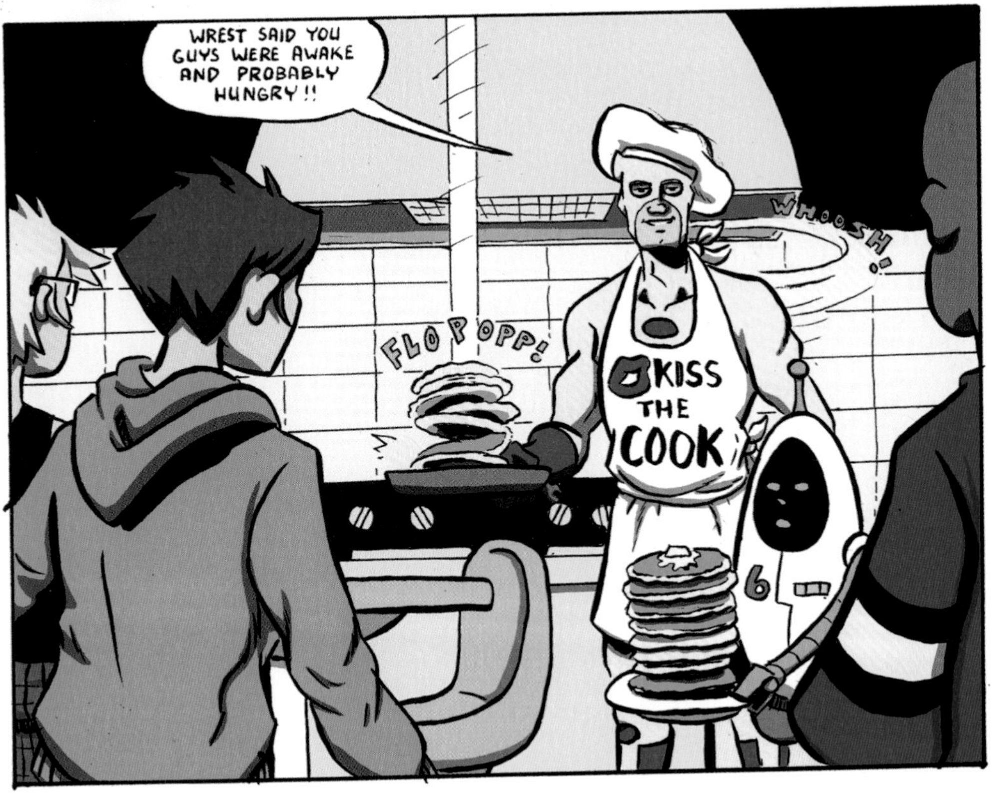
WREST SAID YOU GUYS WERE AWAKE AND PROBABLY HUNGRY!!
WHOOSH!
FLOPOPP!
KISS THE COOK

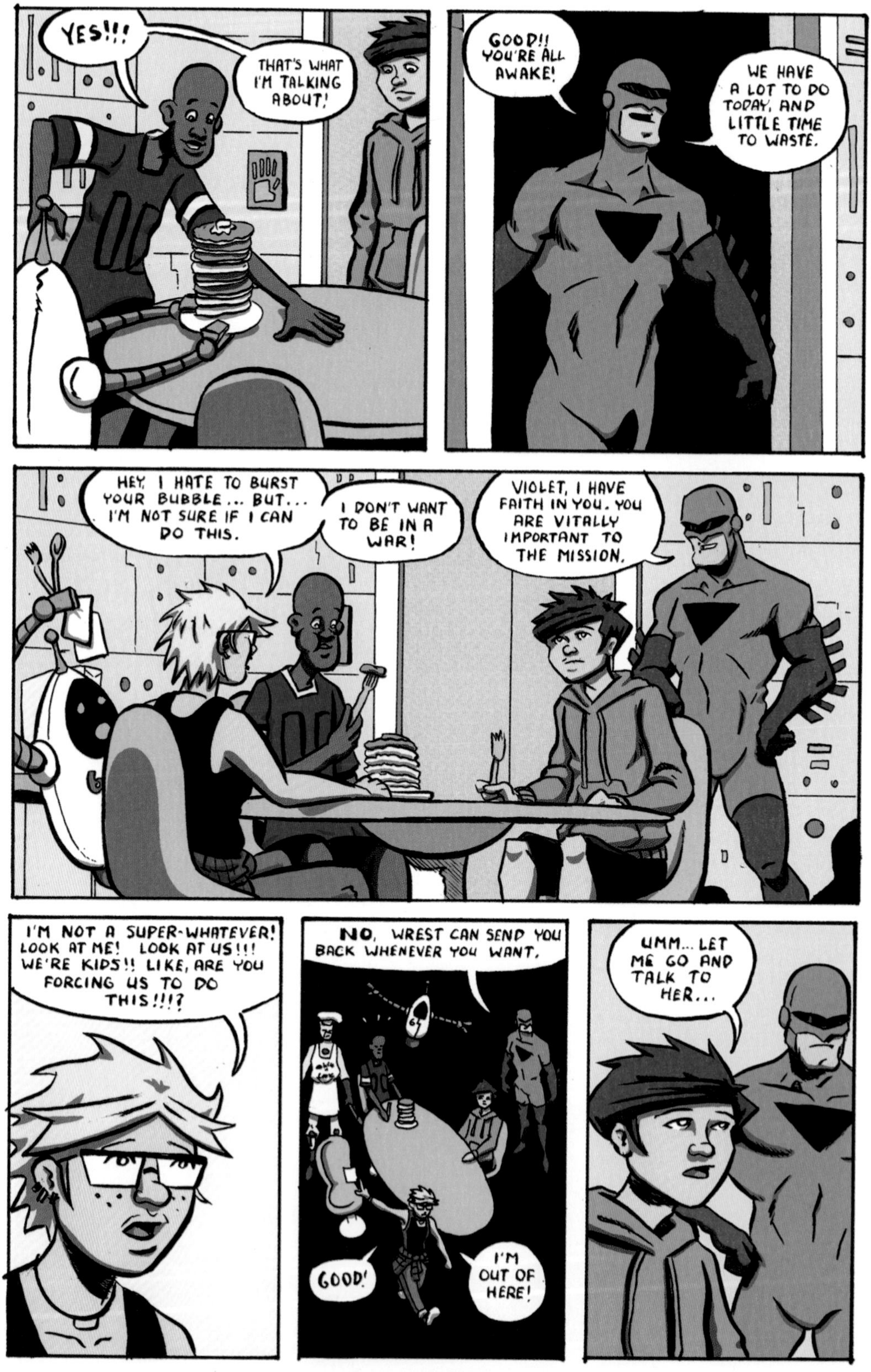
YES!!!
THAT'S WHAT I'M TALKING ABOUT!
GOOD!! YOU'RE ALL AWAKE!
WE HAVE A LOT TO DO TODAY, AND LITTLE TIME TO WASTE.
HEY, I HATE TO BURST YOUR BUBBLE... BUT... I'M NOT SURE IF I CAN DO THIS.
I DON'T WANT TO BE IN A WAR!
VIOLET, I HAVE FAITH IN YOU. YOU ARE VITALLY IMPORTANT TO THE MISSION.
I'M NOT A SUPER-WHATEVER! LOOK AT ME! LOOK AT US!!! WE'RE KIDS!! LIKE, ARE YOU FORCING US TO DO THIS!!!?
NO, WREST CAN SEND YOU BACK WHENEVER YOU WANT.
GOOD!
I'M OUT OF HERE!
UMM... LET ME GO AND TALK TO HER...

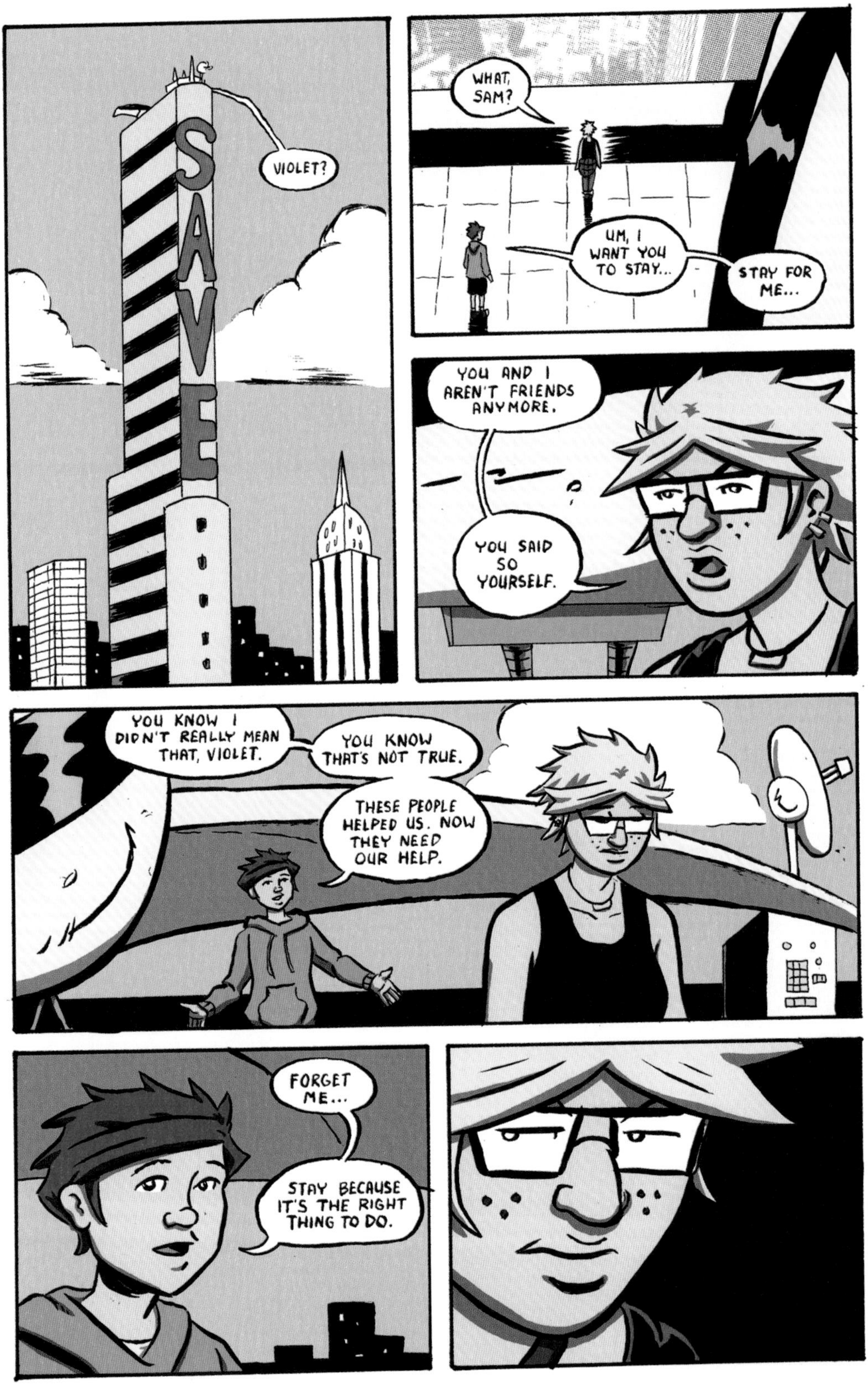
SAVE
VIOLET?
WHAT, SAM?
UM, I WANT YOU TO STAY...
STAY FOR ME...
YOU AND I AREN'T FRIENDS ANYMORE.
YOU SAID SO YOURSELF.
YOU KNOW I DIDN'T REALLY MEAN THAT, VIOLET.
YOU KNOW THAT'S NOT TRUE.
THESE PEOPLE HELPED US. NOW THEY NEED OUR HELP.
FORGET ME...
STAY BECAUSE IT'S THE RIGHT THING TO DO.

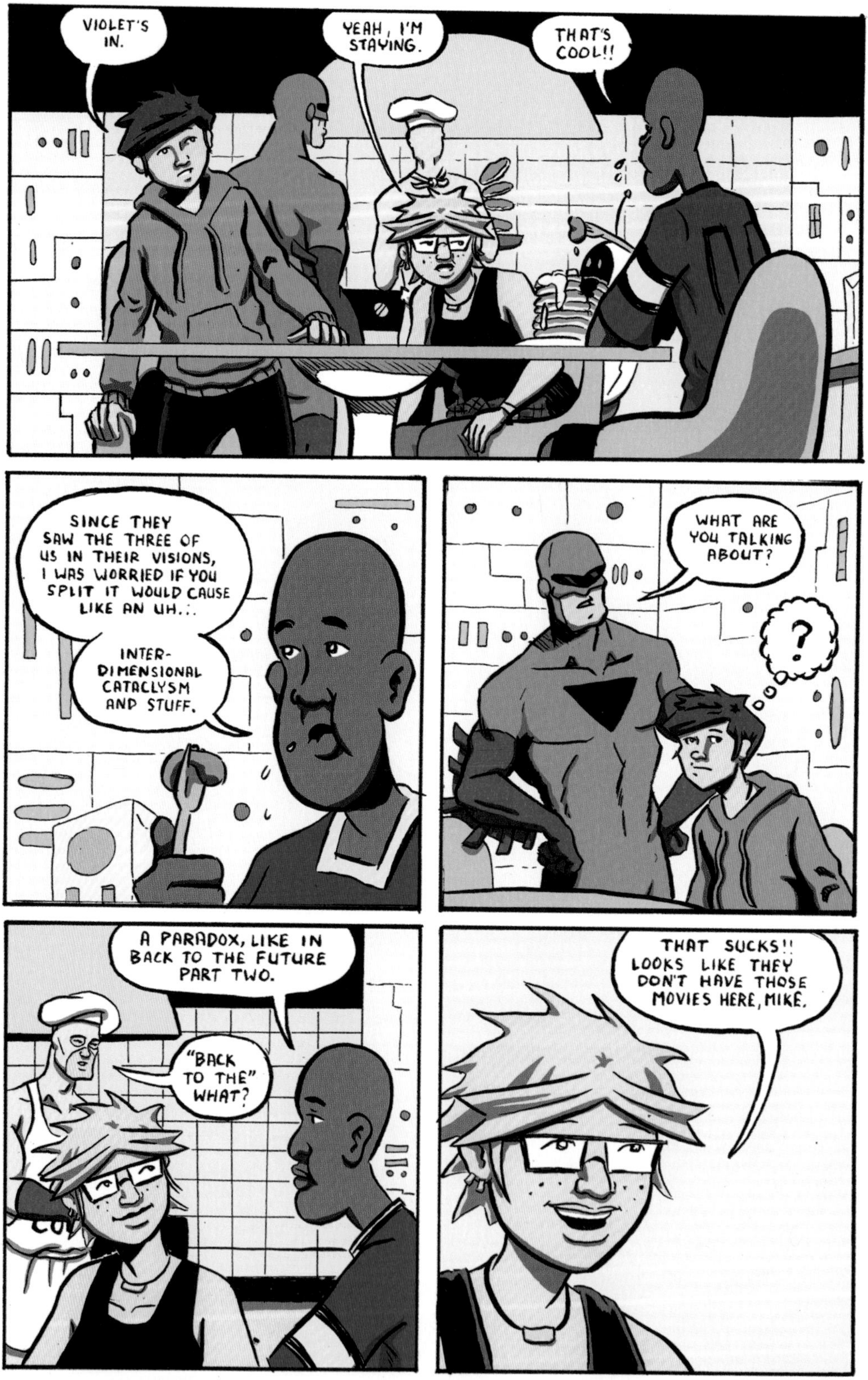
VIOLET'S IN.
YEAH, I'M STAYING.
THAT'S COOL!!
SINCE THEY SAW THE THREE OF US IN THEIR VISIONS, I WAS WORRIED IF YOU SPLIT IT WOULD CAUSE LIKE AN UH...
INTER-DIMENSIONAL CATACLYSM AND STUFF.
WHAT ARE YOU TALKING ABOUT?
?
A PARADOX, LIKE IN BACK TO THE FUTURE PART TWO.
"BACK TO THE" WHAT?
THAT SUCKS!! LOOKS LIKE THEY DON'T HAVE THOSE MOVIES HERE, MIKE.

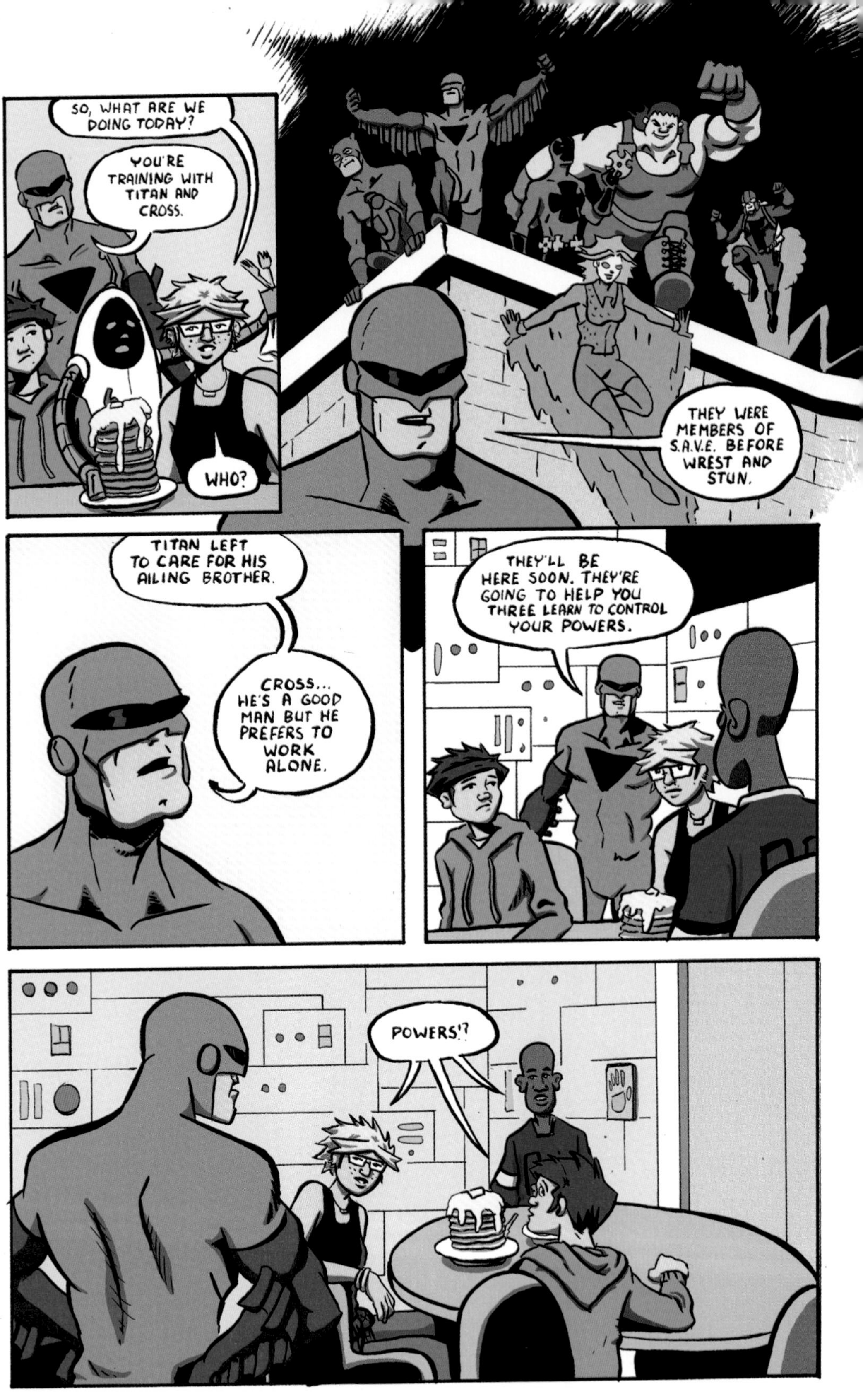
SO, WHAT ARE WE DOING TODAY?
YOU'RE TRAINING WITH TITAN AND CROSS.
WHO?
THEY WERE MEMBERS OF S.A.V.E. BEFORE WREST AND STUN.
TITAN LEFT TO CARE FOR HIS AILING BROTHER.
CROSS... HE'S A GOOD MAN BUT HE PREFERS TO WORK ALONE.
THEY'LL BE HERE SOON. THEY'RE GOING TO HELP YOU THREE LEARN TO CONTROL YOUR POWERS.
POWERS!?

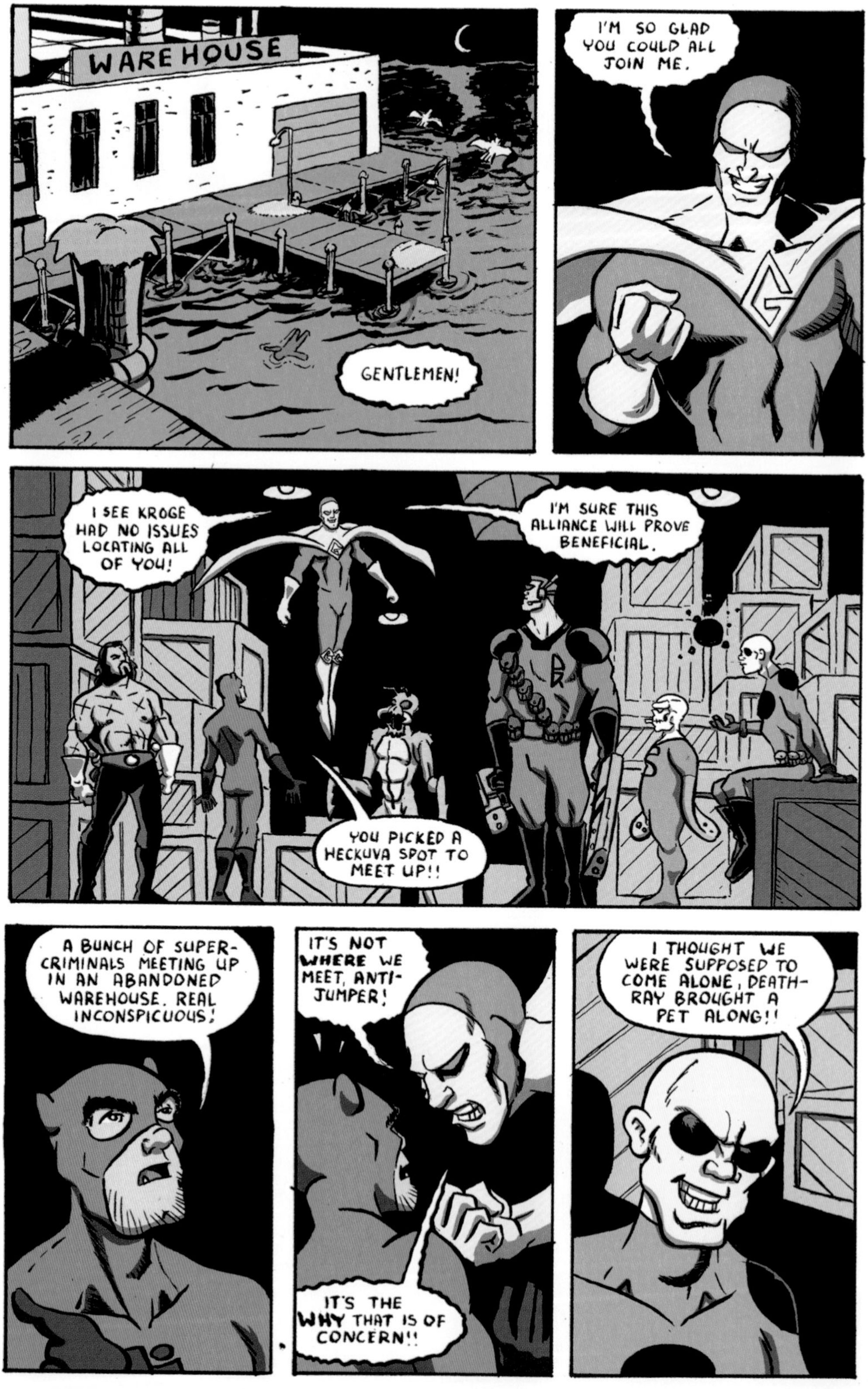
WAREHOUSE
GENTLEMEN!
I'M SO GLAD YOU COULD ALL JOIN ME.
I SEE KROGE HAD NO ISSUES LOCATING ALL OF YOU!
I'M SURE THIS ALLIANCE WILL PROVE BENEFICIAL.
YOU PICKED A HECKUVA SPOT TO MEET UP!!
A BUNCH OF SUPER-CRIMINALS MEETING UP IN AN ABANDONED WAREHOUSE. REAL INCONSPICUOUS!
IT'S NOT WHERE WE MEET, ANTI-JUMPER!
IT'S THE WHY THAT IS OF CONCERN!!
I THOUGHT WE WERE SUPPOSED TO COME ALONE, DEATH-RAY BROUGHT A PET ALONG!!

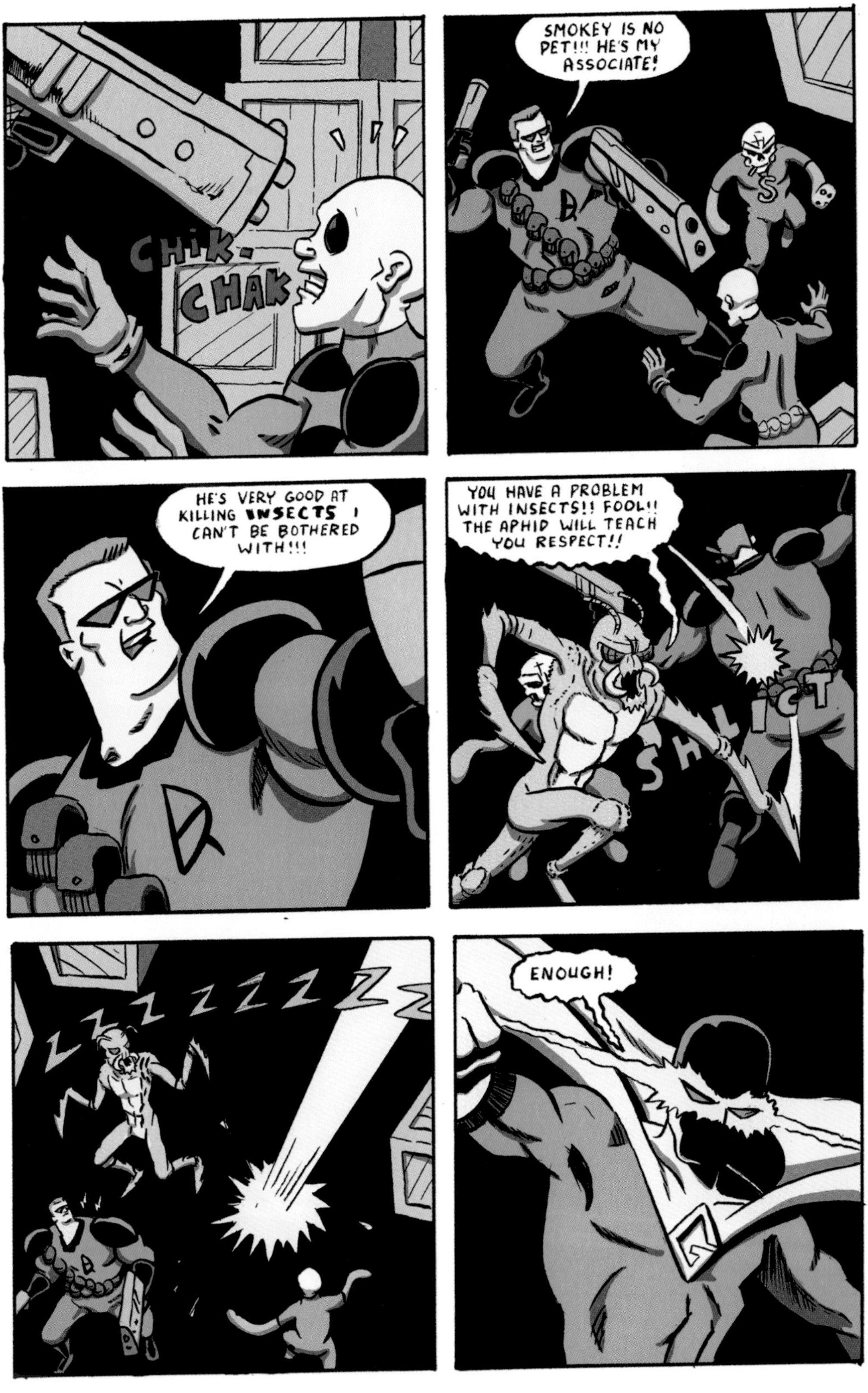
CHIK-CHAK
SMOKEY IS NO PET!!! HE'S MY ASSOCIATE!
HE'S VERY GOOD AT KILLING INSECTS I CAN'T BE BOTHERED WITH!!!
YOU HAVE A PROBLEM WITH INSECTS!! FOOL!! THE APHID WILL TEACH YOU RESPECT!!
SHLICT
ZZZZZZZZZ
ENOUGH!

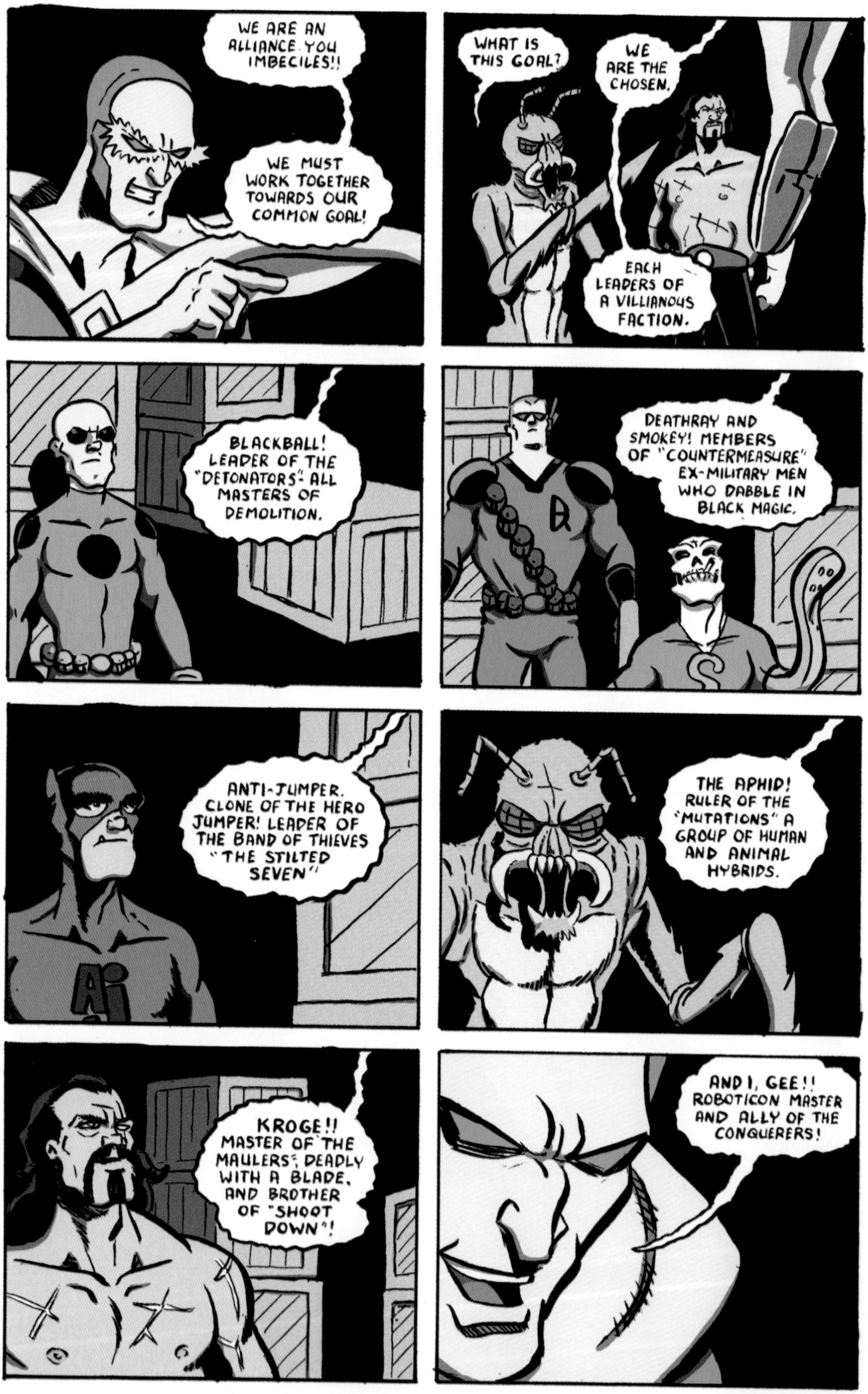
WE ARE AN ALLIANCE YOU IMBECILES!!
WE MUST WORK TOGETHER TOWARDS OUR COMMON GOAL!
WHAT IS THIS GOAL?
WE ARE THE CHOSEN.
EACH LEADERS OF A VILLIANOUS FACTION.
BLACKBALL! LEADER OF THE "DETONATORS" ALL MASTERS OF DEMOLITION.
DEATHRAY AND SMOKEY! MEMBERS OF "COUNTERMEASURE" EX-MILITARY MEN WHO DABBLE IN BLACK MAGIC.
ANTI-JUMPER. CLONE OF THE HERO JUMPER! LEADER OF THE BAND OF THIEVES "THE STILTED SEVEN"
THE APHID! RULER OF THE "MUTATIONS" A GROUP OF HUMAN AND ANIMAL HYBRIDS.
KROGE!! MASTER OF THE MAULERS", DEADLY WITH A BLADE, AND BROTHER OF "SHOOT DOWN"!
AND I, GEE!! ROBOTICON MASTER AND ALLY OF THE CONQUERERS!

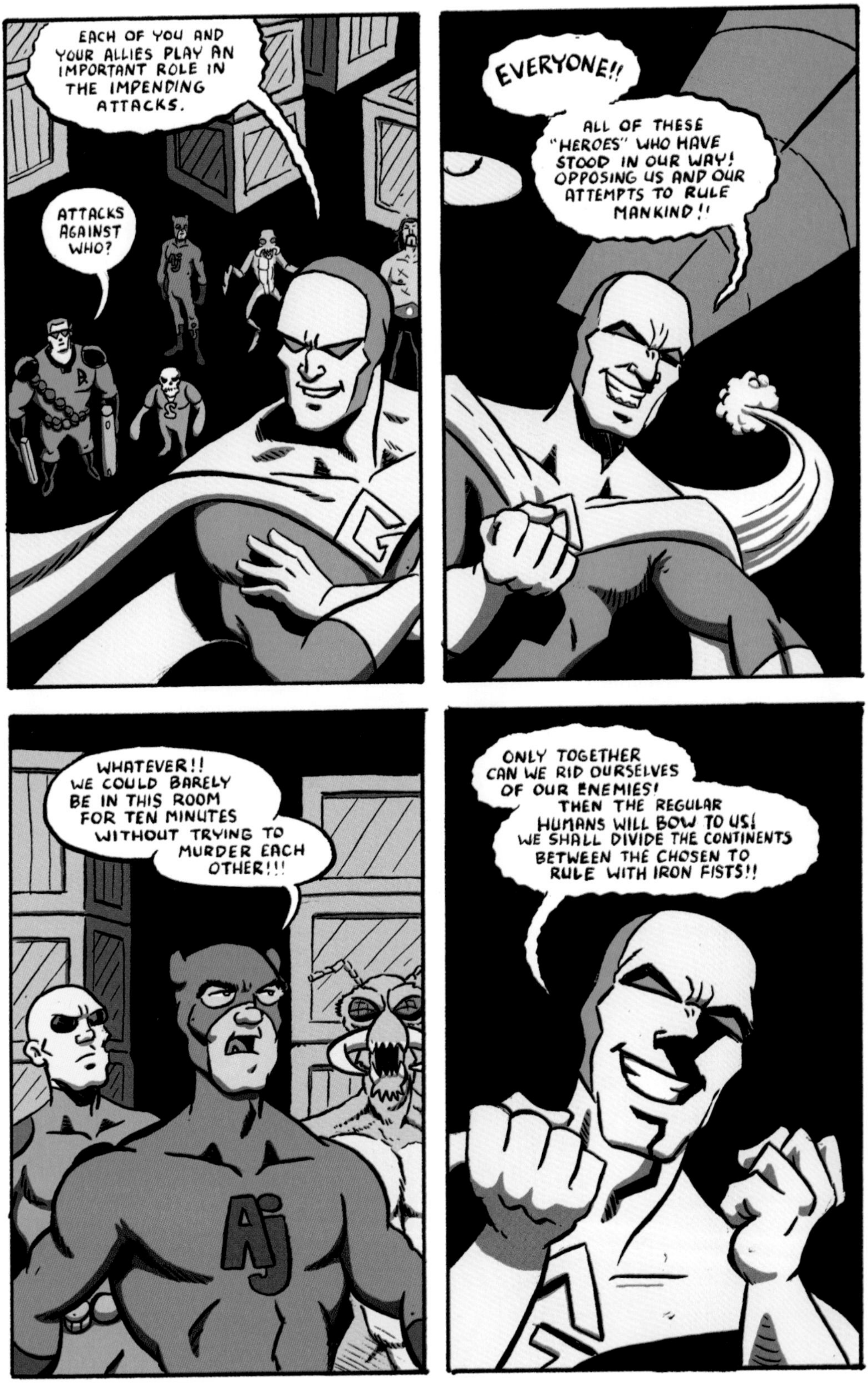

EACH OF YOU AND YOUR ALLIES PLAY AN IMPORTANT ROLE IN THE IMPENDING ATTACKS.
ATTACKS AGAINST WHO?
EVERYONE!!
ALL OF THESE "HEROES" WHO HAVE STOOD IN OUR WAY! OPPOSING US AND OUR ATTEMPTS TO RULE MANKIND!!
WHATEVER!! WE COULD BARELY BE IN THIS ROOM FOR TEN MINUTES WITHOUT TRYING TO MURDER EACH OTHER!!!
ONLY TOGETHER CAN WE RID OURSELVES OF OUR ENEMIES! THEN THE REGULAR HUMANS WILL BOW TO US! WE SHALL DIVIDE THE CONTINENTS BETWEEN THE CHOSEN TO RULE WITH IRON FISTS!!

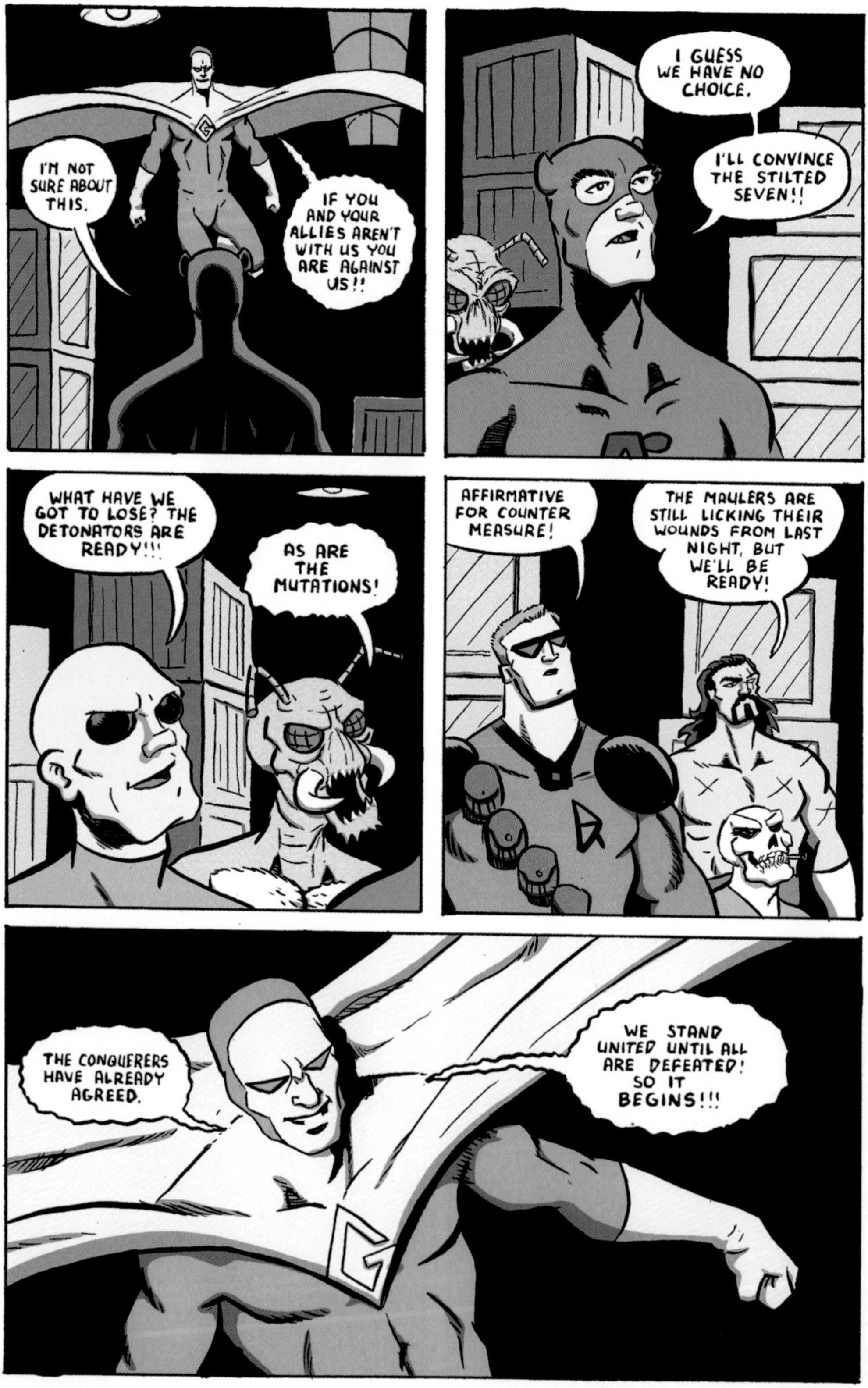
I'M NOT SURE ABOUT THIS.
IF YOU AND YOUR ALLIES AREN'T WITH US YOU ARE AGAINST US!!
I GUESS WE HAVE NO CHOICE.
I'LL CONVINCE THE STILTED SEVEN!!
WHAT HAVE WE GOT TO LOSE? THE DETONATORS ARE READY!!!
AS ARE THE MUTATIONS!
AFFIRMATIVE FOR COUNTER MEASURE!
THE MAULERS ARE STILL LICKING THEIR WOUNDS FROM LAST NIGHT, BUT WE'LL BE READY!
THE CONQUERERS HAVE ALREADY AGREED.
WE STAND UNITED UNTIL ALL ARE DEFEATED! SO IT BEGINS!!!

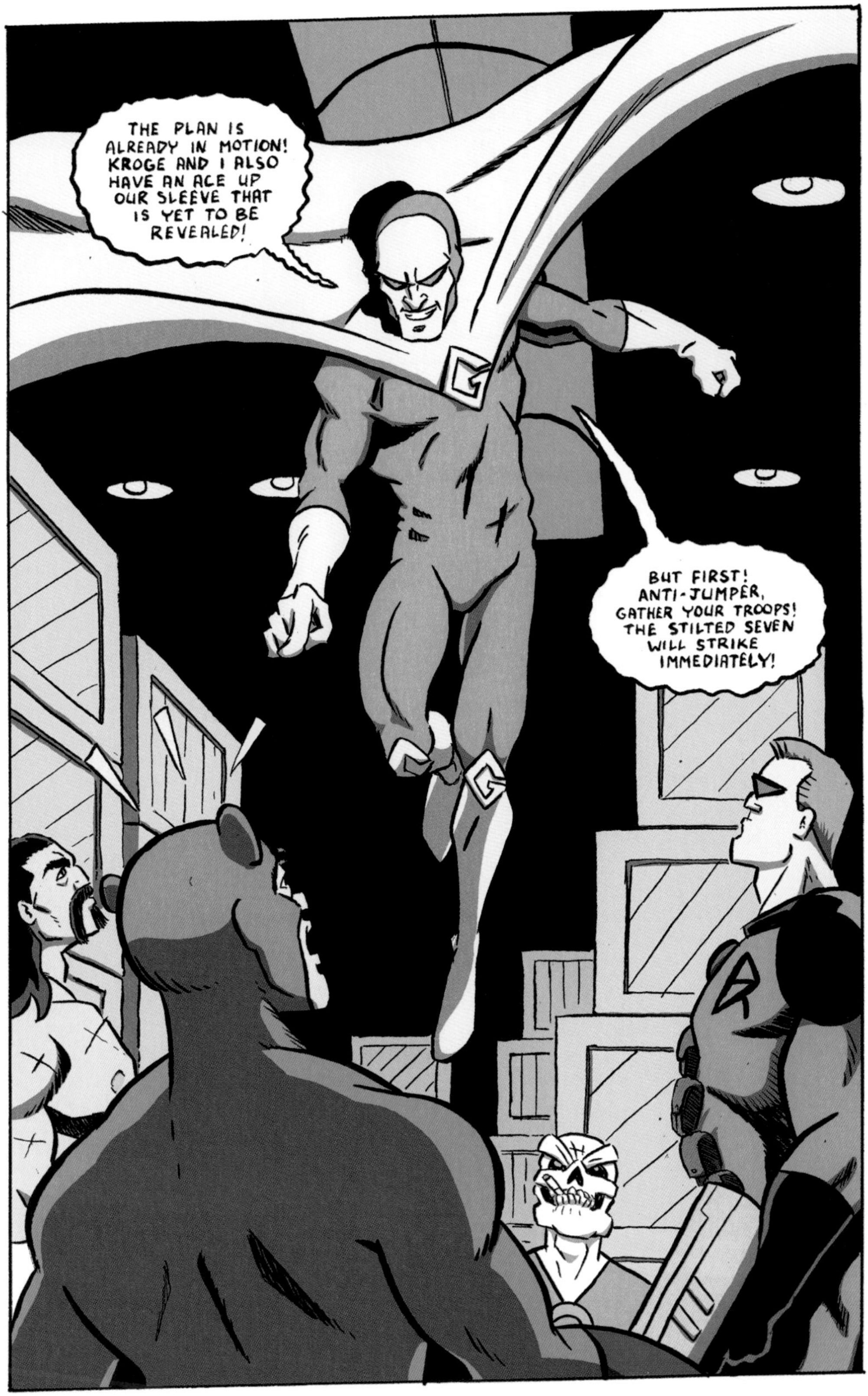
THE PLAN IS ALREADY IN MOTION! KROGE AND I ALSO HAVE AN ACE UP OUR SLEEVE THAT IS YET TO BE REVEALED!
BUT FIRST! ANTI-JUMPER, GATHER YOUR TROOPS! THE STILTED SEVEN WILL STRIKE IMMEDIATELY!

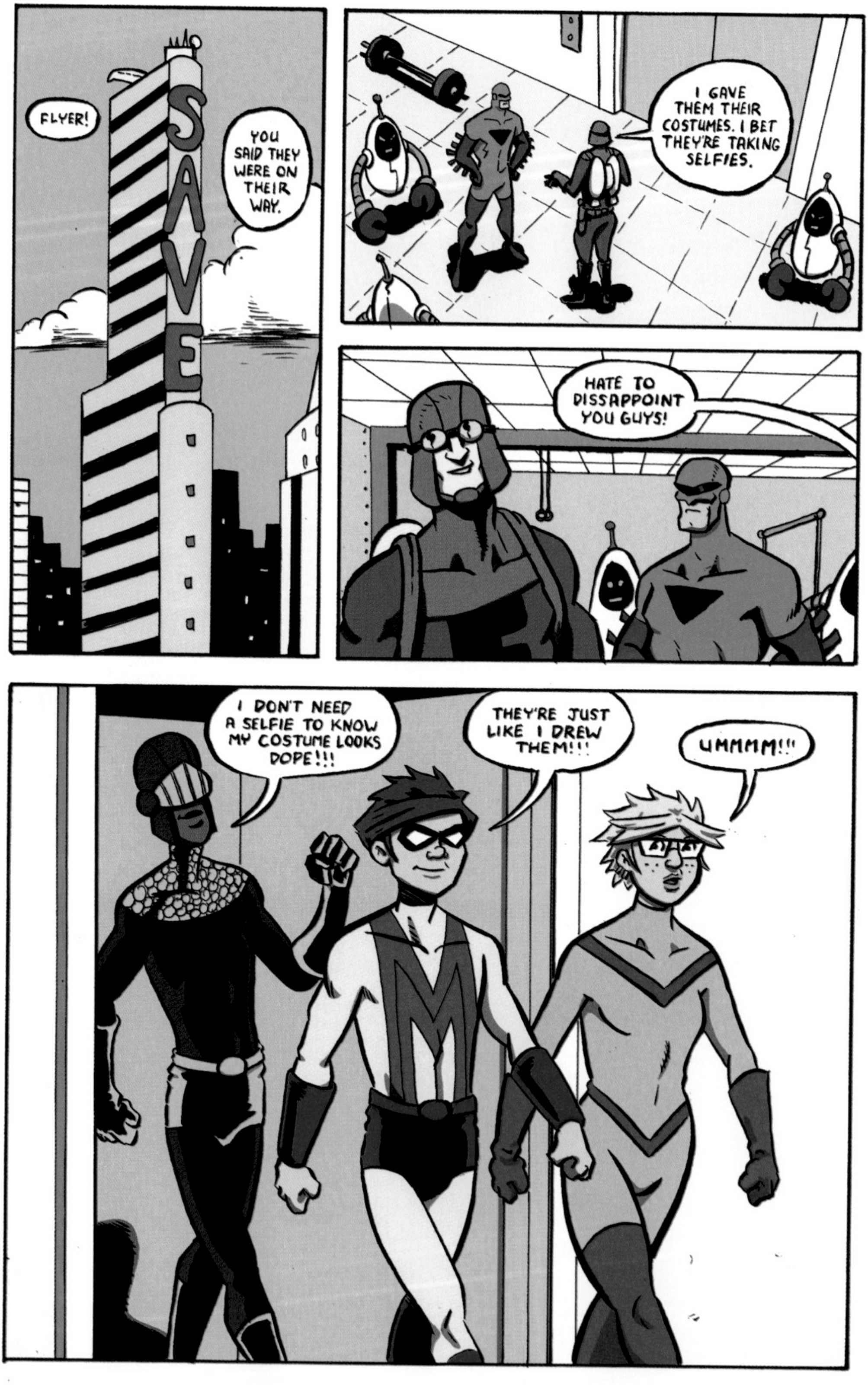
FLYER!
YOU SAID THEY WERE ON THEIR WAY.
I GAVE THEM THEIR COSTUMES. I BET THEY'RE TAKING SELFIES.
HATE TO DISSAPPOINT YOU GUYS!
I DON'T NEED A SELFIE TO KNOW MY COSTUME LOOKS DOPE!!!
THEY'RE JUST LIKE I DREW THEM!!!
UMMMM!!!

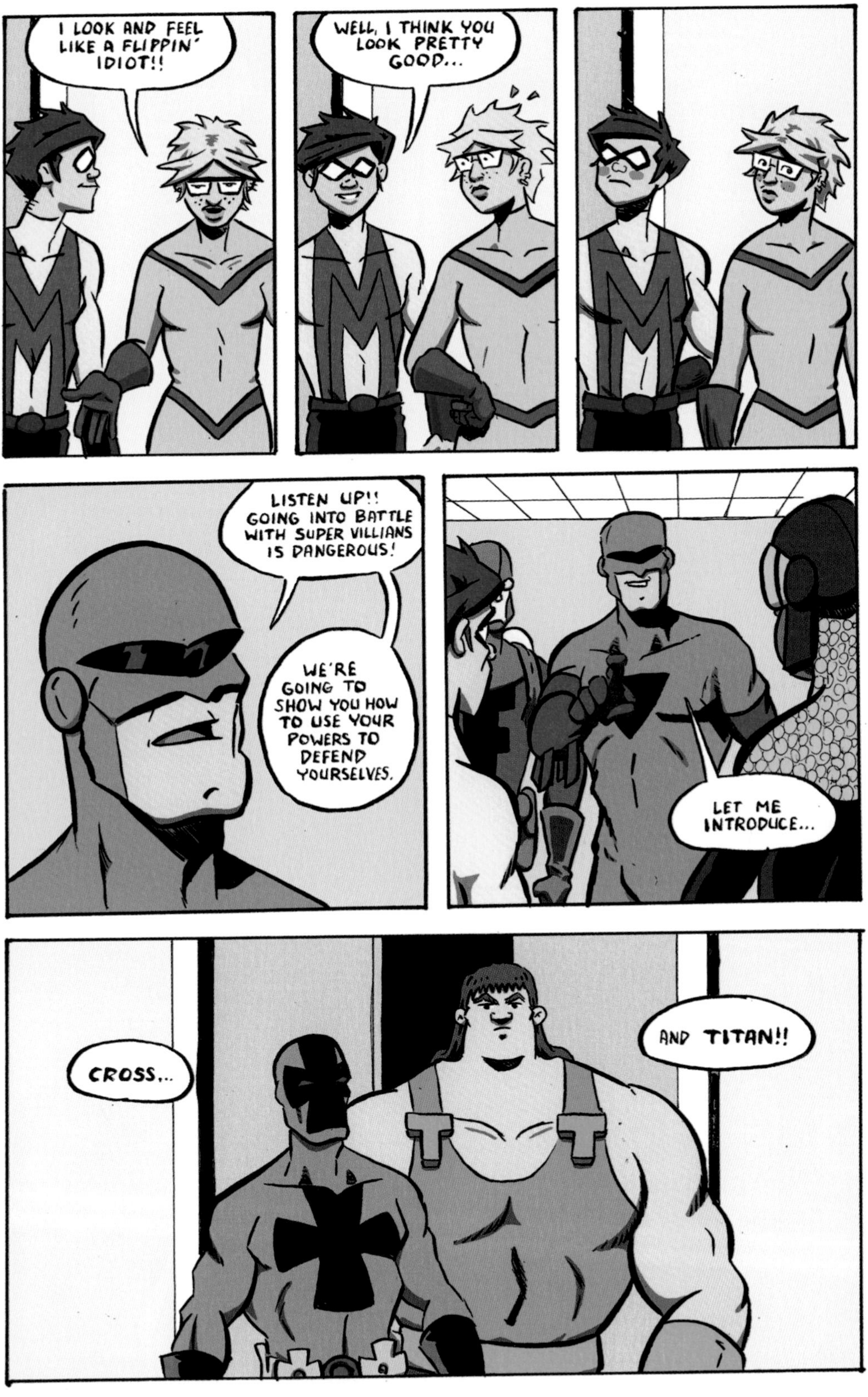
I LOOK AND FEEL LIKE A FLIPPIN' IDIOT!!
WELL, I THINK YOU LOOK PRETTY GOOD...
LISTEN UP!! GOING INTO BATTLE WITH SUPER VILLIANS IS DANGEROUS!
WE'RE GOING TO SHOW YOU HOW TO USE YOUR POWERS TO DEFEND YOURSELVES.
LET ME INTRODUCE...
CROSS...
AND TITAN!!

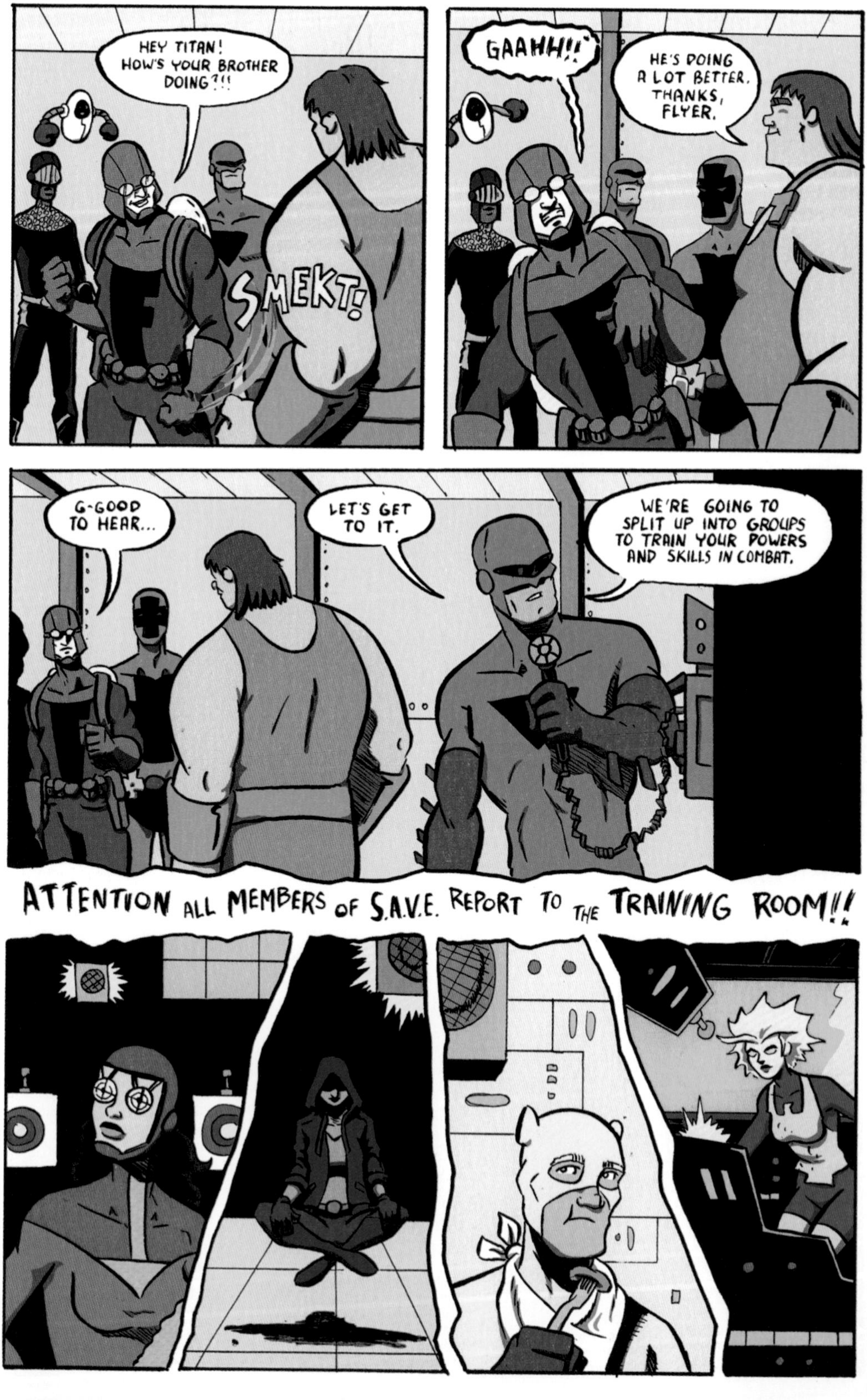
HEY TITAN! HOW'S YOUR BROTHER DOING?!!
SMEKT!
GAAHH!!
HE'S DOING A LOT BETTER. THANKS, FLYER.
G-GOOD TO HEAR...
LET'S GET TO IT.
WE'RE GOING TO SPLIT UP INTO GROUPS TO TRAIN YOUR POWERS AND SKILLS IN COMBAT.
ATTENTION ALL MEMBERS OF S.A.V.E. REPORT TO THE TRAINING ROOM!!

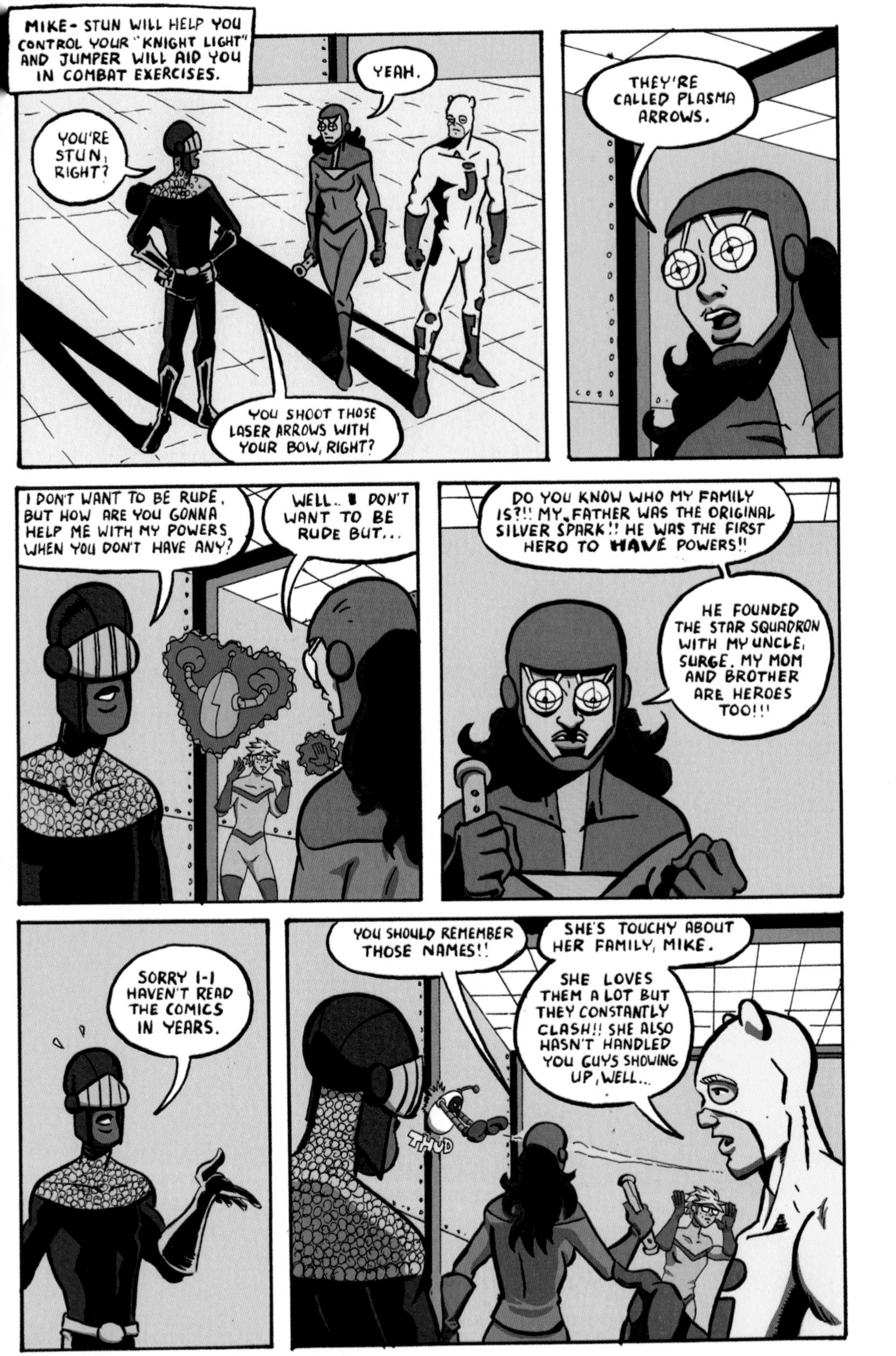
MIKE- STUN WILL HELP YOU CONTROL YOUR "KNIGHT LIGHT" AND JUMPER WILL AID YOU IN COMBAT EXERCISES.
YOU'RE STUN, RIGHT?
YEAH.
YOU SHOOT THOSE LASER ARROWS WITH YOUR BOW, RIGHT?
THEY'RE CALLED PLASMA ARROWS.
I DON'T WANT TO BE RUDE, BUT HOW ARE YOU GONNA HELP ME WITH MY POWERS WHEN YOU DON'T HAVE ANY?
WELL.. I DON'T WANT TO BE RUDE BUT...
DO YOU KNOW WHO MY FAMILY IS?!! MY FATHER WAS THE ORIGINAL SILVER SPARK!! HE WAS THE FIRST HERO TO HAVE POWERS!!
HE FOUNDED THE STAR SQUADRON WITH MY UNCLE, SURGE. MY MOM AND BROTHER ARE HEROES TOO!!!
SORRY I-I HAVEN'T READ THE COMICS IN YEARS.
YOU SHOULD REMEMBER THOSE NAMES!!
SHE'S TOUCHY ABOUT HER FAMILY, MIKE.
SHE LOVES THEM A LOT BUT THEY CONSTANTLY CLASH!! SHE ALSO HASN'T HANDLED YOU GUYS SHOWING UP, WELL...
THUD

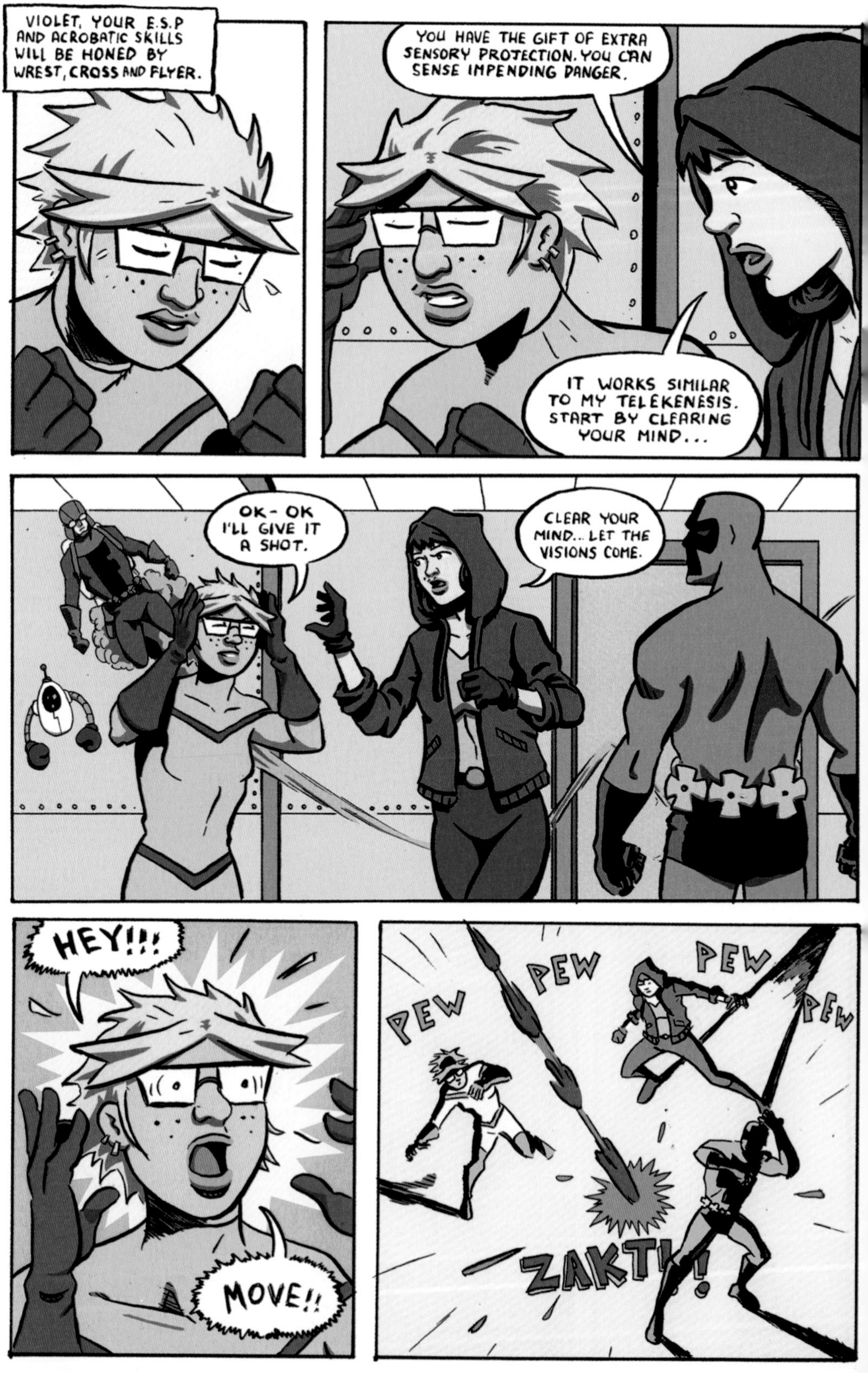
VIOLET, YOUR E.S.P AND ACROBATIC SKILLS WILL BE HONED BY WREST, CROSS AND FLYER.
YOU HAVE THE GIFT OF EXTRA SENSORY PROTECTION. YOU CAN SENSE IMPENDING DANGER.
IT WORKS SIMILAR TO MY TELEKENESIS. START BY CLEARING YOUR MIND...
OK- OK I'LL GIVE IT A SHOT.
CLEAR YOUR MIND... LET THE VISIONS COME.
HEY!!!
MOVE!!
PEW
PEW
PEW
PEW
ZAKT!!

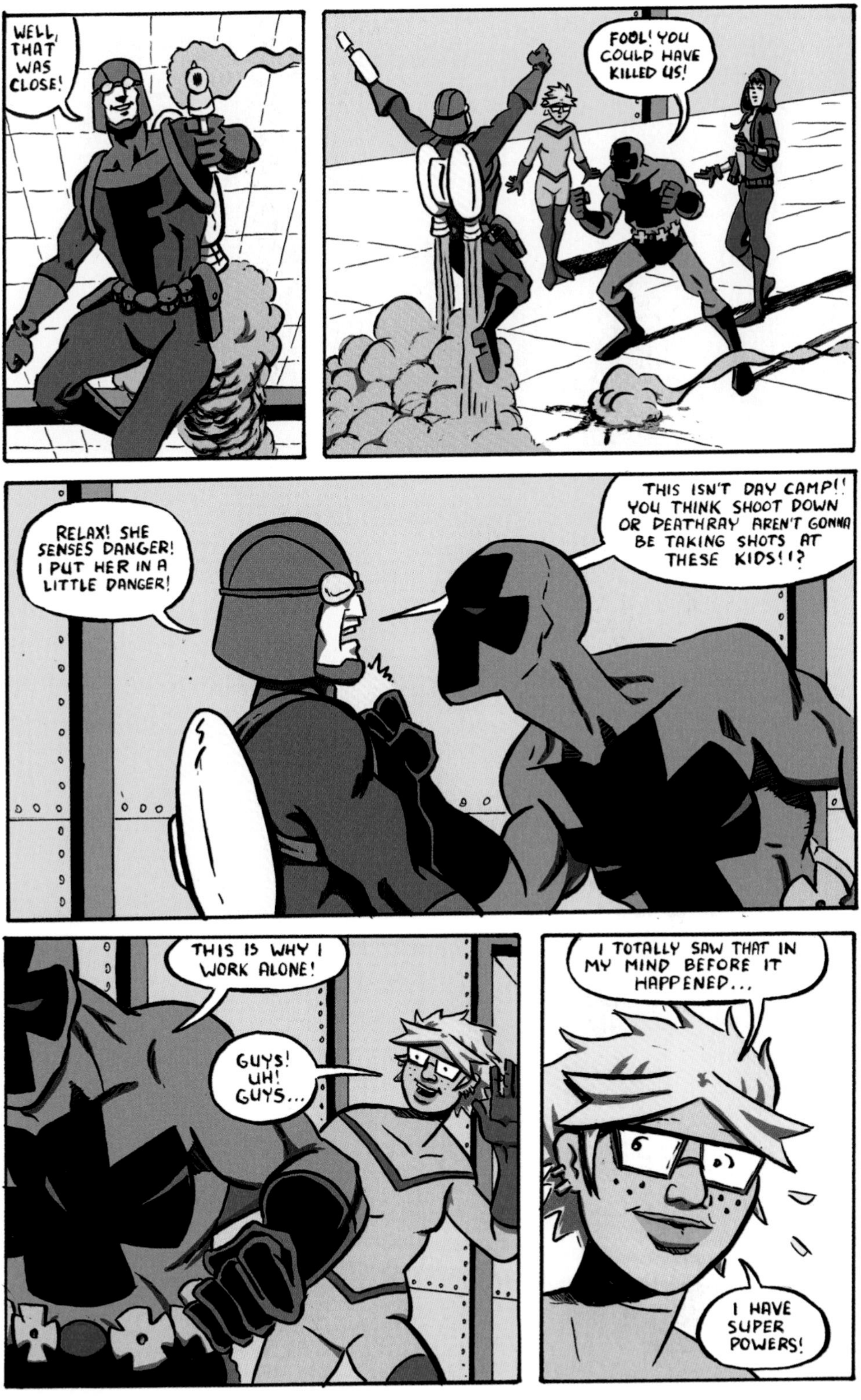
WELL, THAT WAS CLOSE!
FOOL! YOU COULD HAVE KILLED US!
RELAX! SHE SENSES DANGER! I PUT HER IN A LITTLE DANGER!
THIS ISN'T DAY CAMP!! YOU THINK SHOOT DOWN OR DEATHRAY AREN'T GONNA BE TAKING SHOTS AT THESE KIDS!!?
THIS IS WHY I WORK ALONE!
GUYS! UH! GUYS...
I TOTALLY SAW THAT IN MY MIND BEFORE IT HAPPENED...
I HAVE SUPER POWERS!

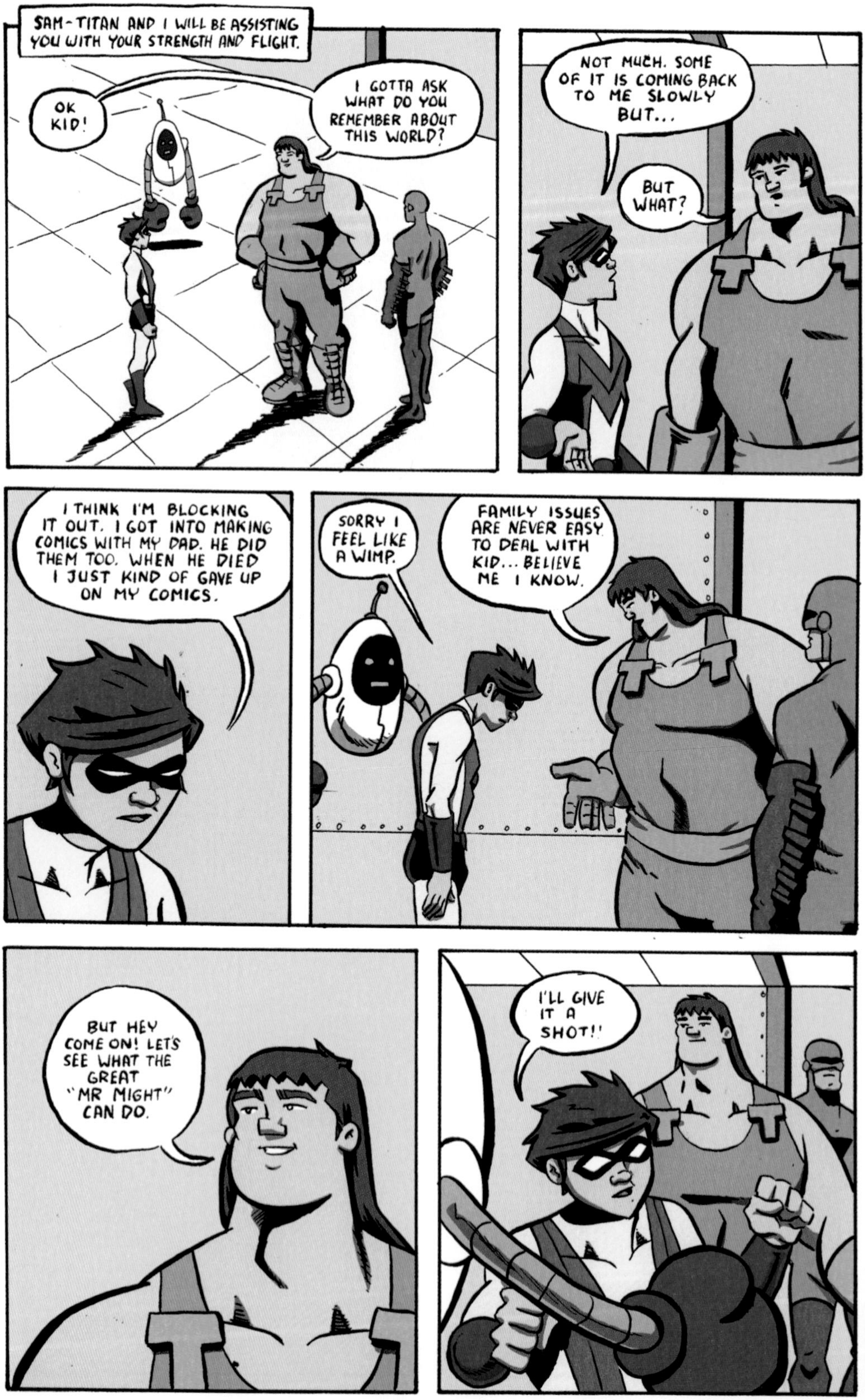
SAM-TITAN AND I WILL BE ASSISTING YOU WITH YOUR STRENGTH AND FLIGHT.
OK KID!
I GOTTA ASK WHAT DO YOU REMEMBER ABOUT THIS WORLD?
NOT MUCH. SOME OF IT IS COMING BACK TO ME SLOWLY BUT...
BUT WHAT?
I THINK I'M BLOCKING IT OUT. I GOT INTO MAKING COMICS WITH MY DAD. HE DID THEM TOO. WHEN HE DIED I JUST KIND OF GAVE UP ON MY COMICS.
SORRY I FEEL LIKE A WIMP.
FAMILY ISSUES ARE NEVER EASY TO DEAL WITH KID... BELIEVE ME I KNOW.
BUT HEY COME ON! LET'S SEE WHAT THE GREAT "MR MIGHT" CAN DO.
I'LL GIVE IT A SHOT!!

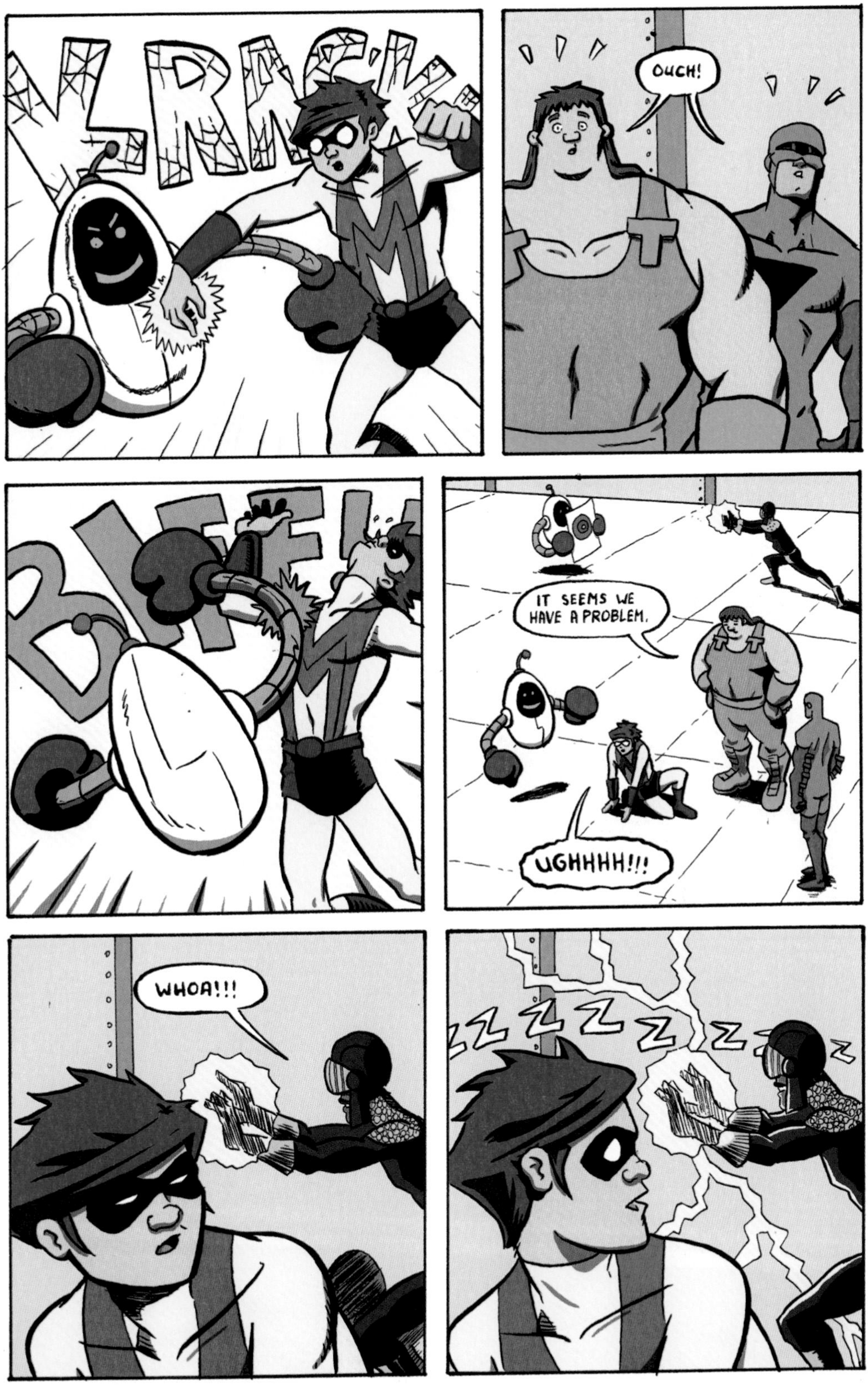
KRACK
OUCH!
IT SEEMS WE HAVE A PROBLEM.
UGHHHH!!!
WHOA!!!
ZZZZZZZZ

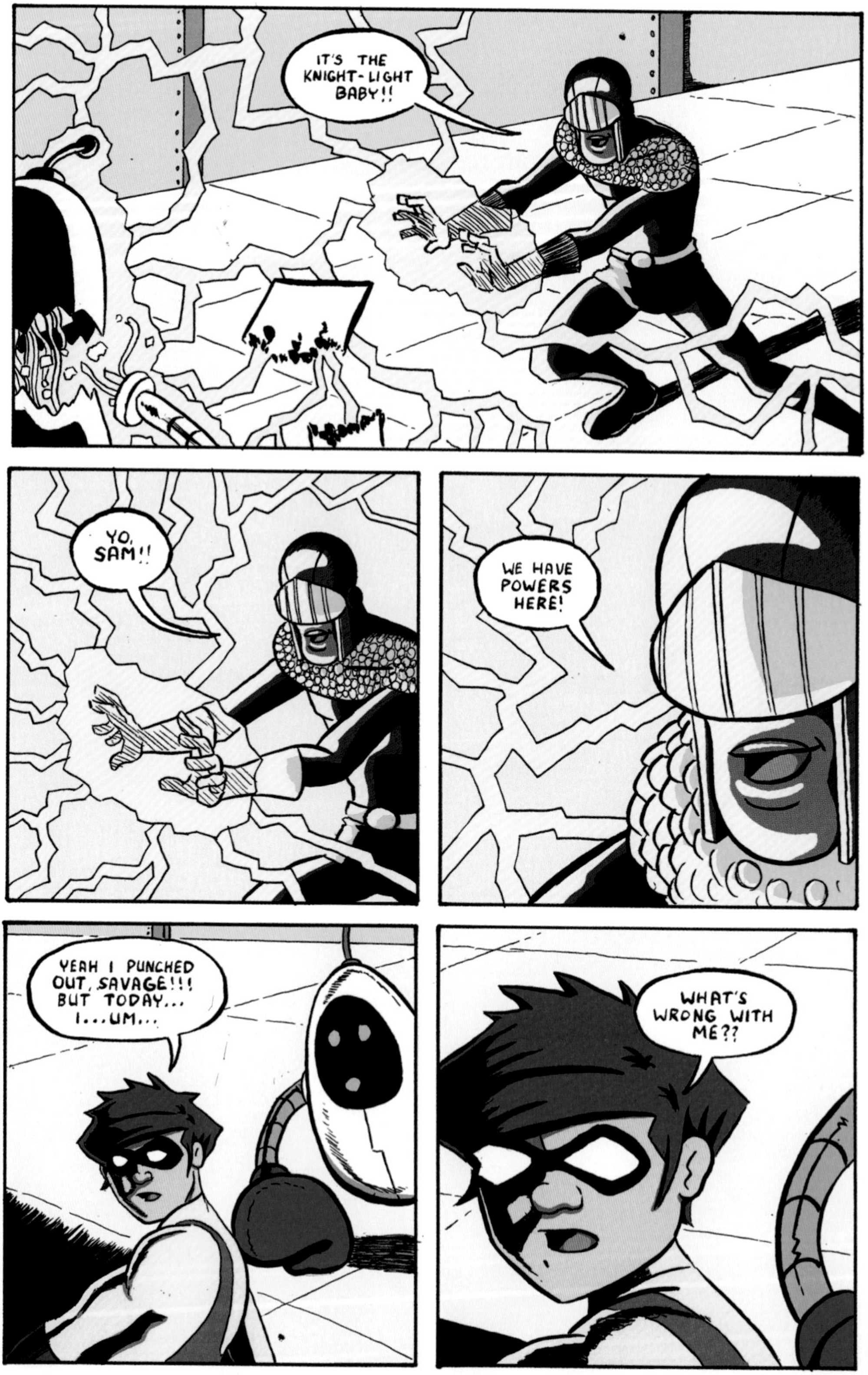
IT'S THE KNIGHT-LIGHT BABY!!
YO, SAM!!
WE HAVE POWERS HERE!
YEAH I PUNCHED OUT, SAVAGE!!! BUT TODAY... I...UM...
WHAT'S WRONG WITH ME??

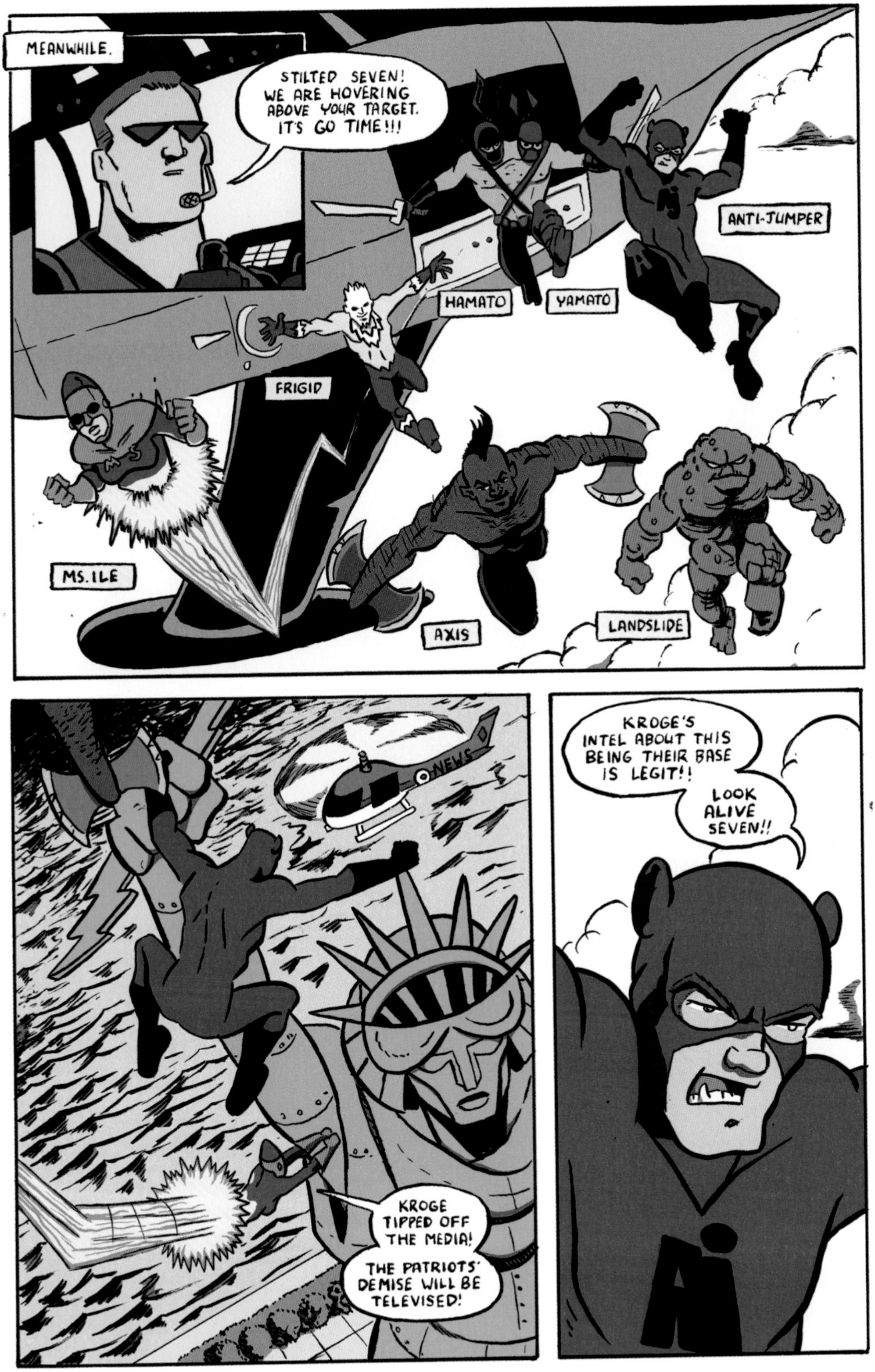

MEANWHILE.
STILTED SEVEN! WE ARE HOVERING ABOVE YOUR TARGET. IT'S GO TIME!!!
ANTI-JUMPER
HAMATO
YAMATO
FRIGID
MS.ILE
AXIS
LANDSLIDE
NEWS
KROGE TIPPED OFF THE MEDIA!
THE PATRIOTS' DEMISE WILL BE TELEVISED!
KROGE'S INTEL ABOUT THIS BEING THEIR BASE IS LEGIT!!
LOOK ALIVE SEVEN!!

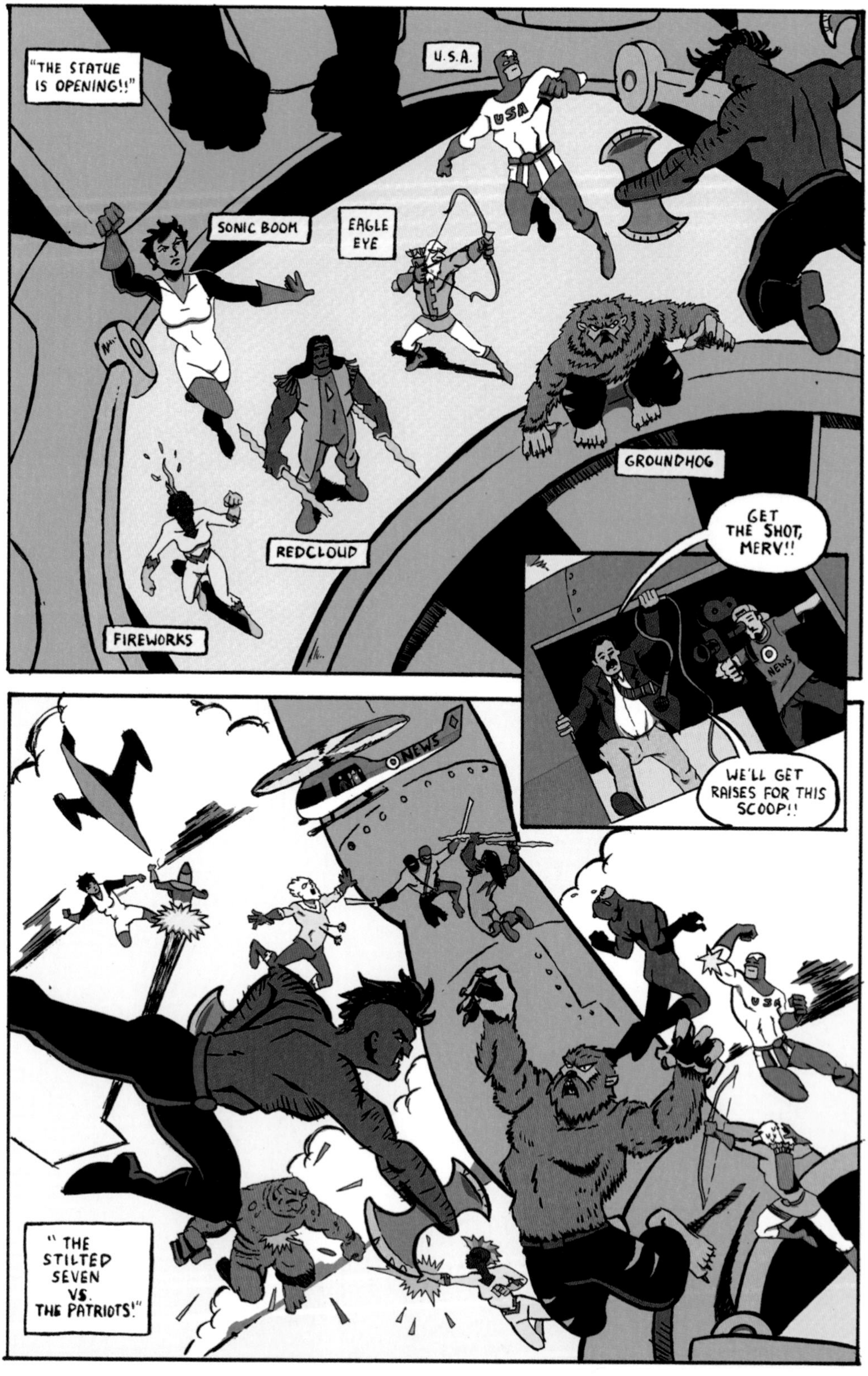
"THE STATUE IS OPENING!!"
U.S.A.
SONIC BOOM
EAGLE EYE
GROUNDHOG
REDCLOUD
FIREWORKS
GET THE SHOT, MERV!!
WE'LL GET RAISES FOR THIS SCOOP!!
NEWS
"THE STILTED SEVEN VS. THE PATRIOTS!"

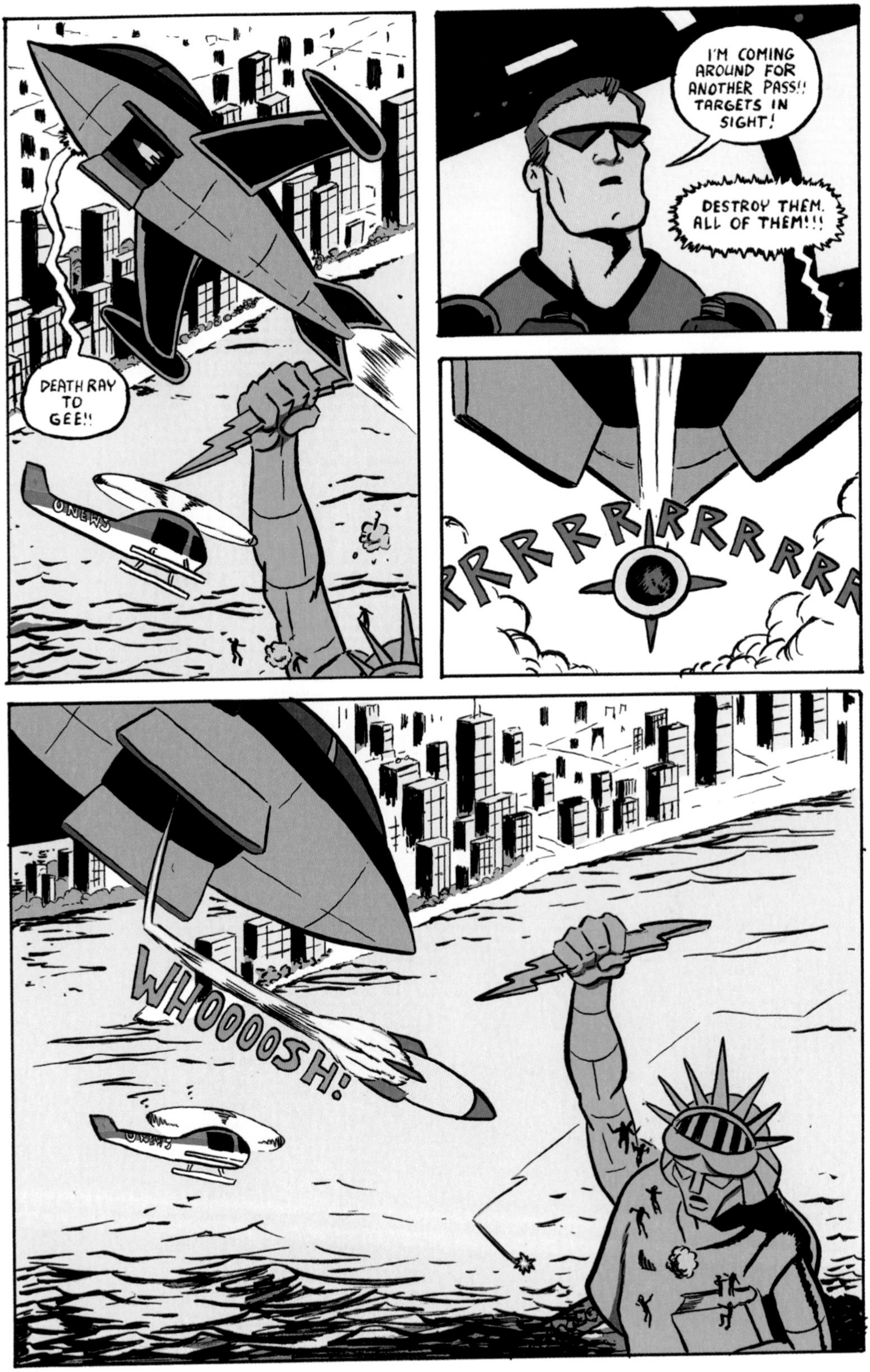
DEATH RAY TO GEE!!
I'M COMING AROUND FOR ANOTHER PASS!! TARGETS IN SIGHT!
DESTROY THEM. ALL OF THEM!!!
RRRRRRRRRRR
WHOOOOOSH!

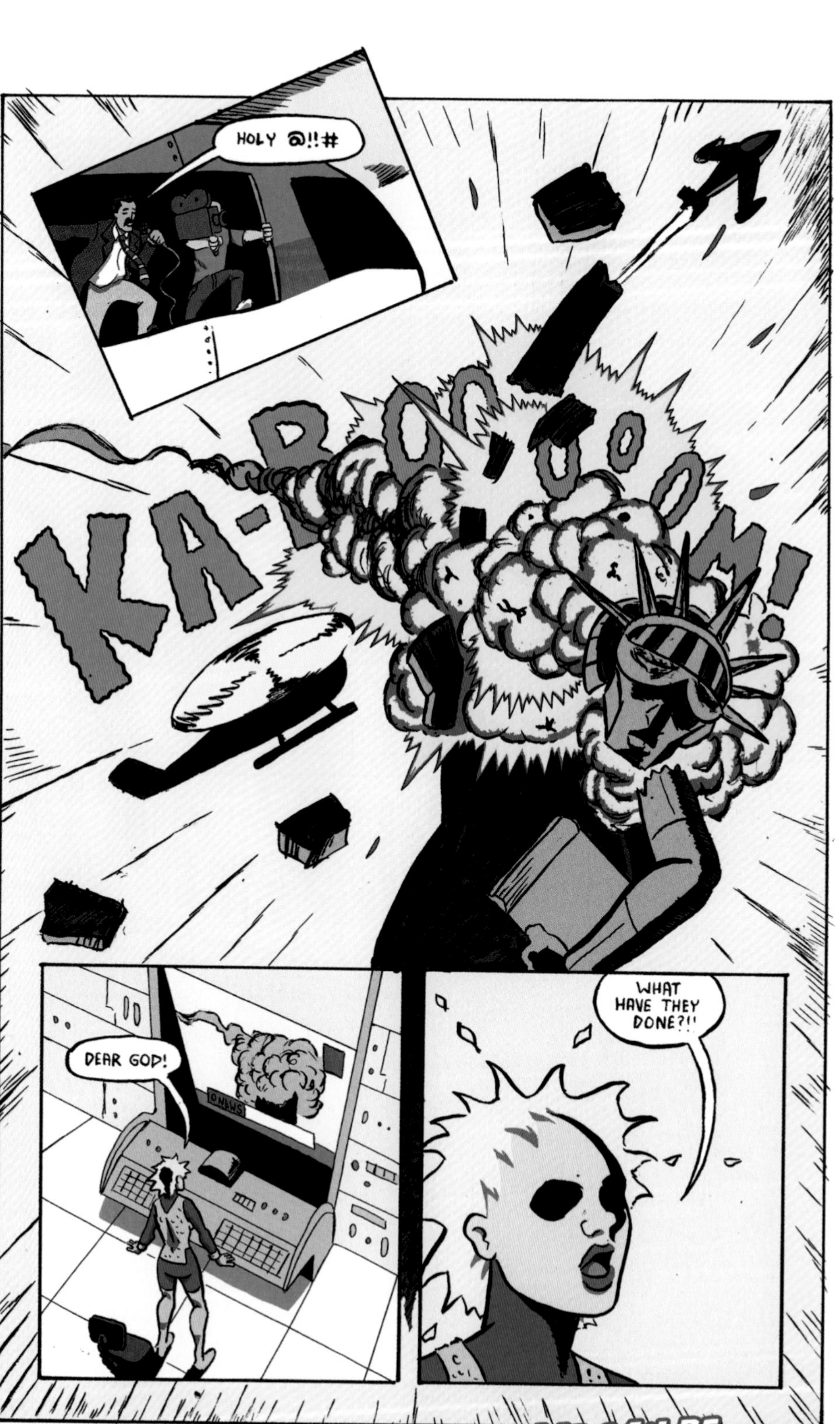

HOLY @!!#
KA-BOOOOOOM!
DEAR GOD!
ONEWS
WHAT HAVE THEY DONE?!!

NEXT: --WE CAN BE HEROES!

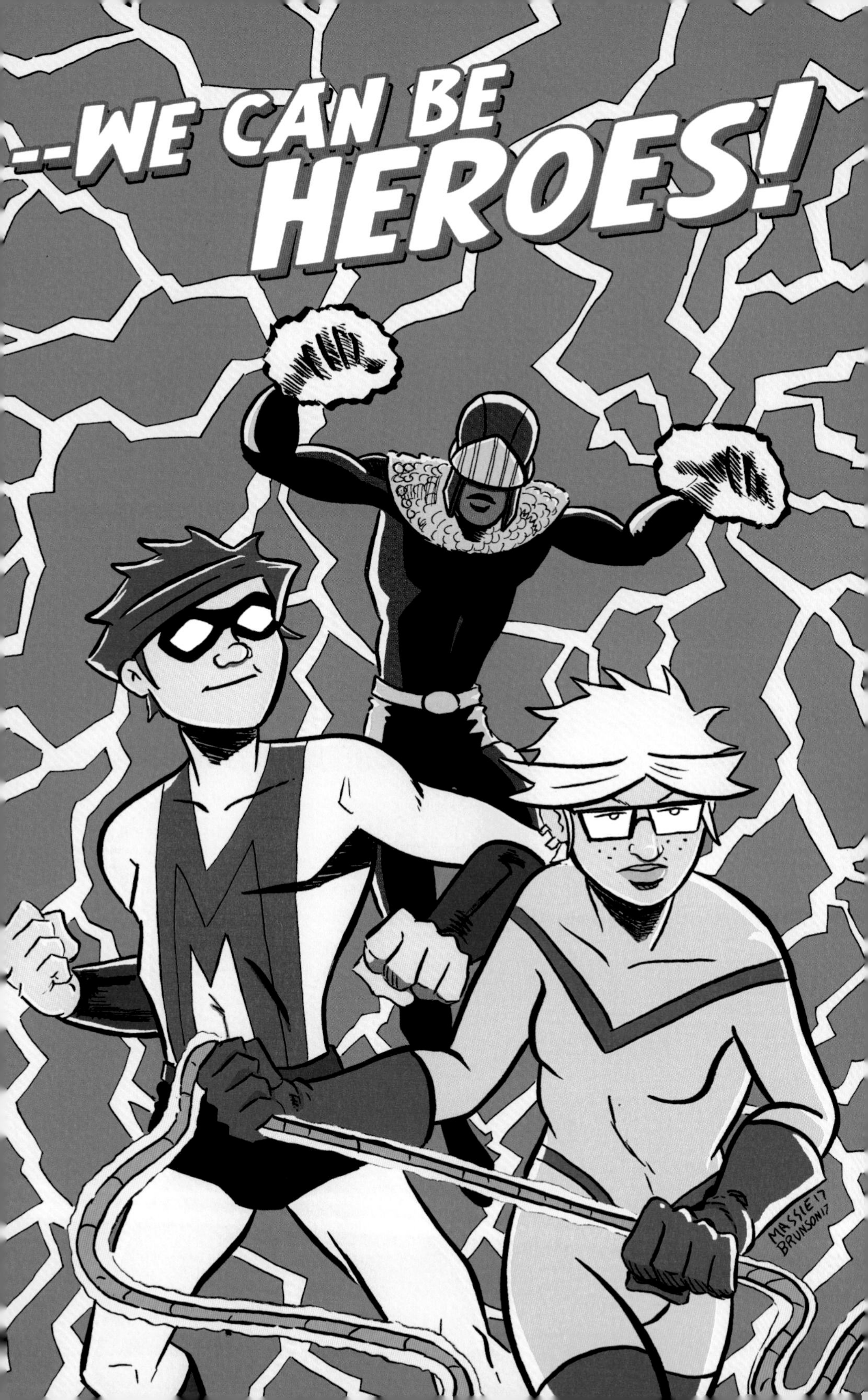
--WE CAN BE
HEROES!
MASSIE17
BRUNSON17

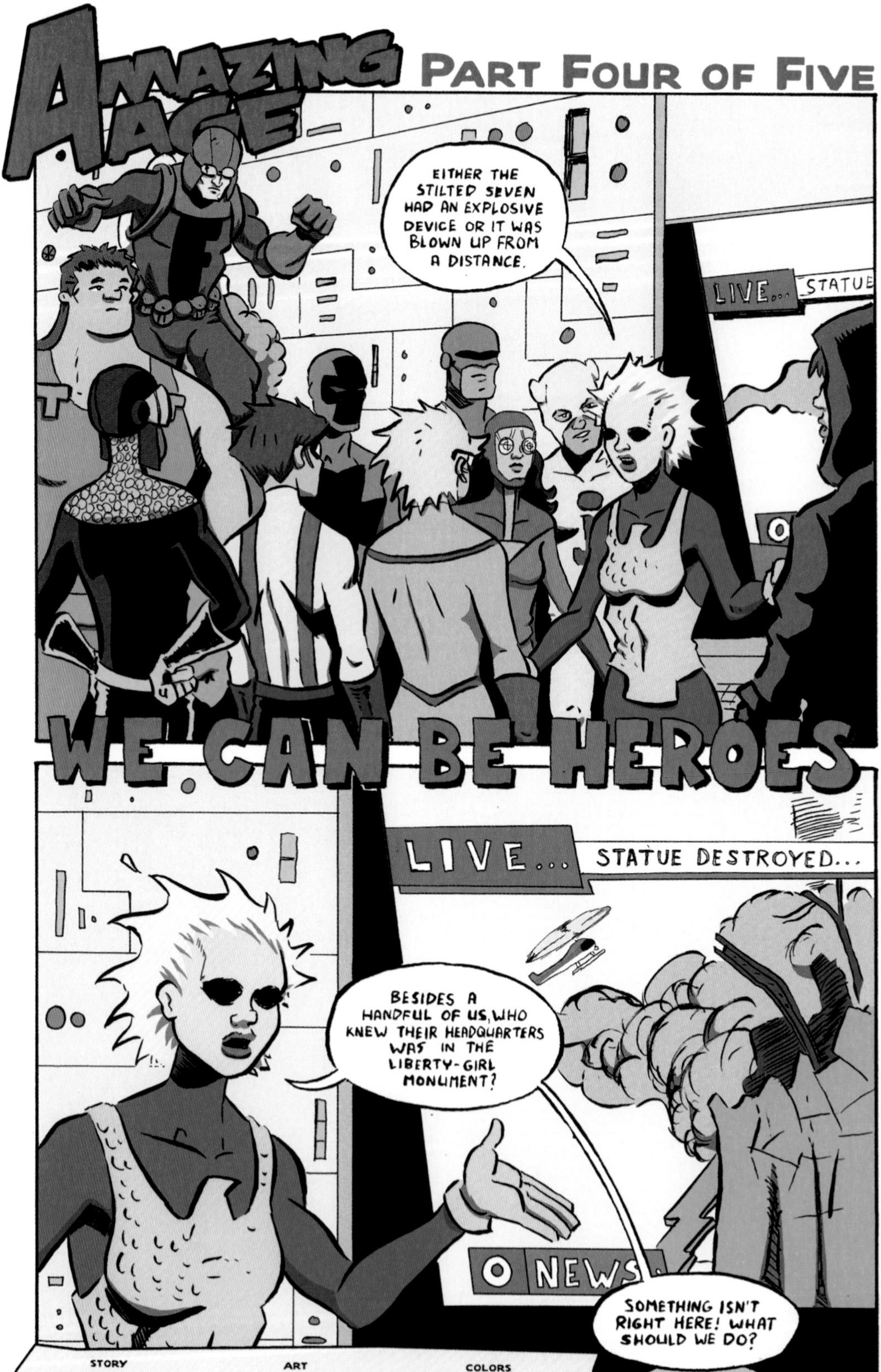
AMAZING AGE
PART FOUR OF FIVE
EITHER THE STILTED SEVEN HAD AN EXPLOSIVE DEVICE OR IT WAS BLOWN UP FROM A DISTANCE.
LIVE... STATUE
WE CAN BE HEROES
LIVE... STATUE DESTROYED...
BESIDES A HANDFUL OF US, WHO KNEW THEIR HEADQUARTERS WAS IN THE LIBERTY-GIRL MONUMENT?
O NEWS
SOMETHING ISN'T RIGHT HERE! WHAT SHOULD WE DO?
STORY
MATTHEW D. SMITH
ART
JEREMY MASSIE
COLORS
CHRISTINE BRUNSON

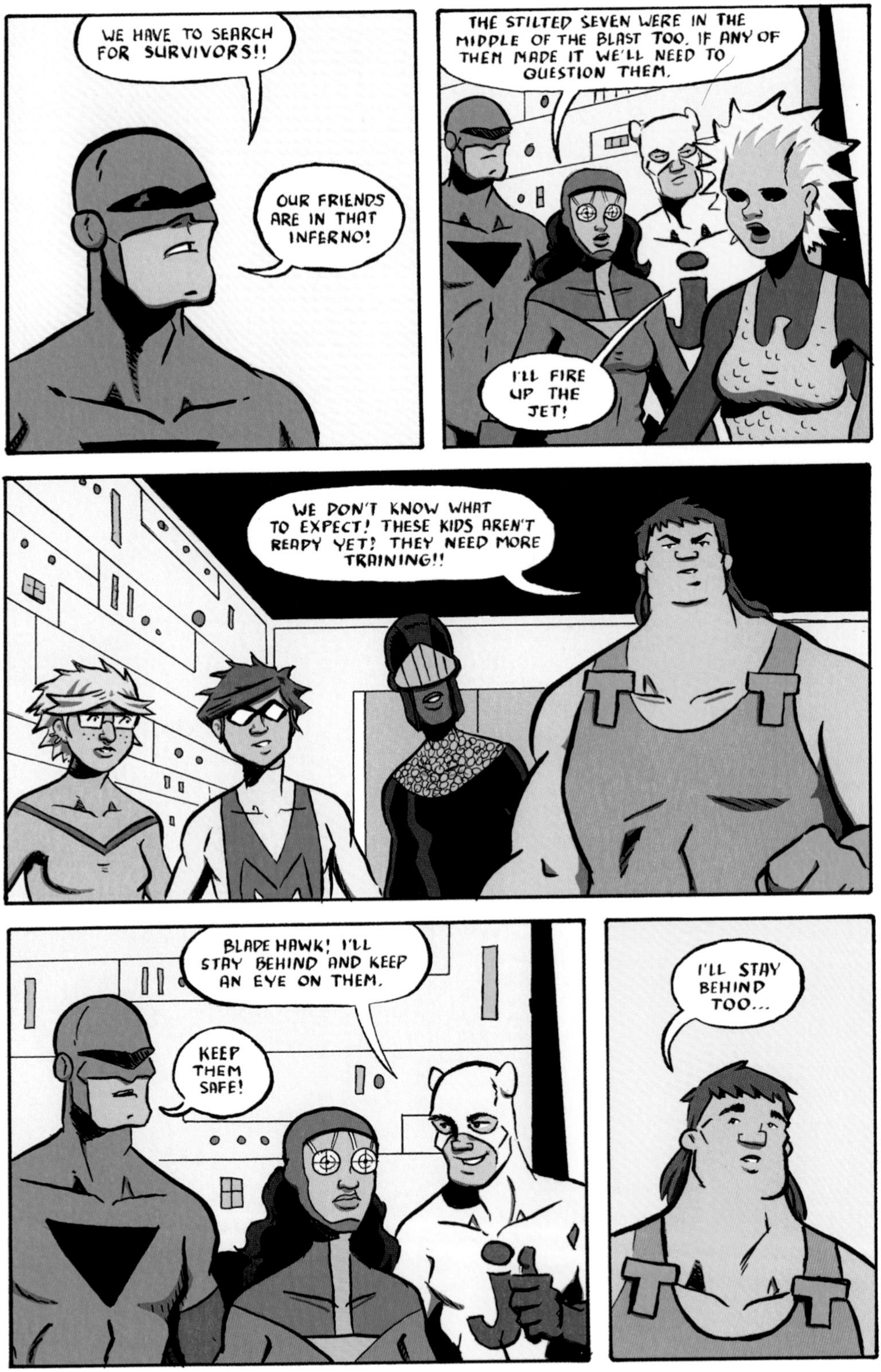
WE HAVE TO SEARCH FOR SURVIVORS!!
OUR FRIENDS ARE IN THAT INFERNO!
THE STILTED SEVEN WERE IN THE MIDDLE OF THE BLAST TOO. IF ANY OF THEM MADE IT WE'LL NEED TO QUESTION THEM.
I'LL FIRE UP THE JET!
WE DON'T KNOW WHAT TO EXPECT! THESE KIDS AREN'T READY YET! THEY NEED MORE TRAINING!!
BLADE HAWK! I'LL STAY BEHIND AND KEEP AN EYE ON THEM.
KEEP THEM SAFE!
I'LL STAY BEHIND TOO...

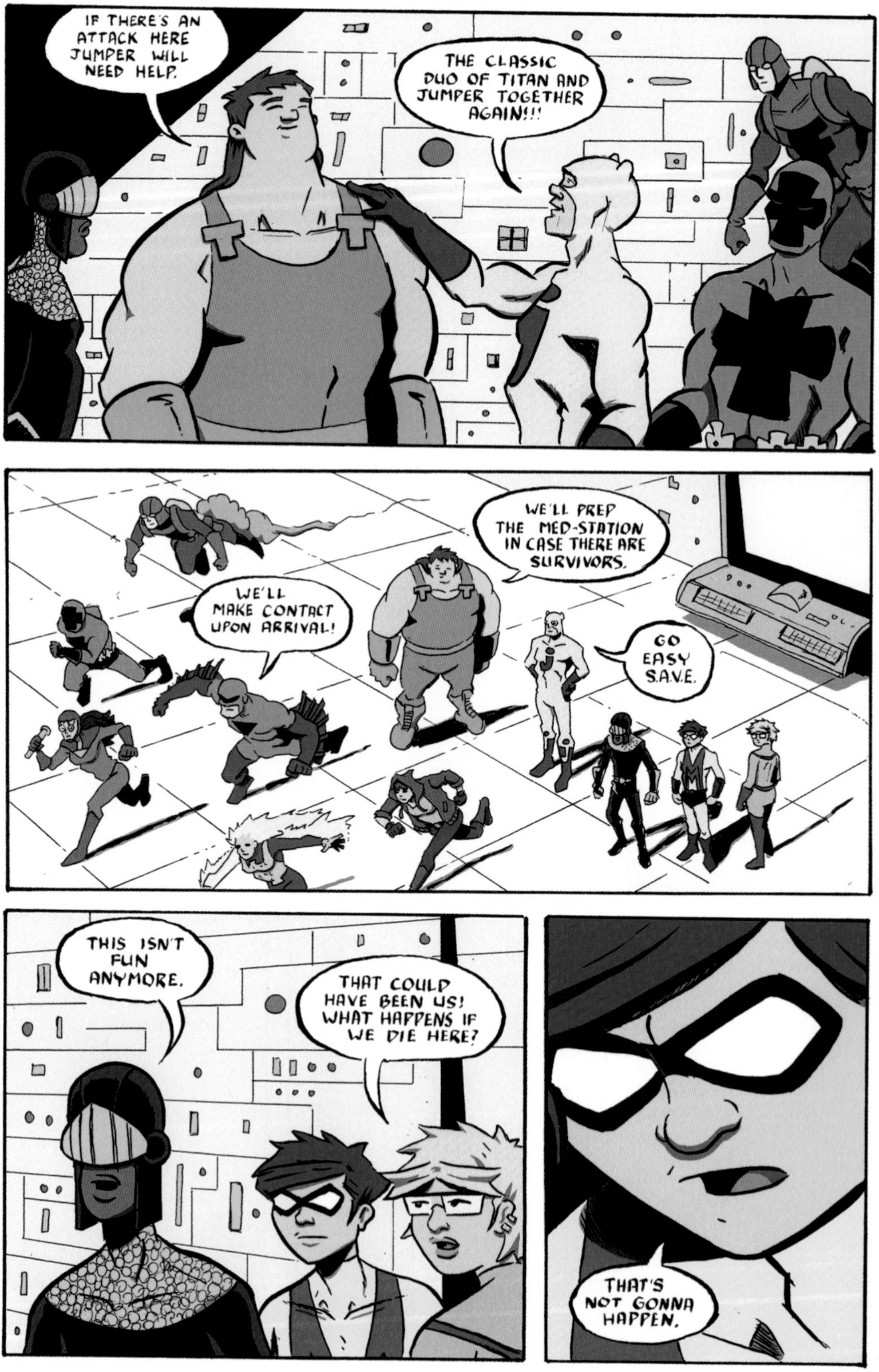
IF THERE'S AN ATTACK HERE JUMPER WILL NEED HELP.
THE CLASSIC DUO OF TITAN AND JUMPER TOGETHER AGAIN!!!
WE'LL MAKE CONTACT UPON ARRIVAL!
WE'LL PREP THE MED-STATION IN CASE THERE ARE SURVIVORS.
GO EASY S.A.V.E.
THIS ISN'T FUN ANYMORE.
THAT COULD HAVE BEEN US! WHAT HAPPENS IF WE DIE HERE?
THAT'S NOT GONNA HAPPEN.

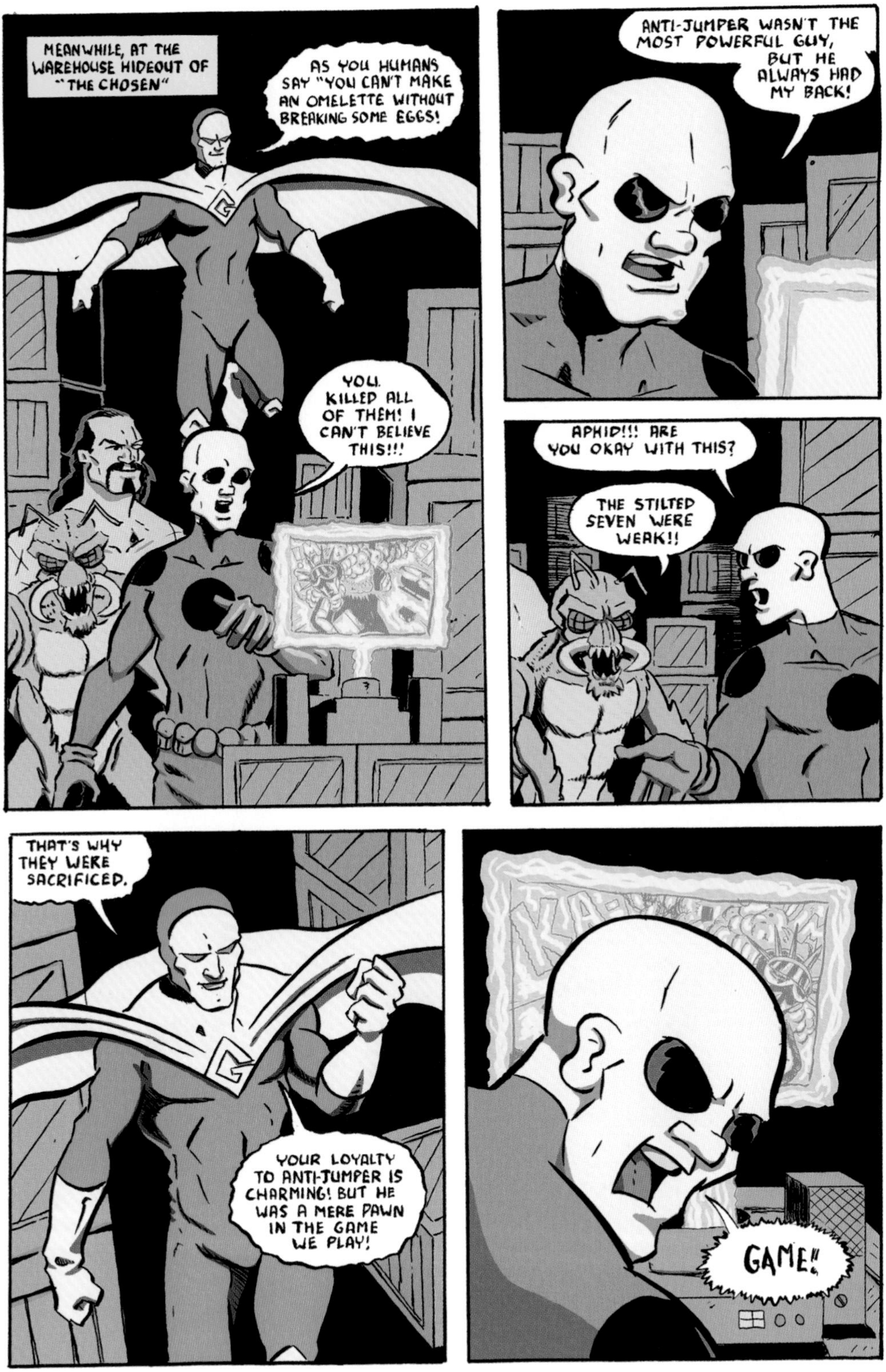
MEANWHILE, AT THE WAREHOUSE HIDEOUT OF "THE CHOSEN"
AS YOU HUMANS SAY "YOU CAN'T MAKE AN OMELETTE WITHOUT BREAKING SOME EGGS!
YOU. KILLED ALL OF THEM! I CAN'T BELIEVE THIS!!!
ANTI-JUMPER WASN'T THE MOST POWERFUL GUY, BUT HE ALWAYS HAD MY BACK!
APHID!!! ARE YOU OKAY WITH THIS?
THE STILTED SEVEN WERE WEAK!!
THAT'S WHY THEY WERE SACRIFICED.
YOUR LOYALTY TO ANTI-JUMPER IS CHARMING! BUT HE WAS A MERE PAWN IN THE GAME WE PLAY!
GAME!!

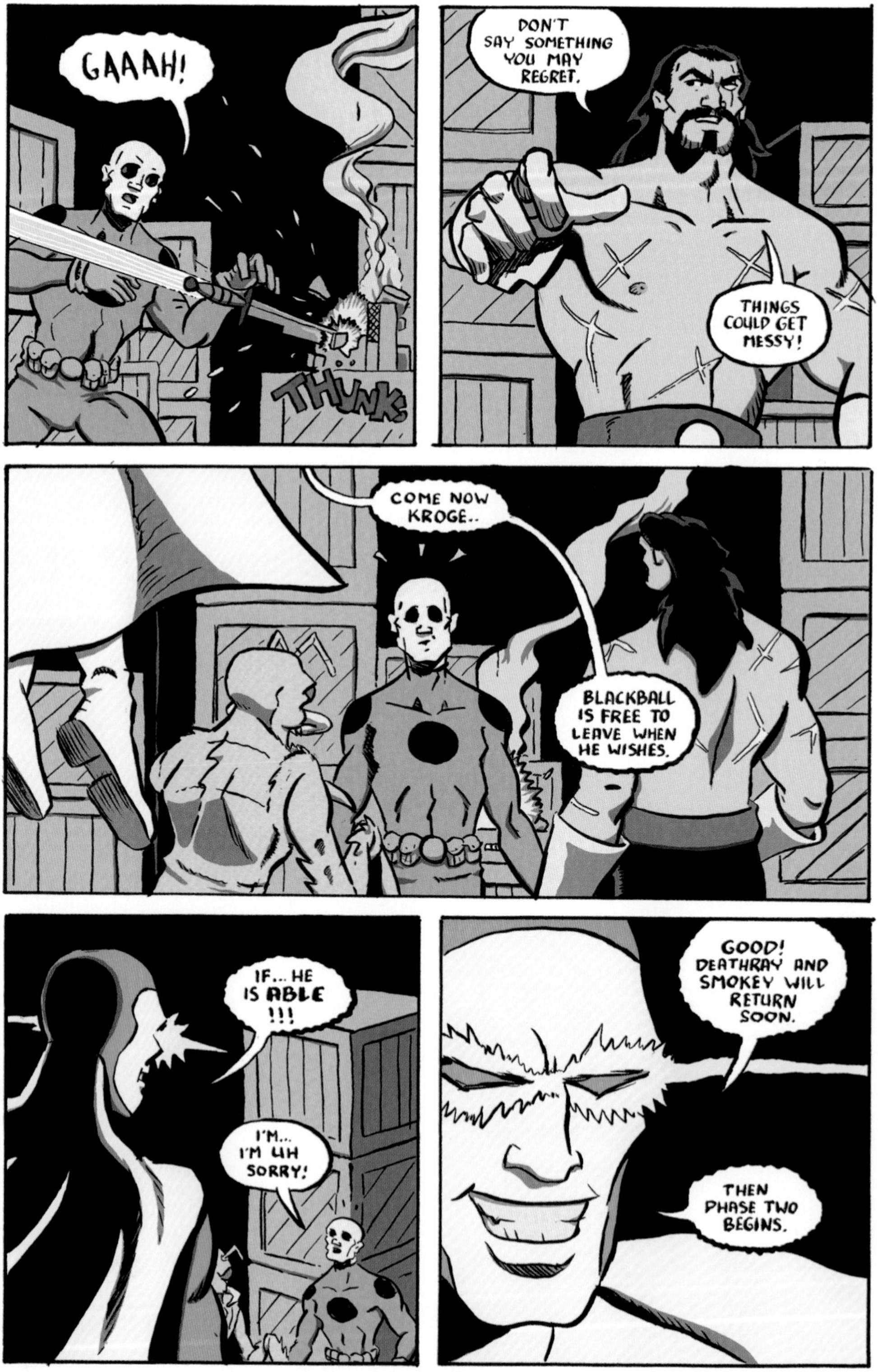
GAAAH!
THUNK!
DON'T SAY SOMETHING YOU MAY REGRET.
THINGS COULD GET MESSY!
COME NOW KROGE..
BLACKBALL IS FREE TO LEAVE WHEN HE WISHES.
IF... HE IS ABLE !!!
I'M... I'M UH SORRY!
GOOD! DEATHRAY AND SMOKEY WILL RETURN SOON.
THEN PHASE TWO BEGINS.

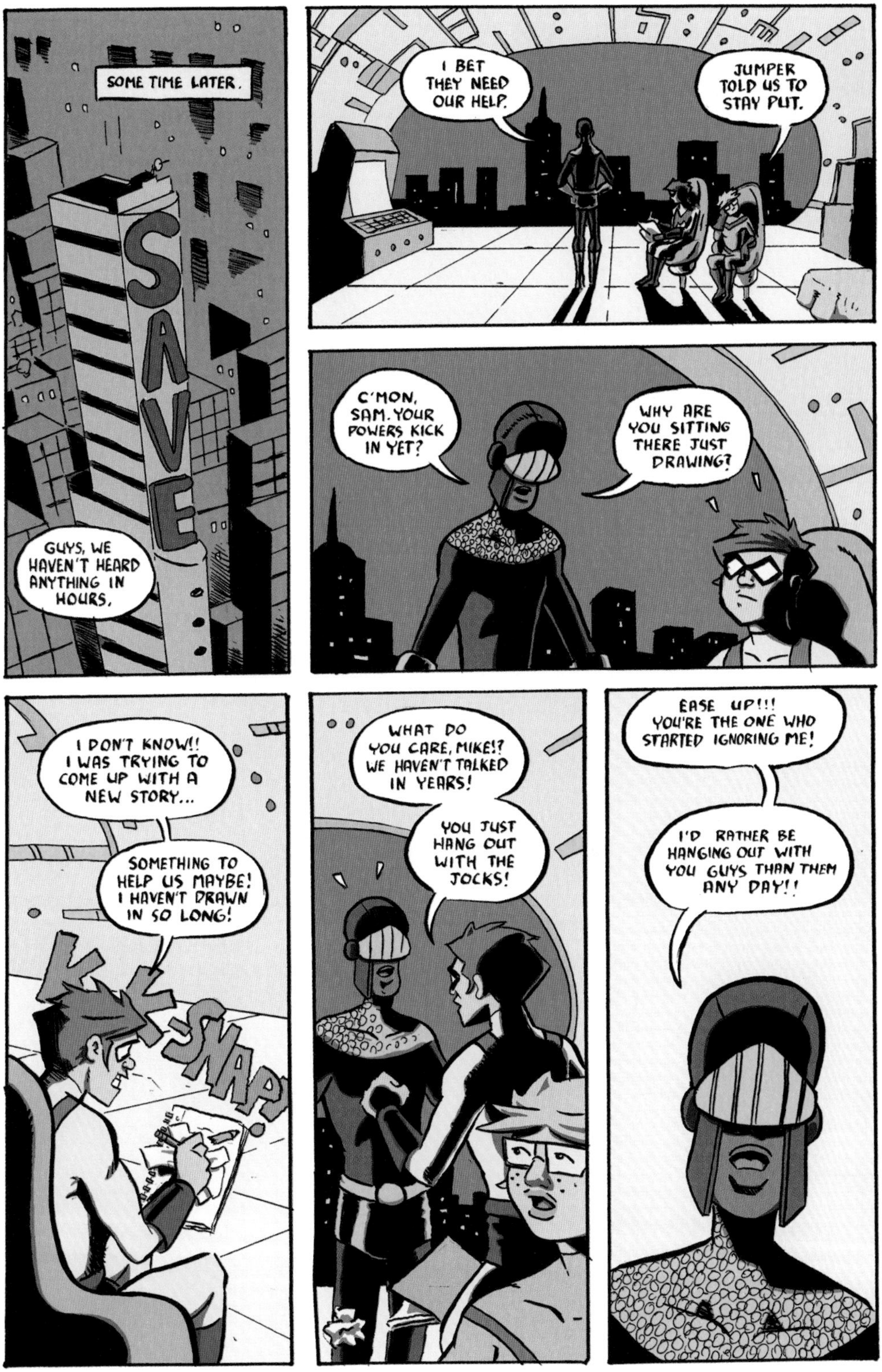
SOME TIME LATER.
SAVE
GUYS, WE HAVEN'T HEARD ANYTHING IN HOURS.
I BET THEY NEED OUR HELP.
JUMPER TOLD US TO STAY PUT.
C'MON, SAM. YOUR POWERS KICK IN YET?
WHY ARE YOU SITTING THERE JUST DRAWING?
I DON'T KNOW!! I WAS TRYING TO COME UP WITH A NEW STORY...
SOMETHING TO HELP US MAYBE! I HAVEN'T DRAWN IN SO LONG!
K-SNAP!
WHAT DO YOU CARE, MIKE!? WE HAVEN'T TALKED IN YEARS!
YOU JUST HANG OUT WITH THE JOCKS!
EASE UP!!! YOU'RE THE ONE WHO STARTED IGNORING ME!
I'D RATHER BE HANGING OUT WITH YOU GUYS THAN THEM ANY DAY!!

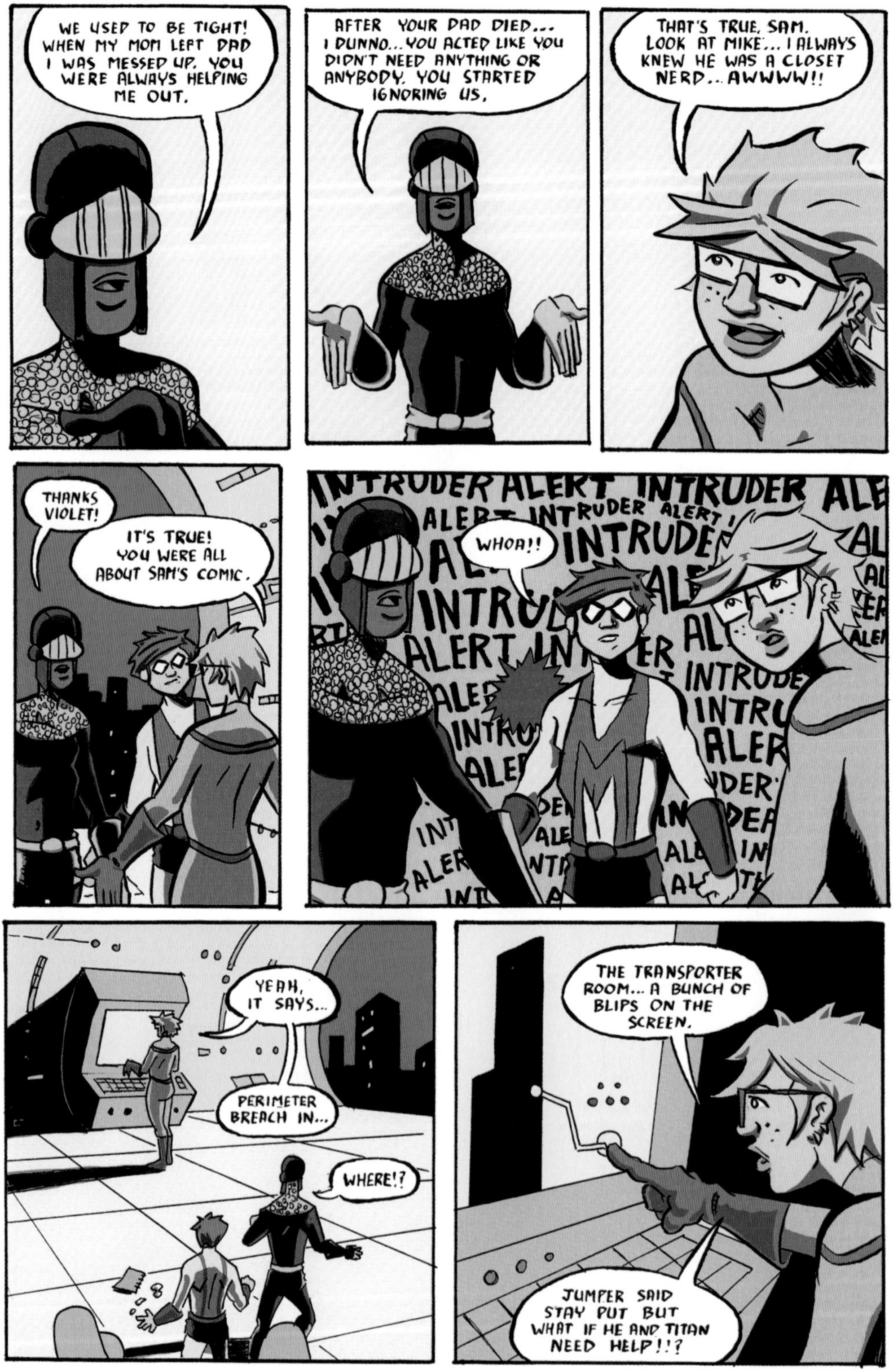
WE USED TO BE TIGHT! WHEN MY MOM LEFT DAD I WAS MESSED UP. YOU WERE ALWAYS HELPING ME OUT.
AFTER YOUR DAD DIED... I DUNNO... YOU ACTED LIKE YOU DIDN'T NEED ANYTHING OR ANYBODY. YOU STARTED IGNORING US.
THAT'S TRUE, SAM. LOOK AT MIKE... I ALWAYS KNEW HE WAS A CLOSET NERD... AWWWW!!
THANKS VIOLET!
IT'S TRUE! YOU WERE ALL ABOUT SAM'S COMIC.
INTRUDER ALERT INTRUDER ALERT
WHOA!!
YEAH, IT SAYS...
PERIMETER BREACH IN...
WHERE!?
THE TRANSPORTER ROOM... A BUNCH OF BLIPS ON THE SCREEN.
JUMPER SAID STAY PUT BUT WHAT IF HE AND TITAN NEED HELP!!?

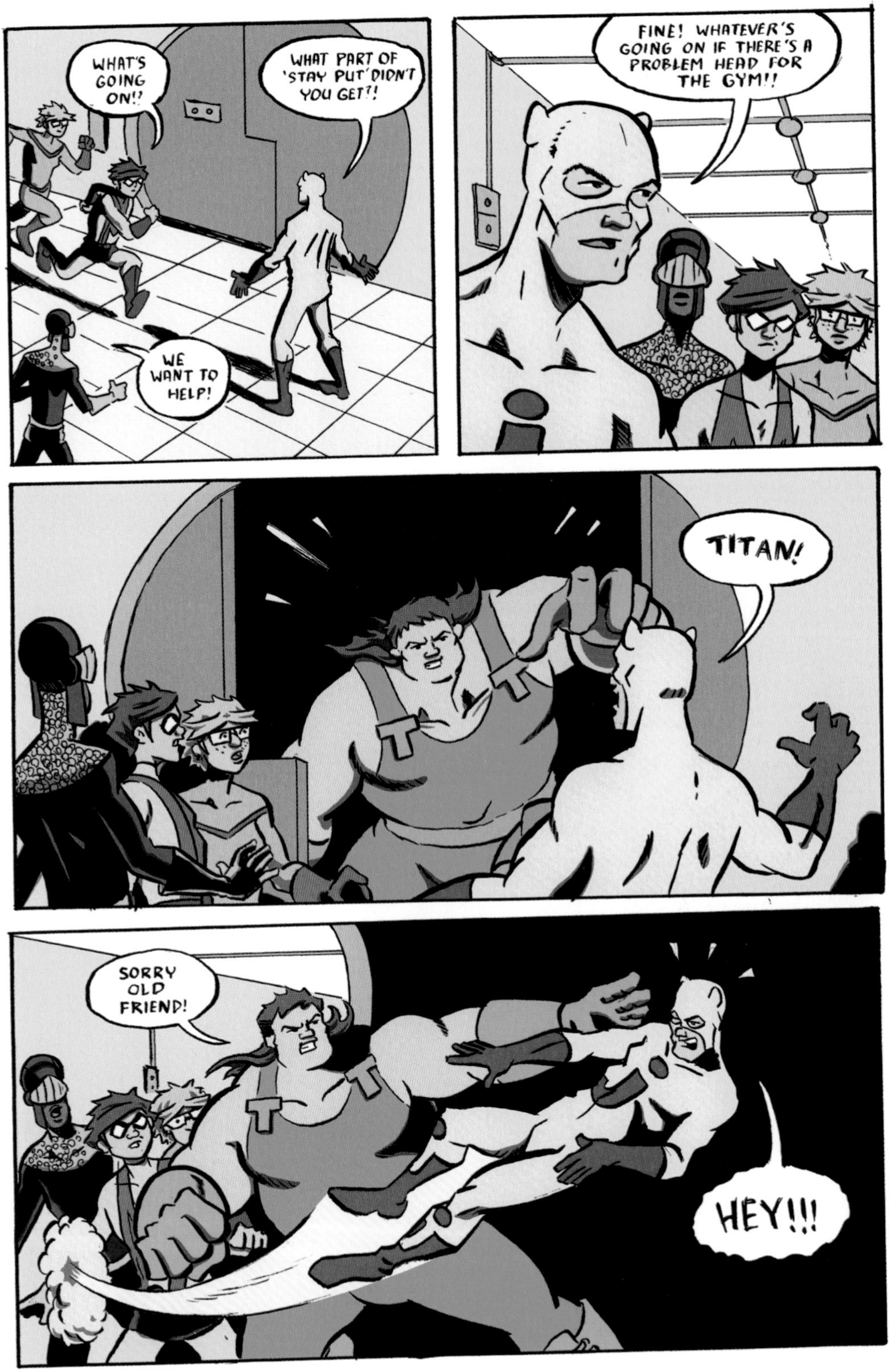
WHAT'S GOING ON!?
WHAT PART OF 'STAY PUT' DIDN'T YOU GET?!
WE WANT TO HELP!
FINE! WHATEVER'S GOING ON IF THERE'S A PROBLEM HEAD FOR THE GYM!!
TITAN!
SORRY OLD FRIEND!
HEY!!!

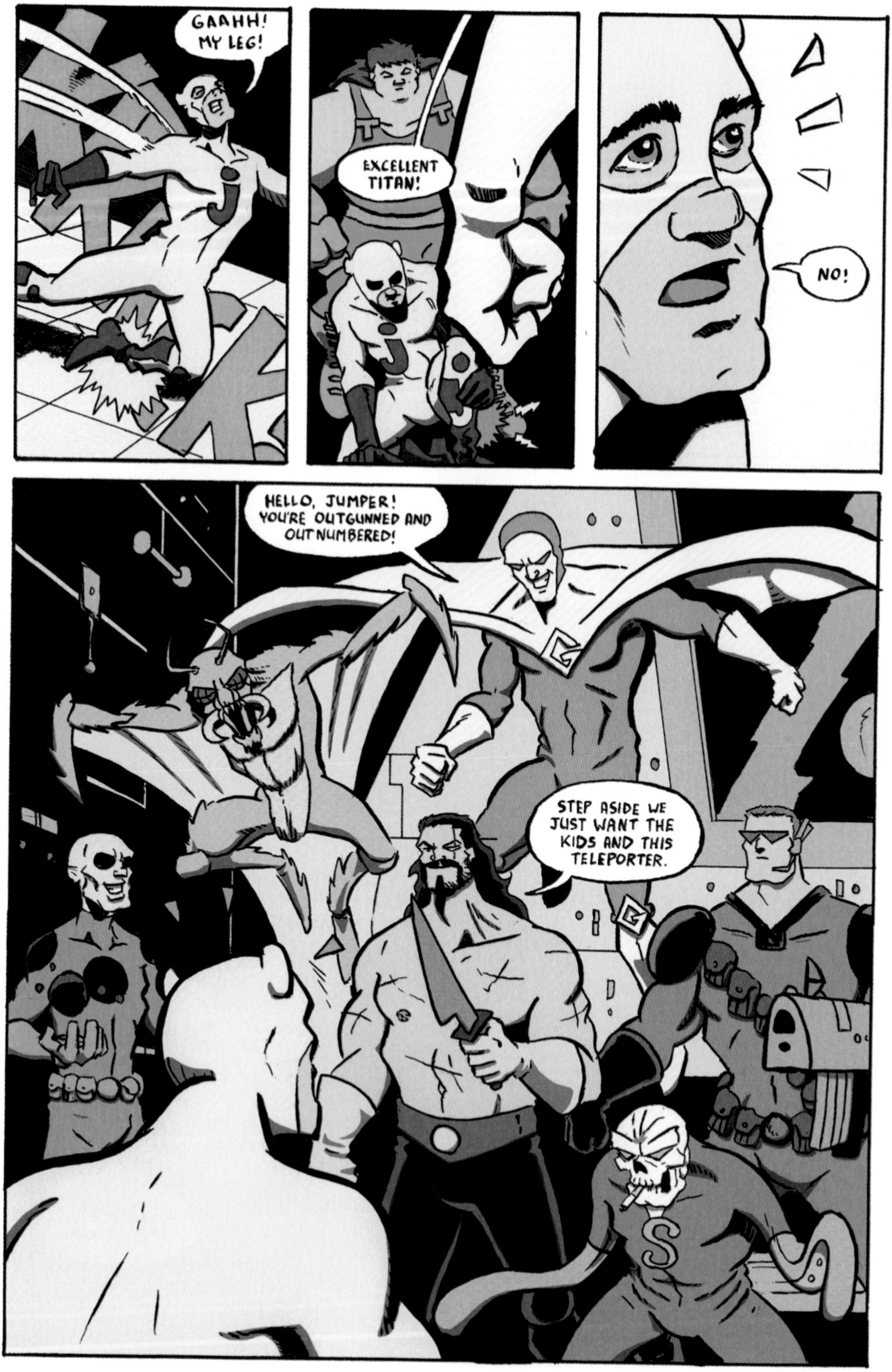
GAAHH! MY LEG!
EXCELLENT TITAN!
NO!
HELLO, JUMPER! YOU'RE OUTGUNNED AND OUTNUMBERED!
STEP ASIDE WE JUST WANT THE KIDS AND THIS TELEPORTER.

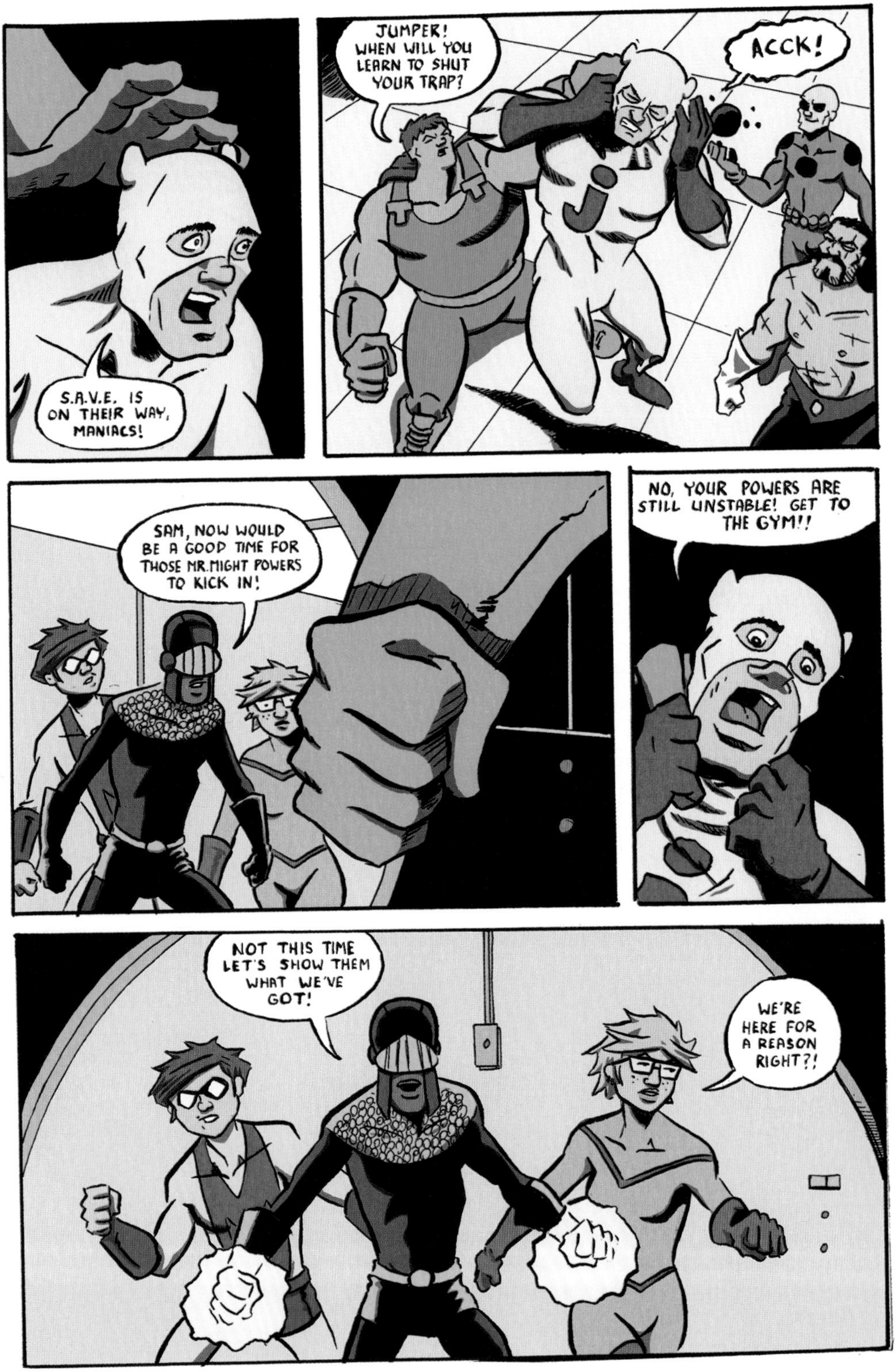
S.A.V.E. IS ON THEIR WAY, MANIACS!
JUMPER! WHEN WILL YOU LEARN TO SHUT YOUR TRAP?
ACCK!
SAM, NOW WOULD BE A GOOD TIME FOR THOSE MR.MIGHT POWERS TO KICK IN!
NO, YOUR POWERS ARE STILL UNSTABLE! GET TO THE GYM!!
NOT THIS TIME LET'S SHOW THEM WHAT WE'VE GOT!
WE'RE HERE FOR A REASON RIGHT?!

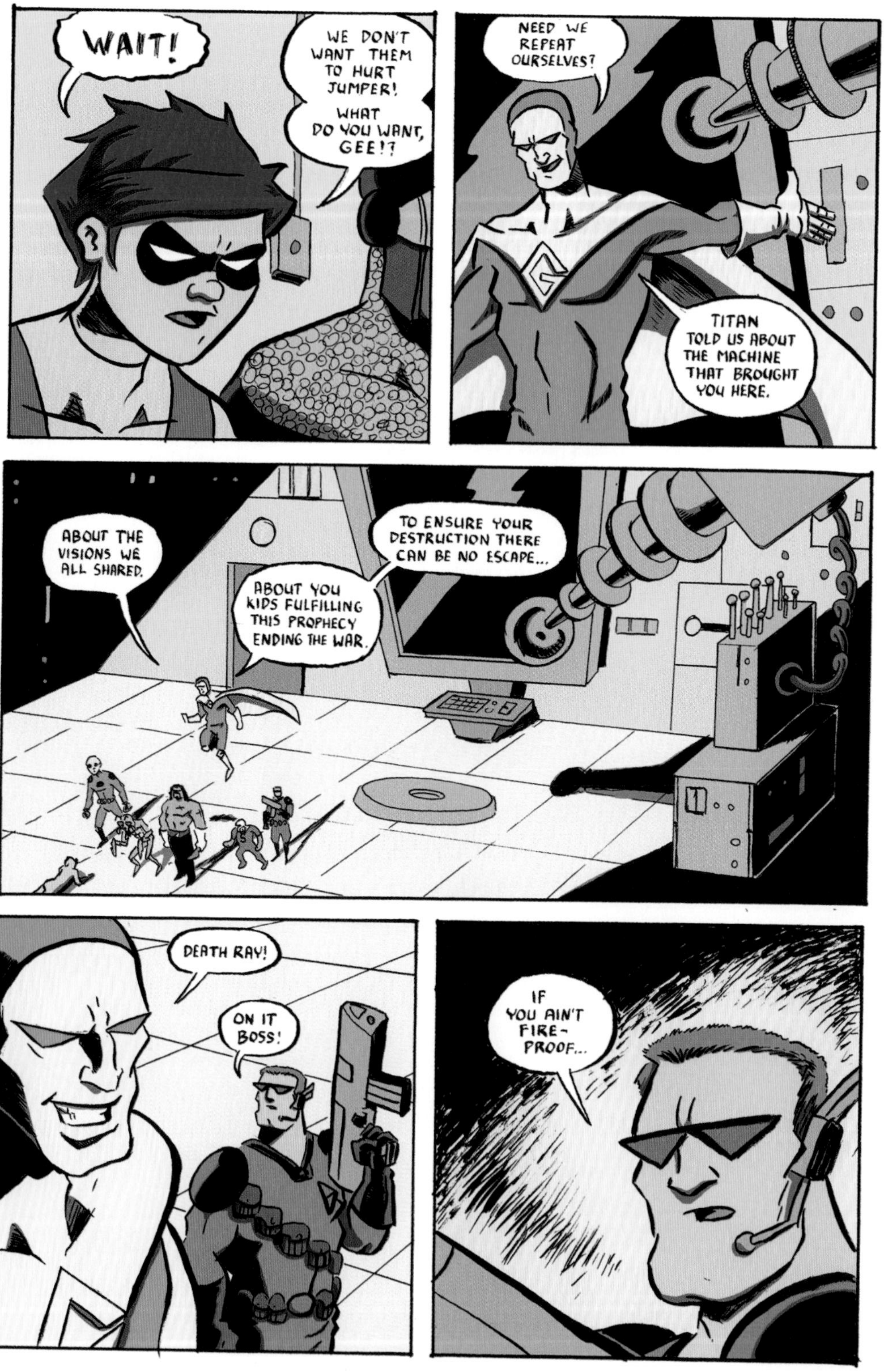
WAIT!
WE DON'T WANT THEM TO HURT JUMPER!
WHAT DO YOU WANT, GEE!?
NEED WE REPEAT OURSELVES?
TITAN TOLD US ABOUT THE MACHINE THAT BROUGHT YOU HERE.
ABOUT THE VISIONS WE ALL SHARED.
ABOUT YOU KIDS FULFILLING THIS PROPHECY ENDING THE WAR.
TO ENSURE YOUR DESTRUCTION THERE CAN BE NO ESCAPE...
DEATH RAY!
ON IT BOSS!
IF YOU AIN'T FIRE-PROOF...

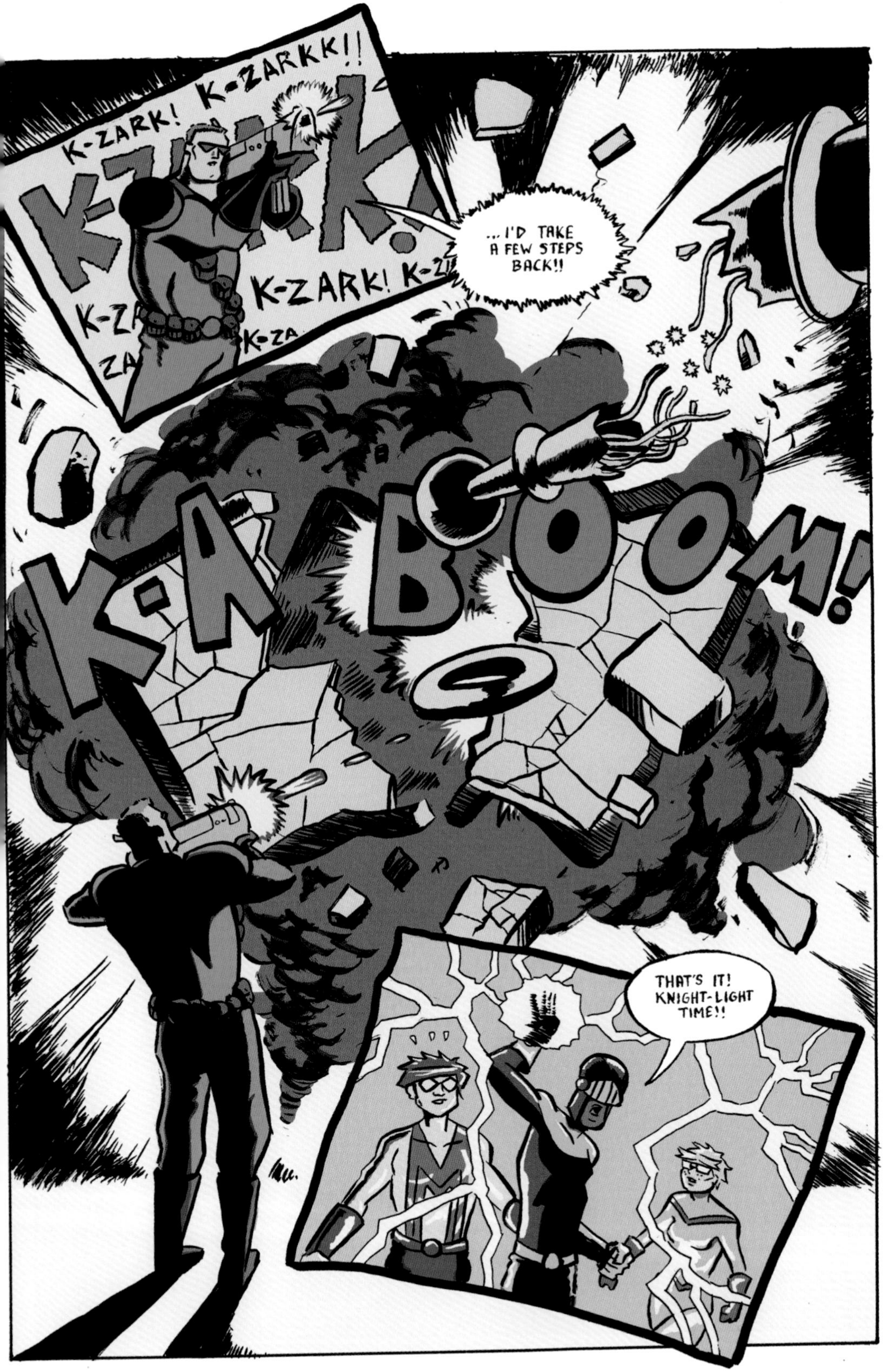
K-ZARK!
K-ZARKK!!
K-ZARK! K-Z
K-ZA
...I'D TAKE A FEW STEPS BACK!!
K-A-BOOM!
THAT'S IT! KNIGHT-LIGHT TIME!!

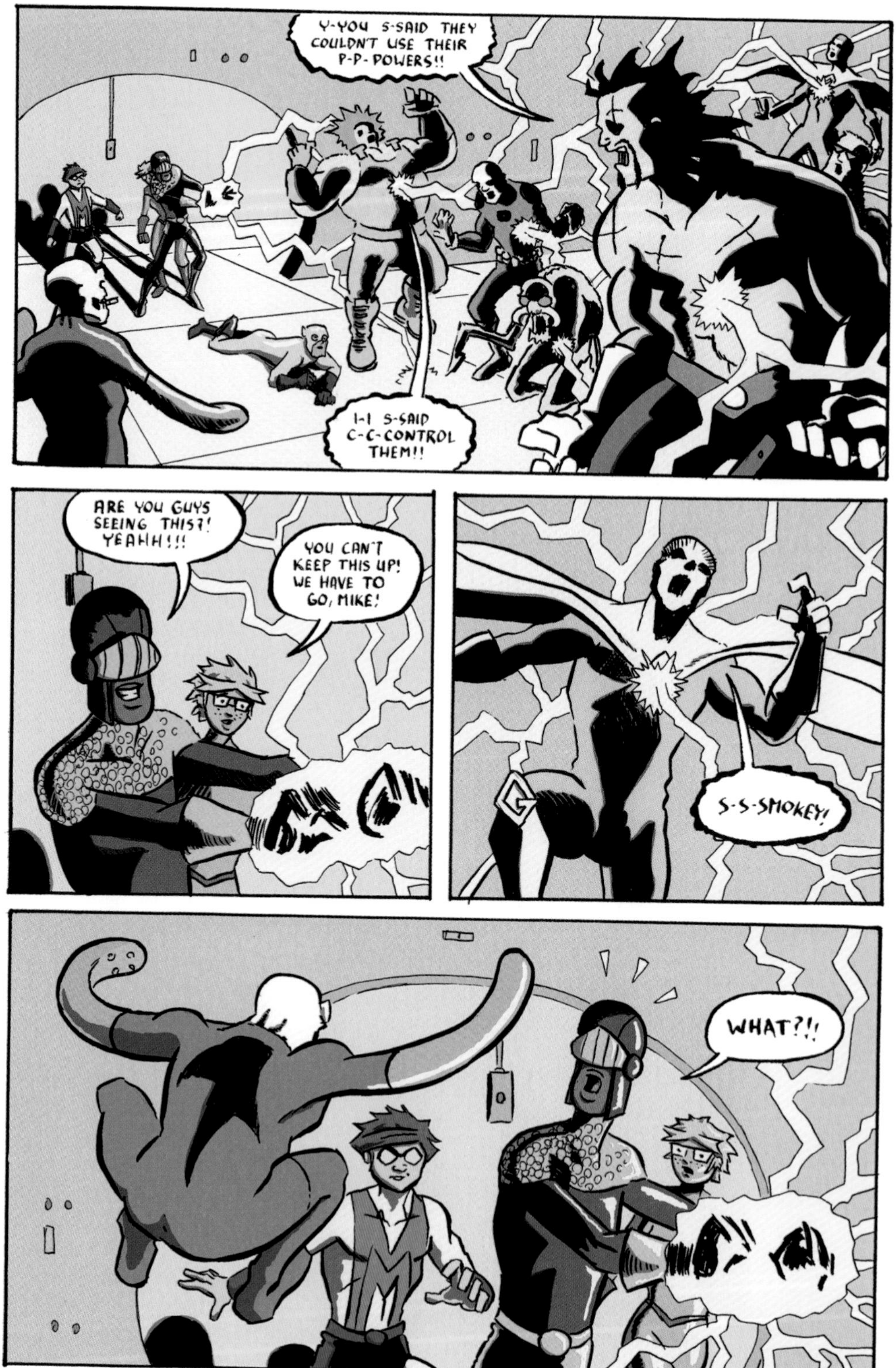
Y-YOU S-SAID THEY COULDN'T USE THEIR P-P-POWERS!!
I-I S-SAID C-C-CONTROL THEM!!
ARE YOU GUYS SEEING THIS?! YEAHH!!!
YOU CAN'T KEEP THIS UP! WE HAVE TO GO, MIKE!
S-S-SMOKEY!
WHAT?!!

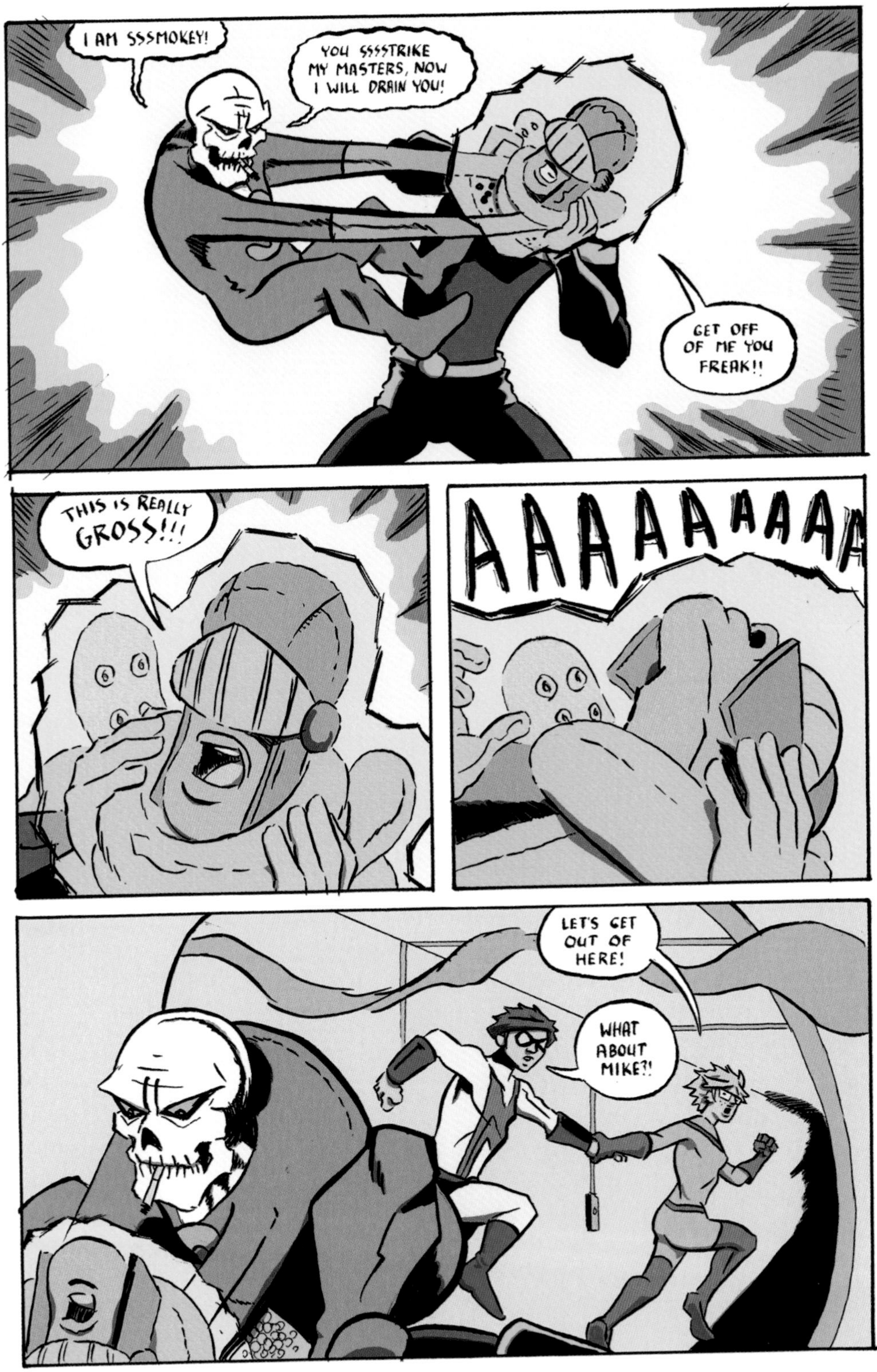
I AM SSSMOKEY!
YOU SSSSTRIKE MY MASTERS, NOW I WILL DRAIN YOU!
GET OFF OF ME YOU FREAK!!
THIS IS REALLY GROSS!!!
AAAAAAAAAA
LET'S GET OUT OF HERE!
WHAT ABOUT MIKE?!

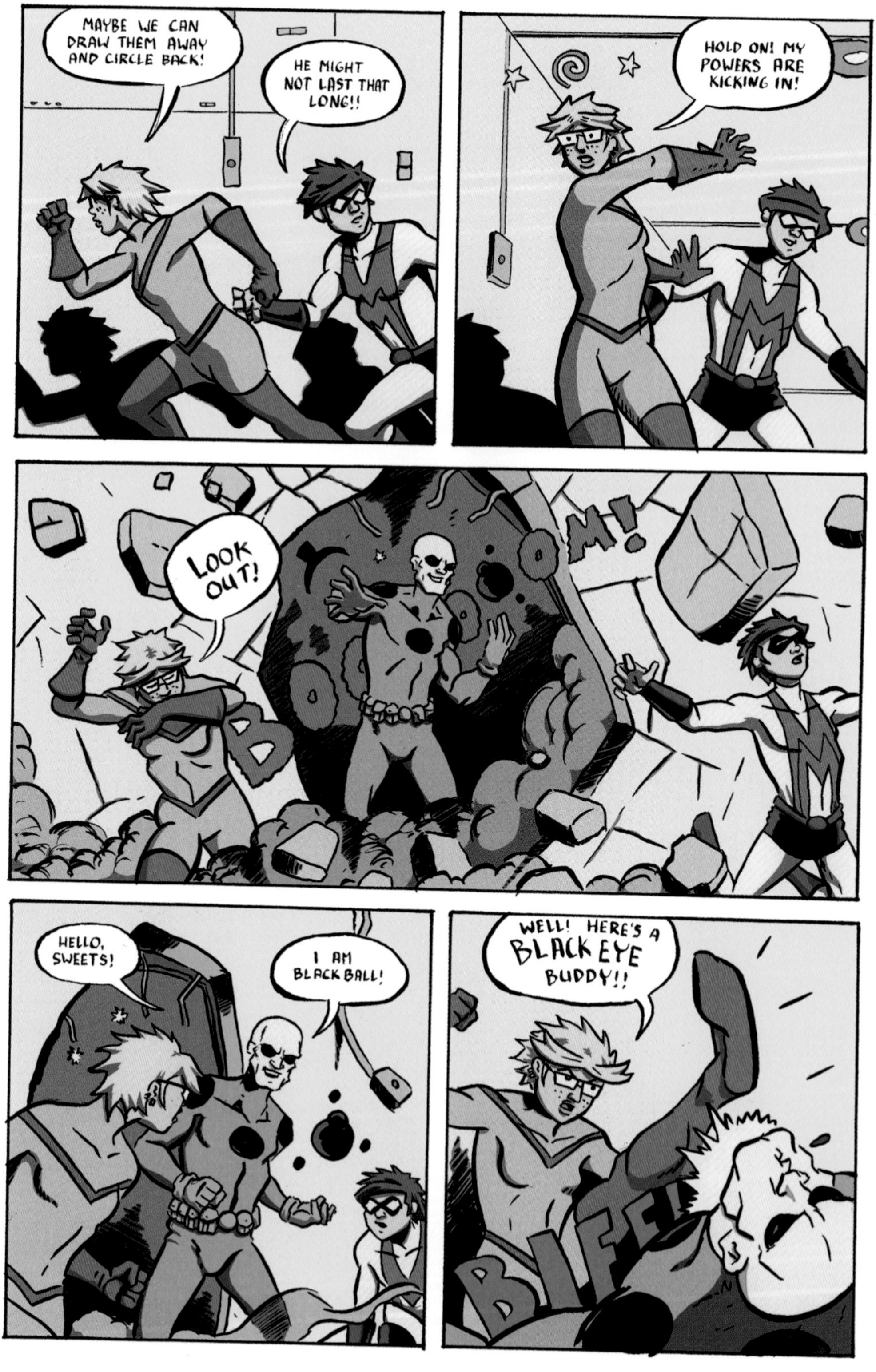
MAYBE WE CAN DRAW THEM AWAY AND CIRCLE BACK!
HE MIGHT NOT LAST THAT LONG!!
HOLD ON! MY POWERS ARE KICKING IN!
LOOK OUT!
BOOOOM!
HELLO, SWEETS!
I AM BLACKBALL!
WELL! HERE'S A BLACK EYE BUDDY!!
BIFF!

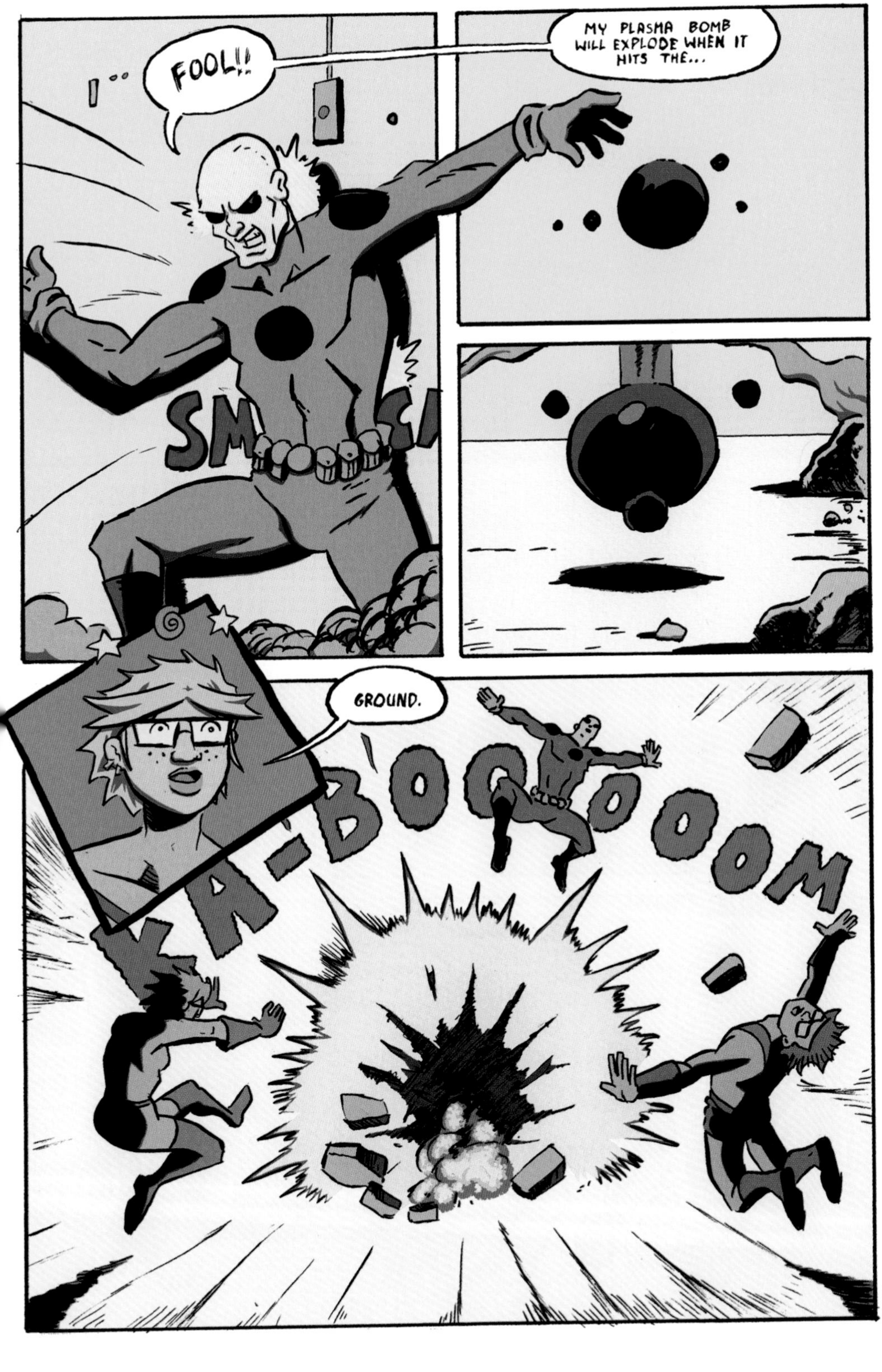
I...
FOOL!!
SMASH
MY PLASMA BOMB WILL EXPLODE WHEN IT HITS THE...
GROUND.
KA-BOOOOOM

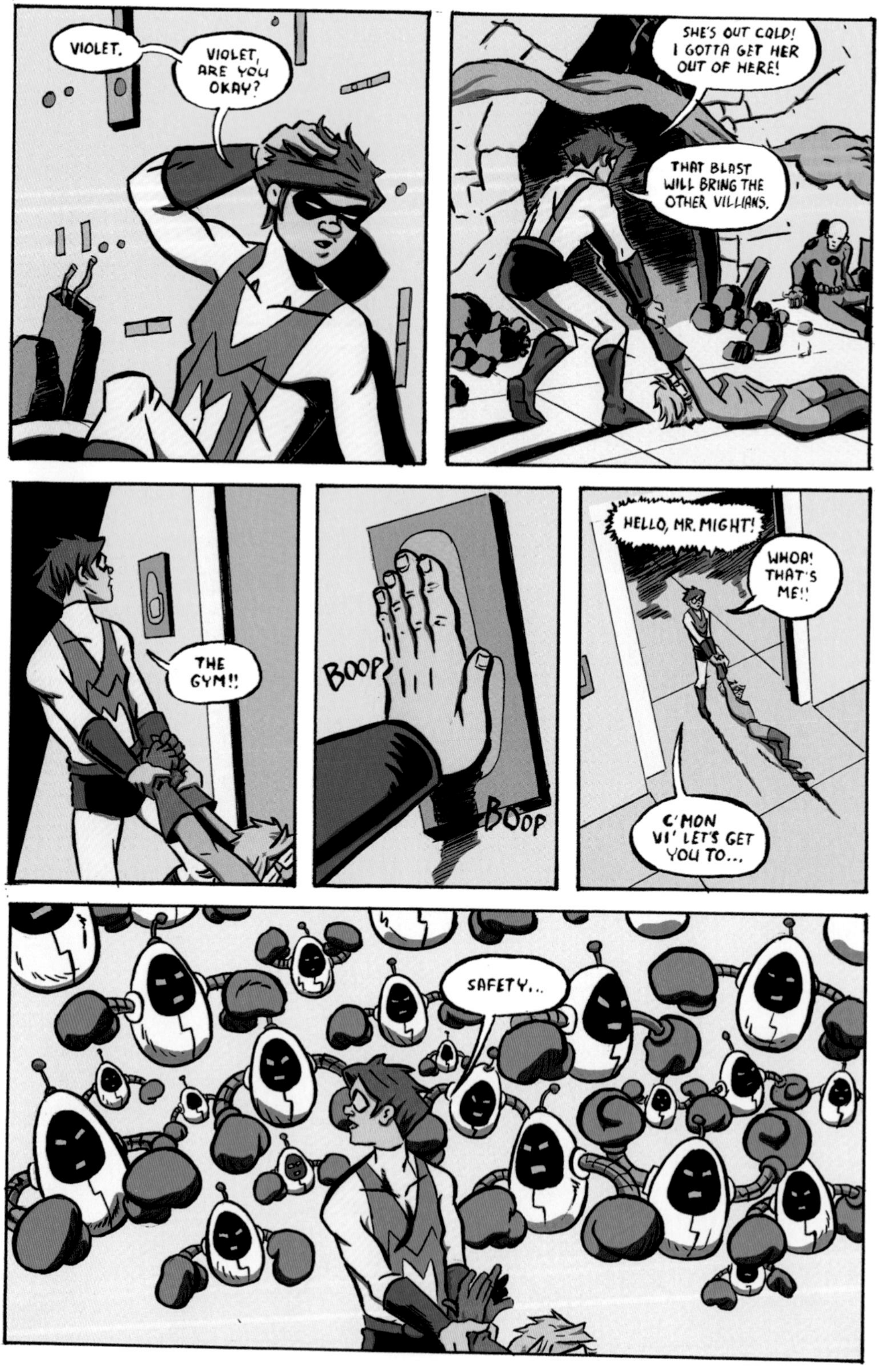
VIOLET.
VIOLET, ARE YOU OKAY?
SHE'S OUT COLD! I GOTTA GET HER OUT OF HERE!
THAT BLAST WILL BRING THE OTHER VILLIANS.
THE GYM!!
BOOP
BOOP
HELLO, MR. MIGHT!
WHOA! THAT'S ME!!
C'MON VI' LET'S GET YOU TO...
SAFETY...

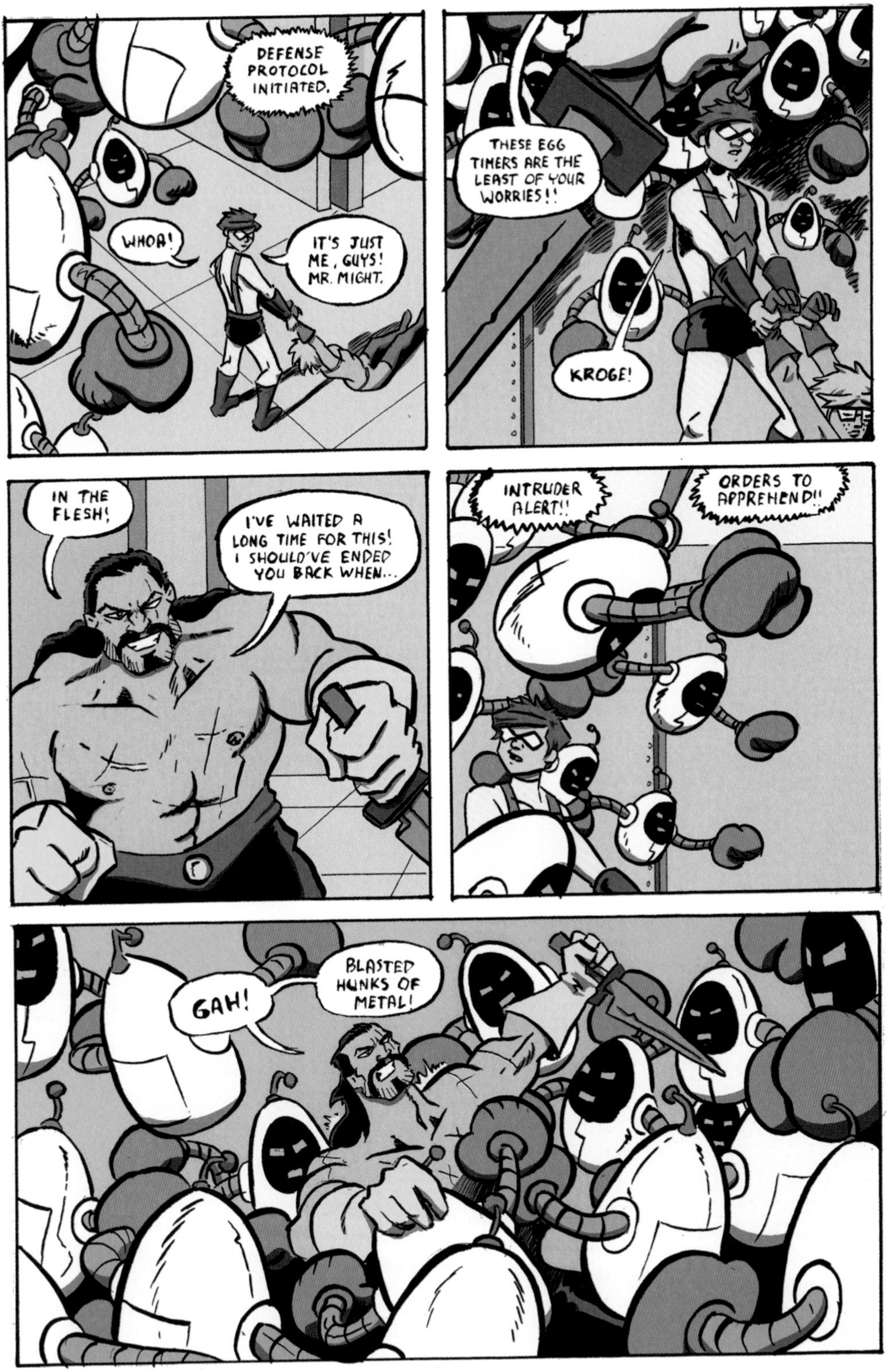
DEFENSE PROTOCOL INITIATED.
WHOA!
IT'S JUST ME, GUYS! MR. MIGHT.
THESE EGG TIMERS ARE THE LEAST OF YOUR WORRIES!!
KROGE!
IN THE FLESH!
I'VE WAITED A LONG TIME FOR THIS! I SHOULD'VE ENDED YOU BACK WHEN...
INTRUDER ALERT!!
ORDERS TO APPREHEND!!
GAH!
BLASTED HUNKS OF METAL!

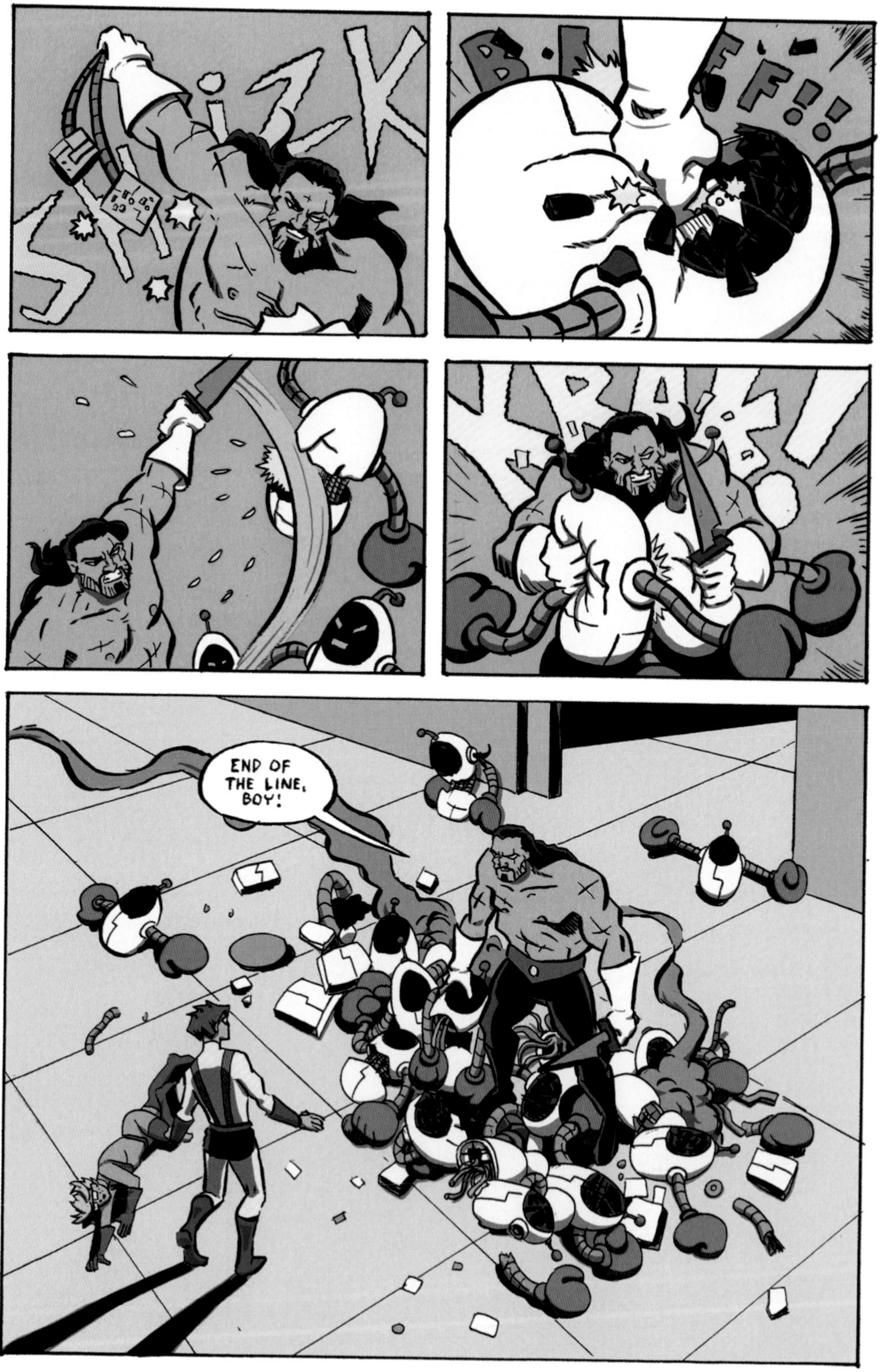
END OF THE LINE, BOY!

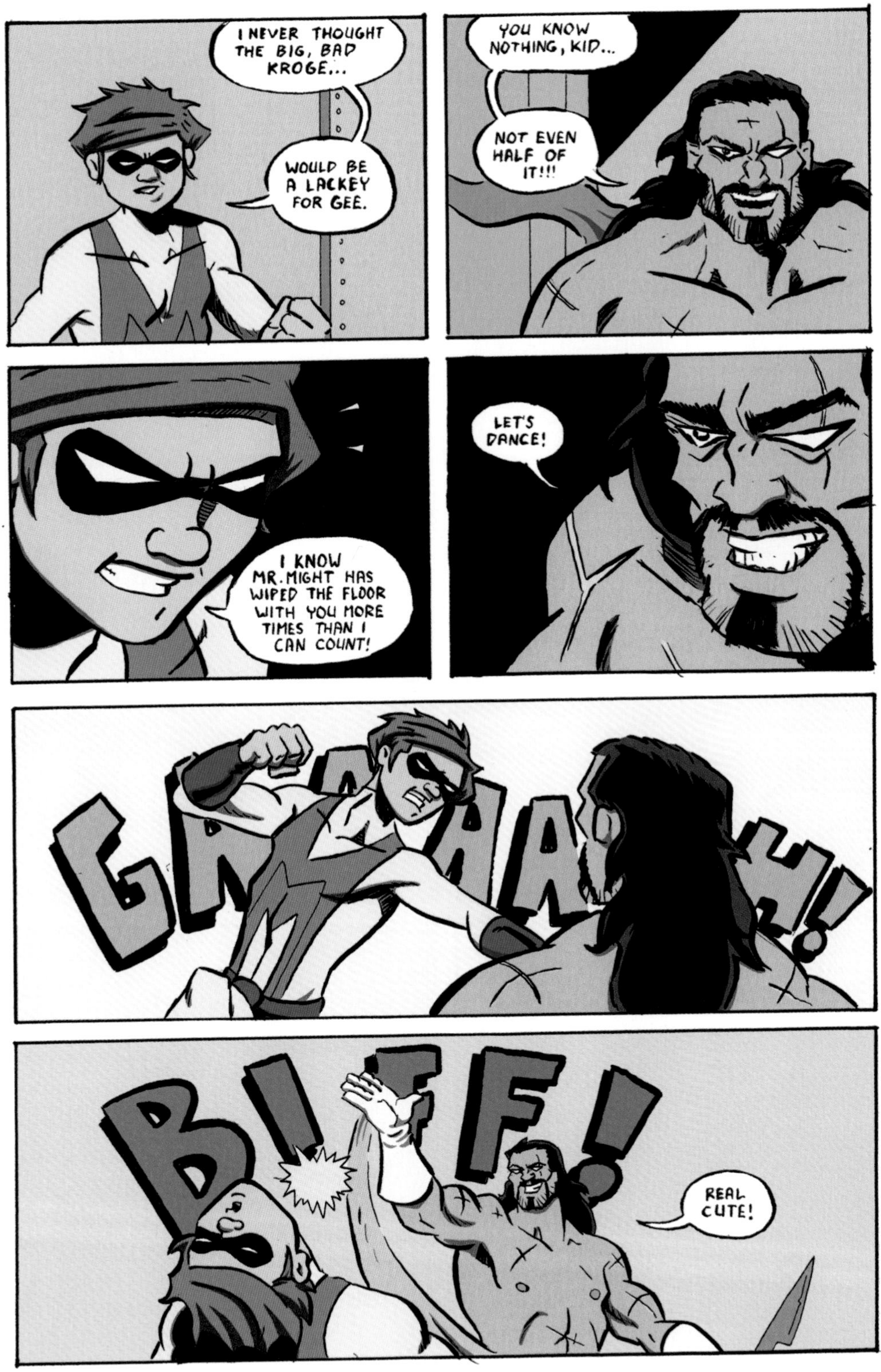
I NEVER THOUGHT THE BIG, BAD KROGE...
WOULD BE A LACKEY FOR GEE.
YOU KNOW NOTHING, KID...
NOT EVEN HALF OF IT!!!
I KNOW MR. MIGHT HAS WIPED THE FLOOR WITH YOU MORE TIMES THAN I CAN COUNT!
LET'S DANCE!
GRAAAH!
BIFF!
REAL CUTE!

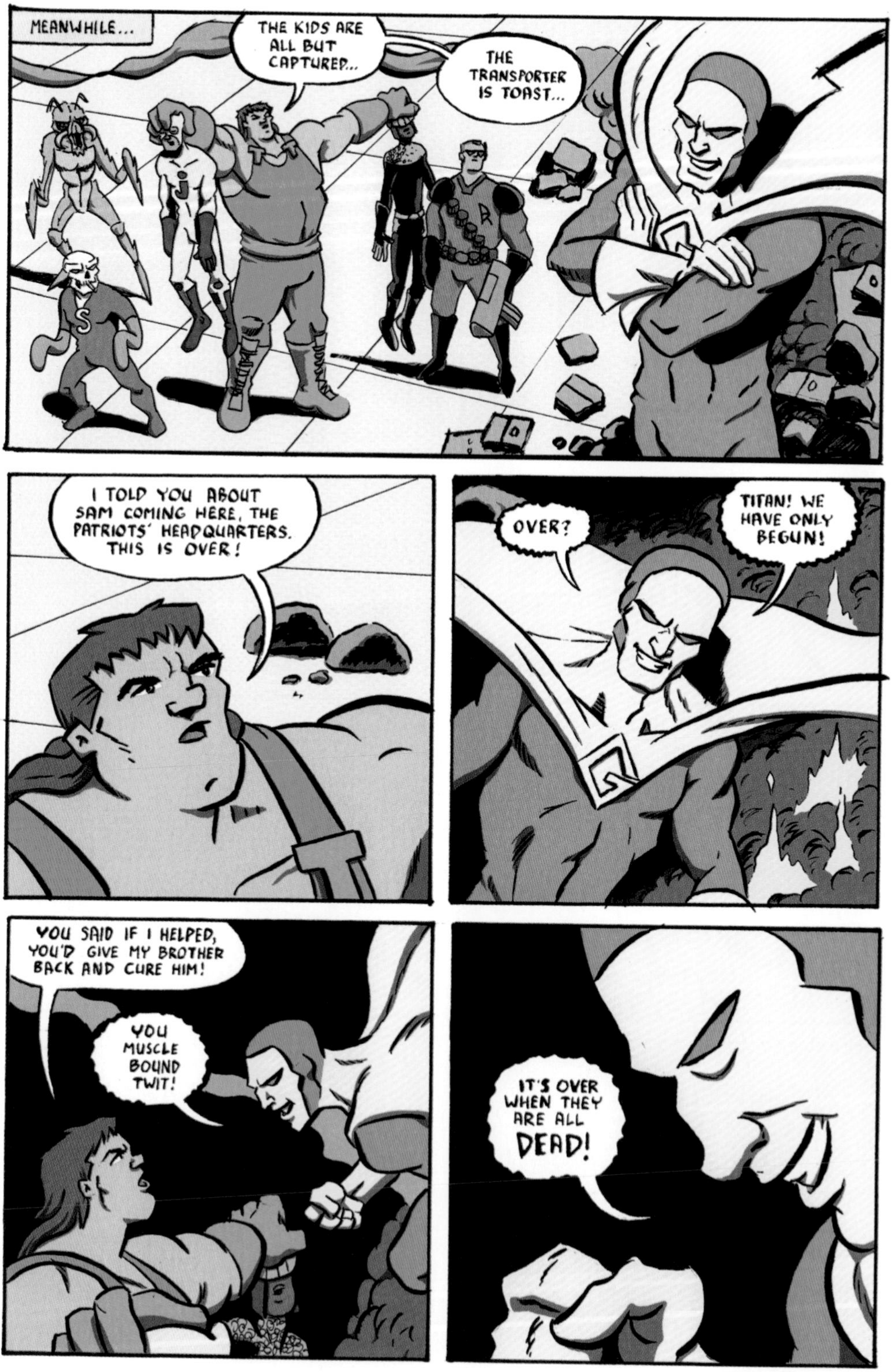
MEANWHILE...
THE KIDS ARE ALL BUT CAPTURED...
THE TRANSPORTER IS TOAST...
I TOLD YOU ABOUT SAM COMING HERE, THE PATRIOTS' HEADQUARTERS. THIS IS OVER!
OVER?
TITAN! WE HAVE ONLY BEGUN!
YOU SAID IF I HELPED, YOU'D GIVE MY BROTHER BACK AND CURE HIM!
YOU MUSCLE BOUND TWIT!
IT'S OVER WHEN THEY ARE ALL DEAD!

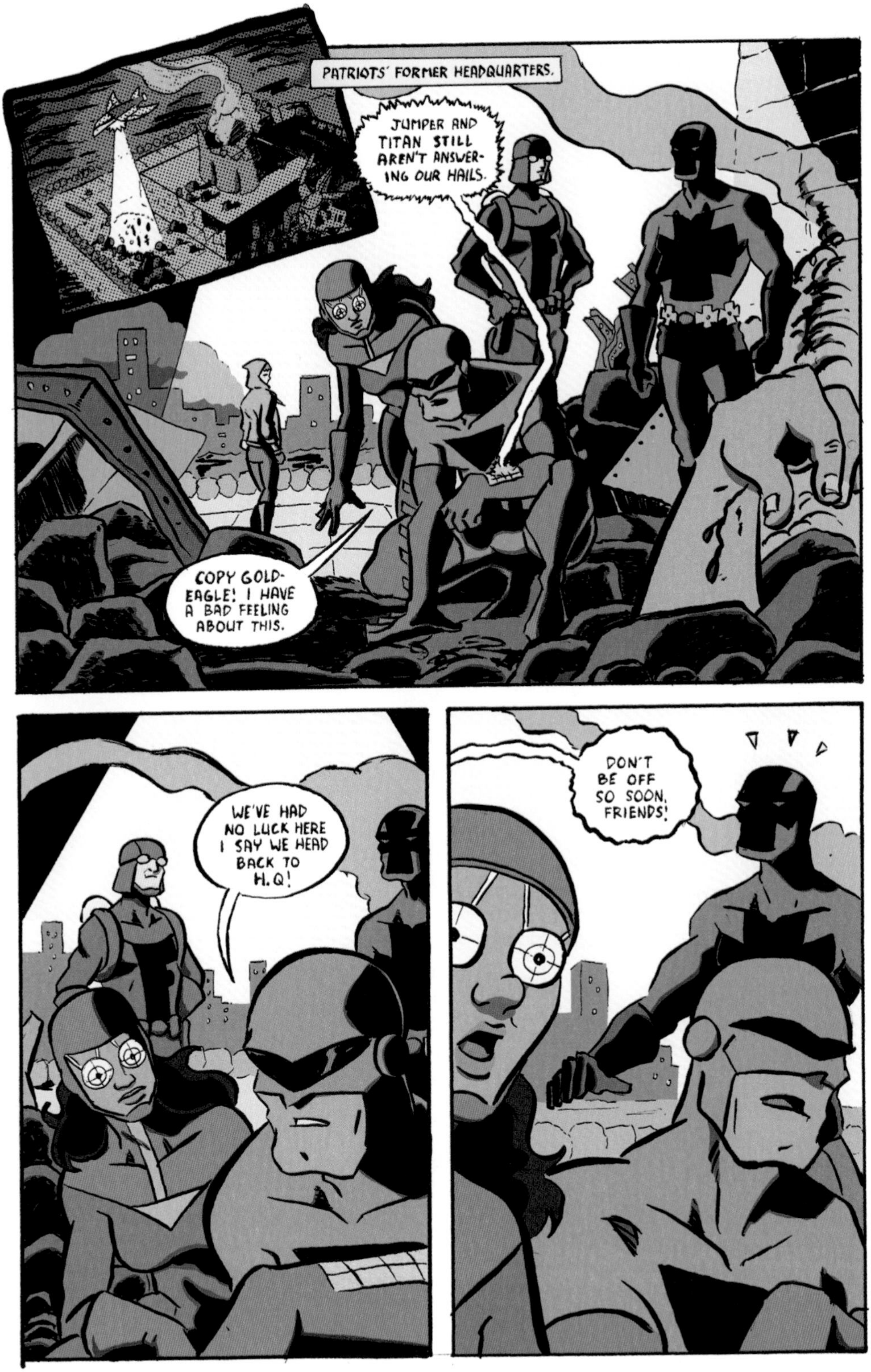
PATRIOTS' FORMER HEADQUARTERS.
JUMPER AND TITAN STILL AREN'T ANSWERING OUR HAILS.
COPY GOLD-EAGLE! I HAVE A BAD FEELING ABOUT THIS.
WE'VE HAD NO LUCK HERE I SAY WE HEAD BACK TO H.Q!
DON'T BE OFF SO SOON, FRIENDS!

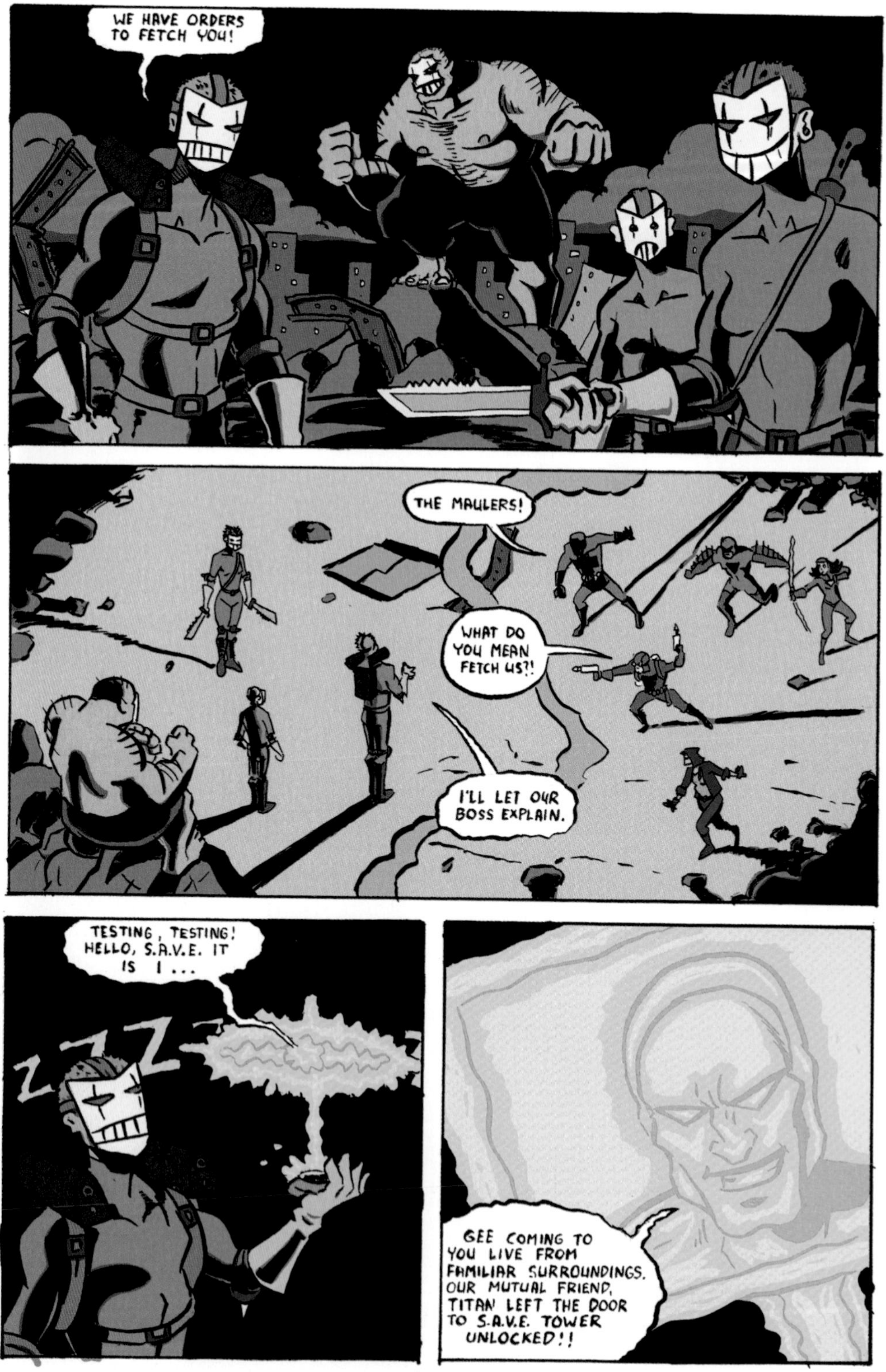
WE HAVE ORDERS TO FETCH YOU!
THE MAULERS!
WHAT DO YOU MEAN FETCH US?!
I'LL LET OUR BOSS EXPLAIN.
TESTING, TESTING! HELLO, S.A.V.E. IT IS I...
GEE COMING TO YOU LIVE FROM FAMILIAR SURROUNDINGS. OUR MUTUAL FRIEND, TITAN LEFT THE DOOR TO S.A.V.E. TOWER UNLOCKED!!

WHILE YOU WERE OUT WE MANAGED TO CAPTURE THESE INTER-DIMENSIONAL BRATS. WANT TO SEE THEM ALIVE AGAIN?!!
I SUGGEST YOU SURRENDER TO THE MAULERS.
I KNOW THAT WAS SHORT AND SWEET BUT YOU GET THE POINT.
TITAN WOULD NEVER BETRAY US! AND WHERE IS JUMPER?!
WE KIDNAPPED TITAN'S SICK BROTHER AND USED HIM FOR LEVERAGE.
JUMPER... HE'S ALIVE.
SO... WHAT'S IT GOING TO BE?
GOLD EAGLE, LAND THE JET AND RENDEZVOUS WITH US... OVER.
WE SURRENDER...
TO BE CONCLUDED...

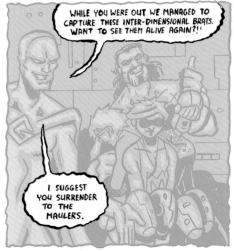

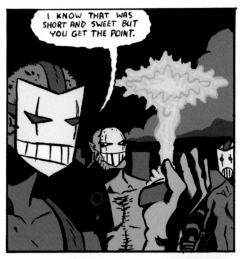

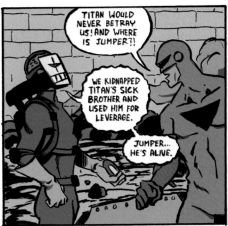

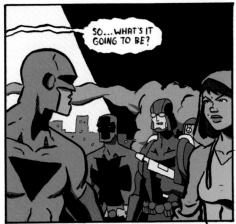

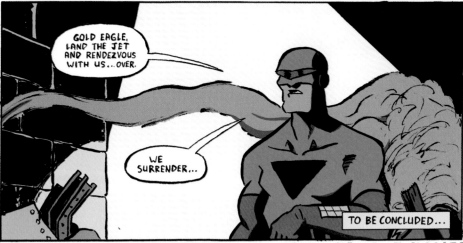

WILL SAM, MIKE, AND VIOLET EVER MAKE IT HOME?

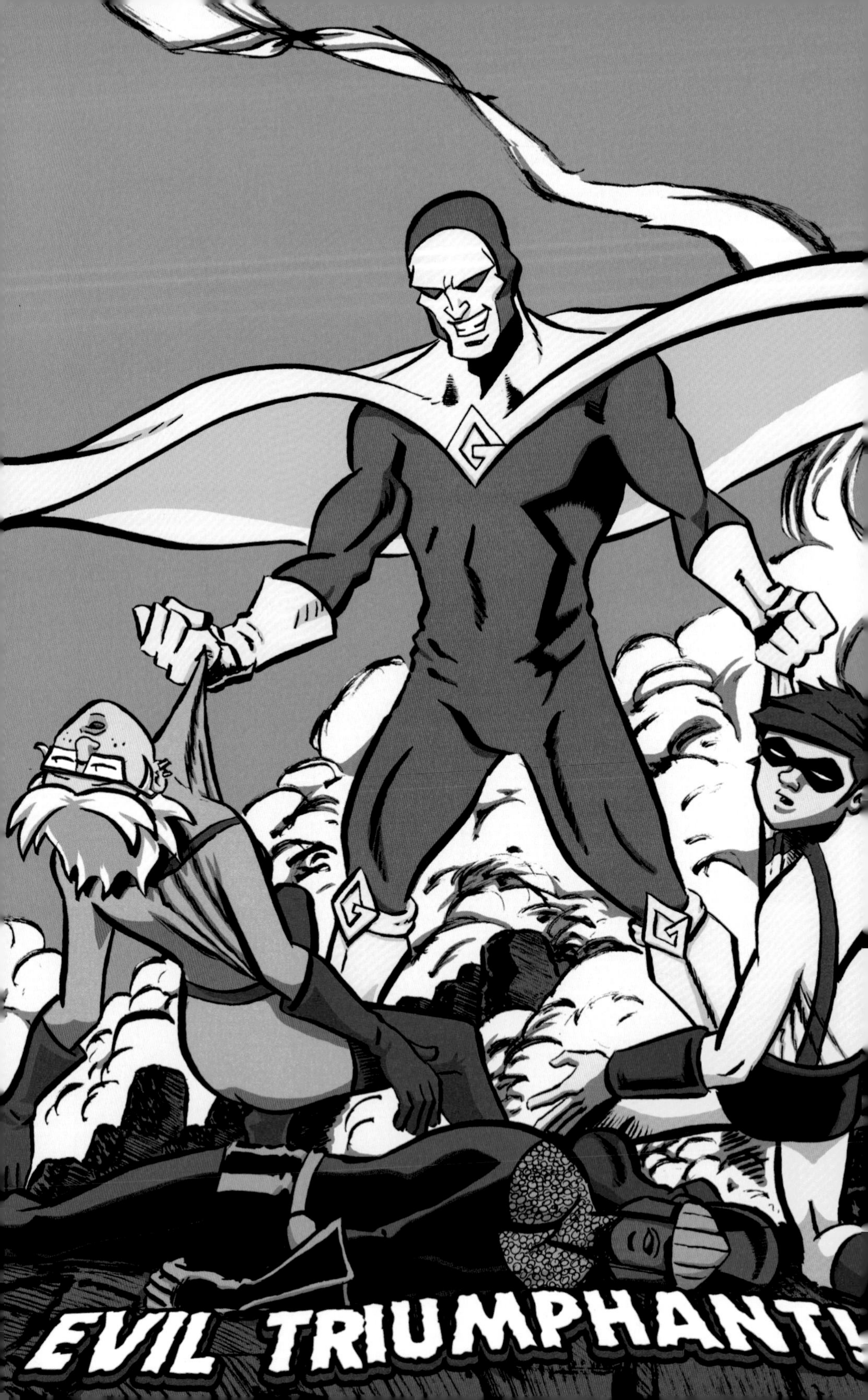
EVIL TRIUMPHANT!

Part Five of Five

Amazing Age

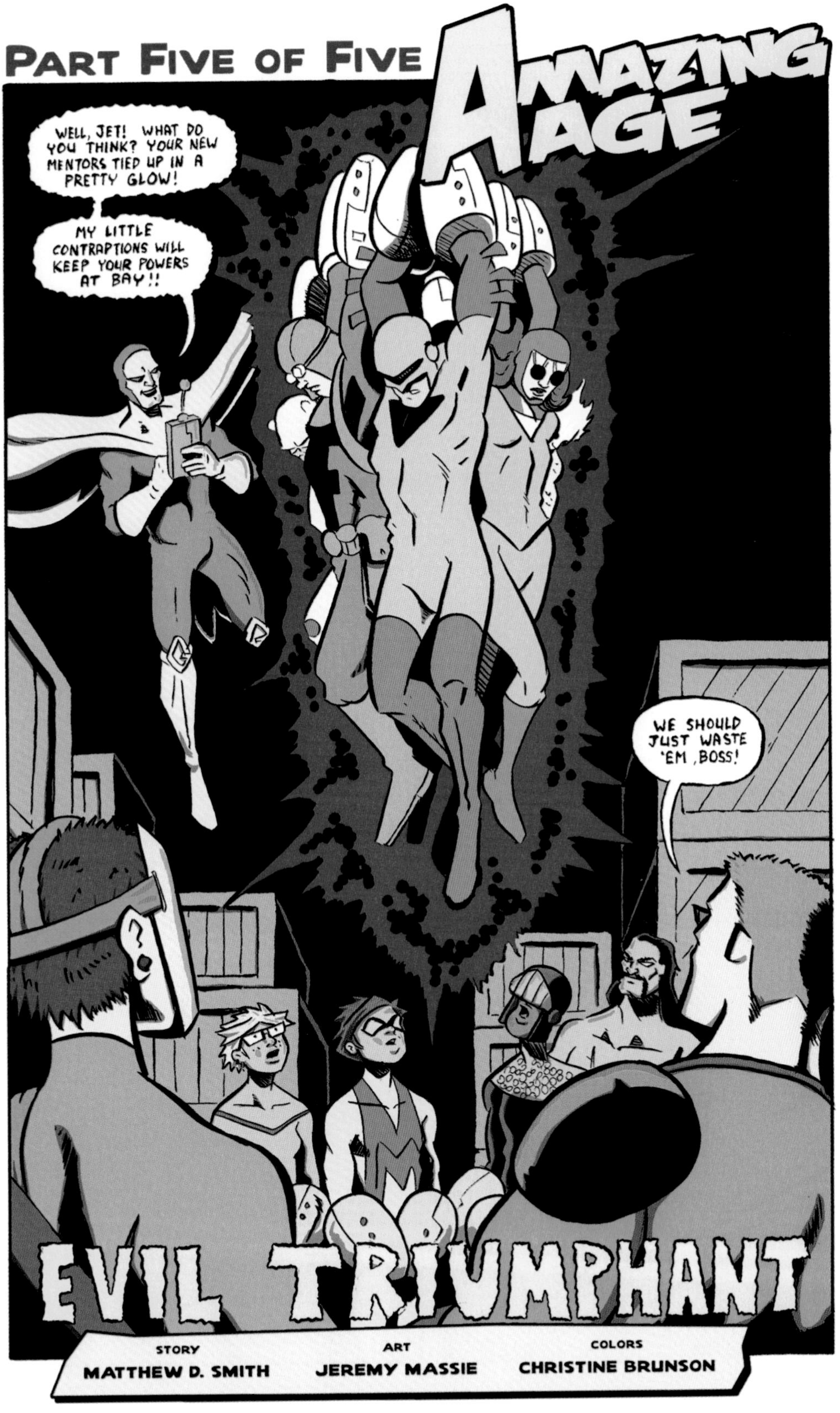
WELL, JET! WHAT DO YOU THINK? YOUR NEW MENTORS TIED UP IN A PRETTY GLOW!
MY LITTLE CONTRAPTIONS WILL KEEP YOUR POWERS AT BAY!!
WE SHOULD JUST WASTE 'EM, BOSS!
EVIL TRIUMPHANT
STORY
MATTHEW D. SMITH
ART
JEREMY MASSIE
COLORS
CHRISTINE BRUNSON

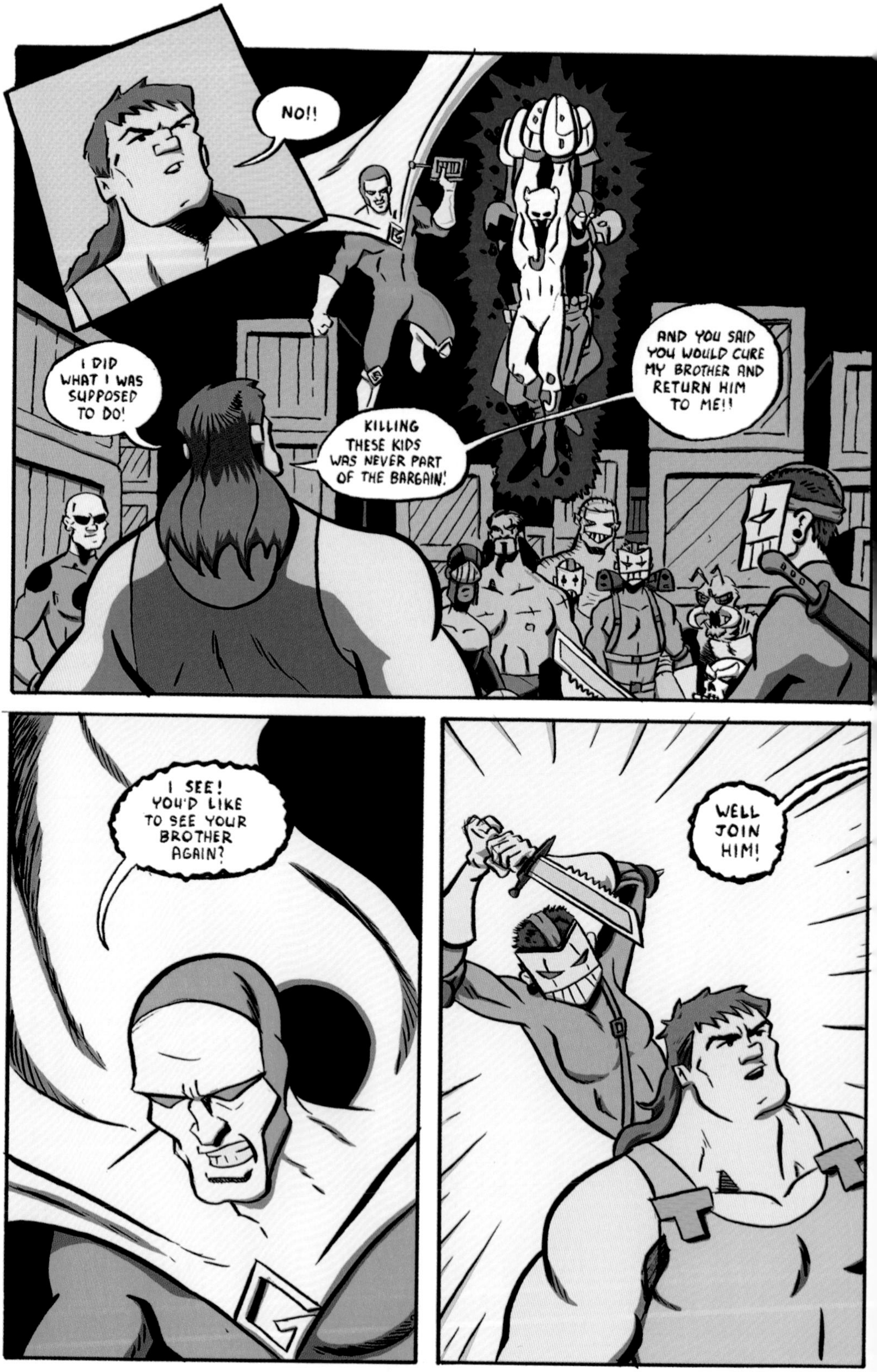
NO!!
I DID WHAT I WAS SUPPOSED TO DO!
KILLING THESE KIDS WAS NEVER PART OF THE BARGAIN!
AND YOU SAID YOU WOULD CURE MY BROTHER AND RETURN HIM TO ME!!
I SEE! YOU'D LIKE TO SEE YOUR BROTHER AGAIN?
WELL JOIN HIM!

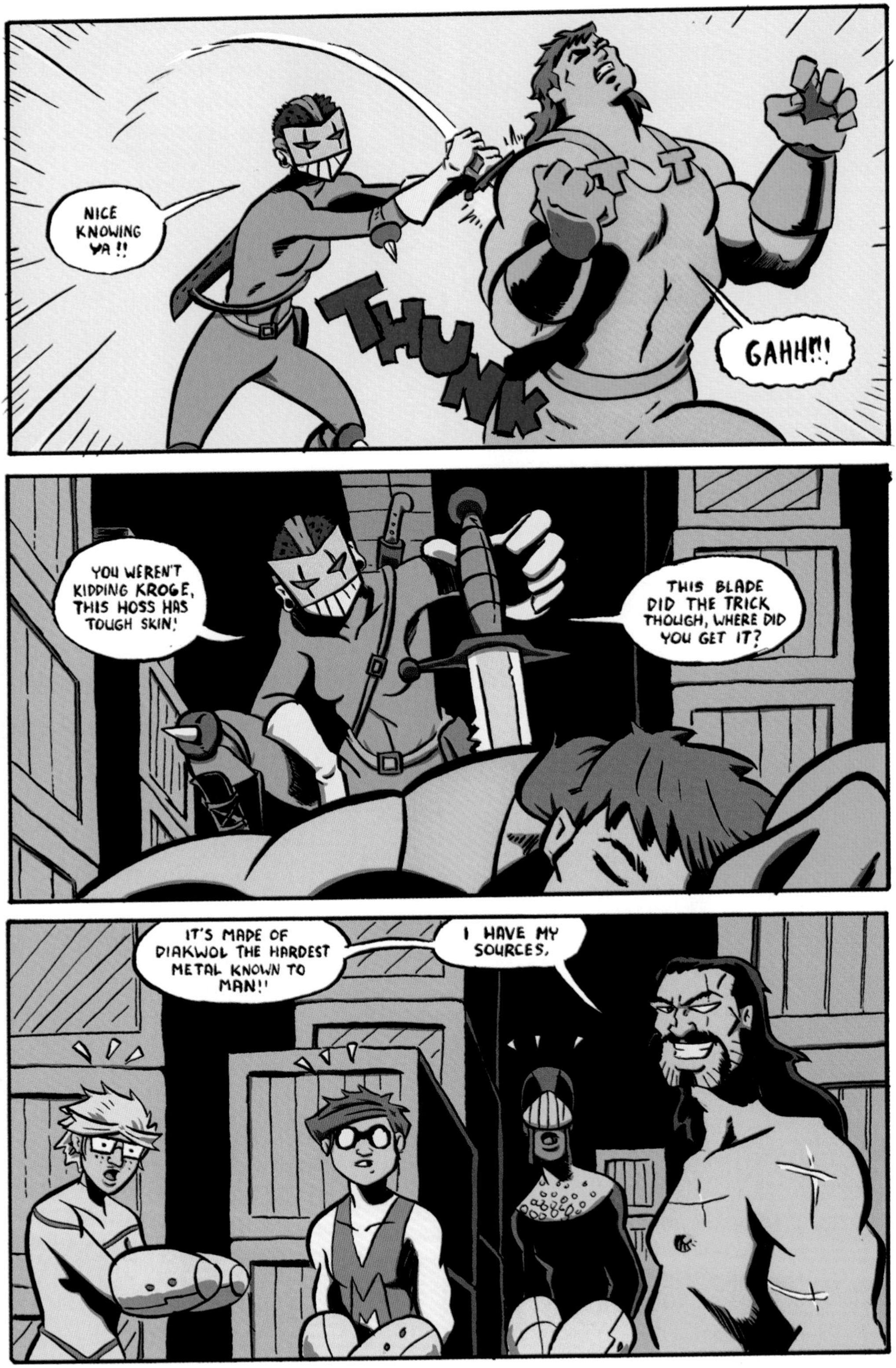
NICE KNOWING YA !!
THUNK
GAHH!!!
YOU WEREN'T KIDDING KROGE, THIS HOSS HAS TOUGH SKIN!
THIS BLADE DID THE TRICK THOUGH, WHERE DID YOU GET IT?
IT'S MADE OF DIAKWOL THE HARDEST METAL KNOWN TO MAN!!
I HAVE MY SOURCES.

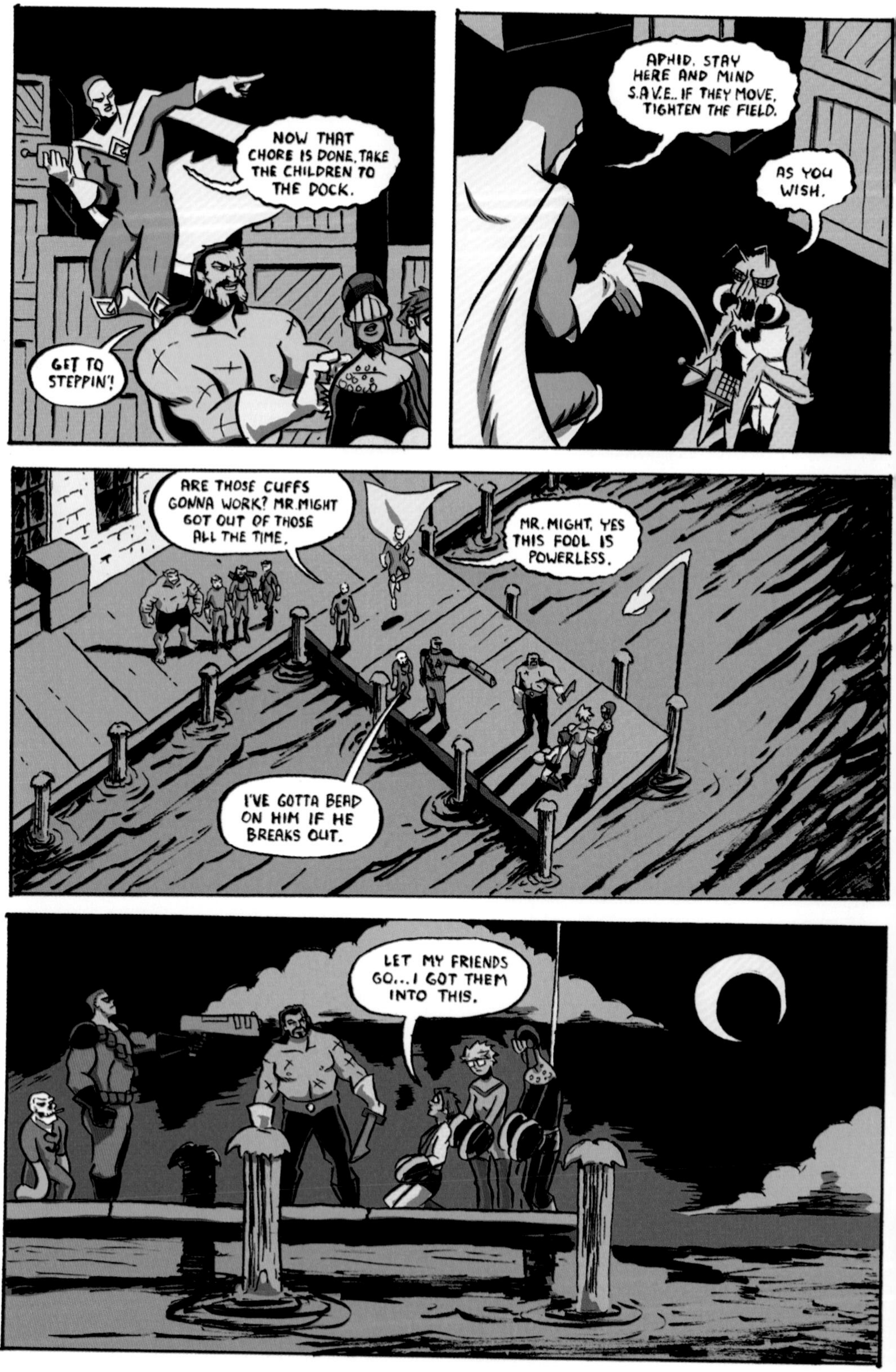
NOW THAT CHORE IS DONE, TAKE THE CHILDREN TO THE DOCK.
GET TO STEPPIN'!
APHID, STAY HERE AND MIND S.A.V.E.. IF THEY MOVE, TIGHTEN THE FIELD.
AS YOU WISH.
ARE THOSE CUFFS GONNA WORK? MR. MIGHT GOT OUT OF THOSE ALL THE TIME.
MR. MIGHT, YES THIS FOOL IS POWERLESS.
I'VE GOTTA BEAD ON HIM IF HE BREAKS OUT.
LET MY FRIENDS GO... I GOT THEM INTO THIS.

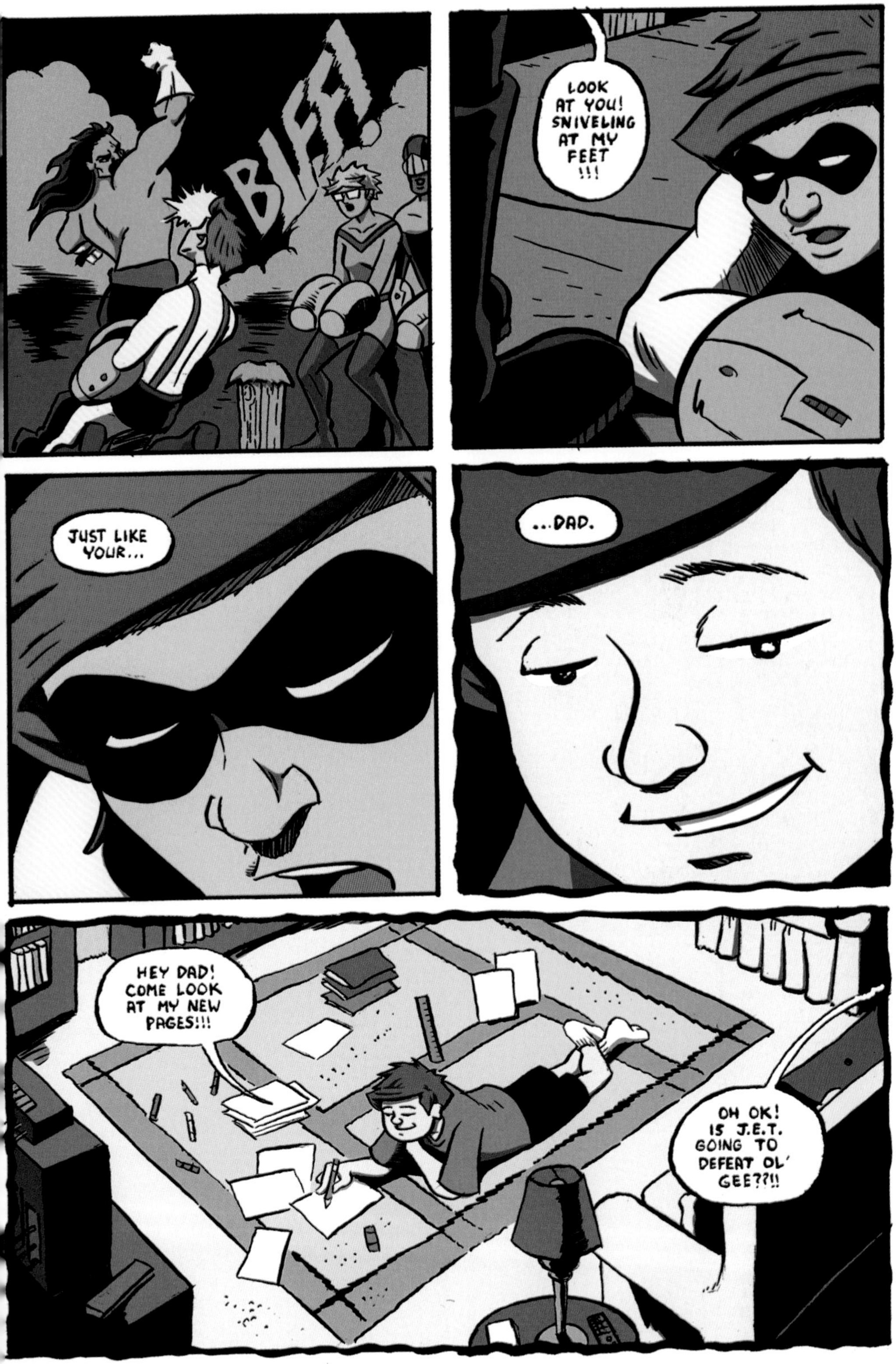
BIFF!
LOOK AT YOU! SNIVELING AT MY FEET !!!
JUST LIKE YOUR...
...DAD.
HEY DAD! COME LOOK AT MY NEW PAGES!!!
OH OK! IS J.E.T. GOING TO DEFEAT OL' GEE??!!

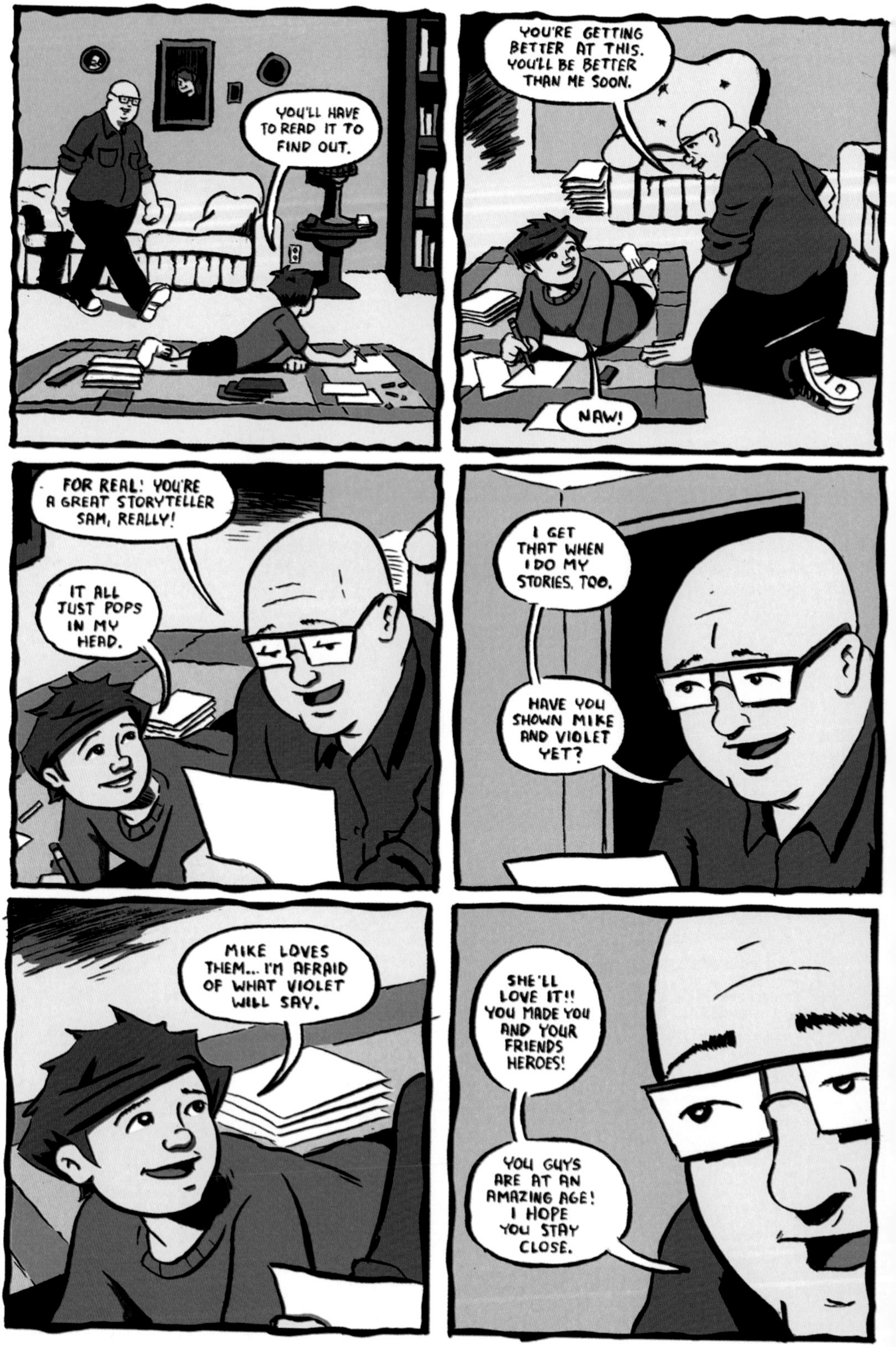
YOU'LL HAVE TO READ IT TO FIND OUT.
YOU'RE GETTING BETTER AT THIS. YOU'LL BE BETTER THAN ME SOON.
NAW!
FOR REAL! YOU'RE A GREAT STORYTELLER SAM, REALLY!
IT ALL JUST POPS IN MY HEAD.
I GET THAT WHEN I DO MY STORIES, TOO.
HAVE YOU SHOWN MIKE AND VIOLET YET?
MIKE LOVES THEM... I'M AFRAID OF WHAT VIOLET WILL SAY.
SHE'LL LOVE IT!! YOU MADE YOU AND YOUR FRIENDS HEROES!
YOU GUYS ARE AT AN AMAZING AGE! I HOPE YOU STAY CLOSE.

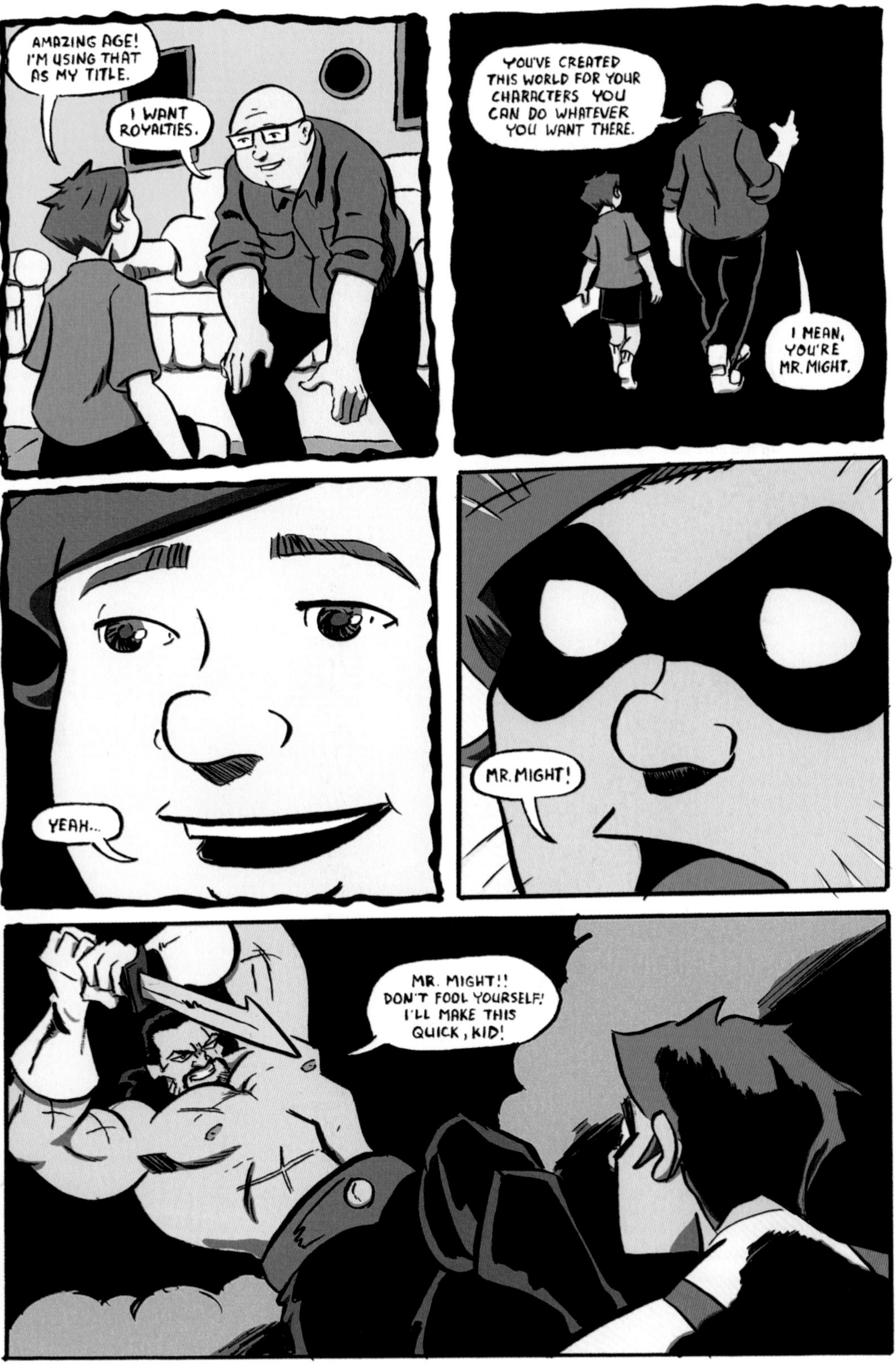
AMAZING AGE! I'M USING THAT AS MY TITLE.
I WANT ROYALTIES.
YOU'VE CREATED THIS WORLD FOR YOUR CHARACTERS YOU CAN DO WHATEVER YOU WANT THERE.
I MEAN, YOU'RE MR. MIGHT.
YEAH...
MR. MIGHT!
MR. MIGHT!! DON'T FOOL YOURSELF! I'LL MAKE THIS QUICK, KID!

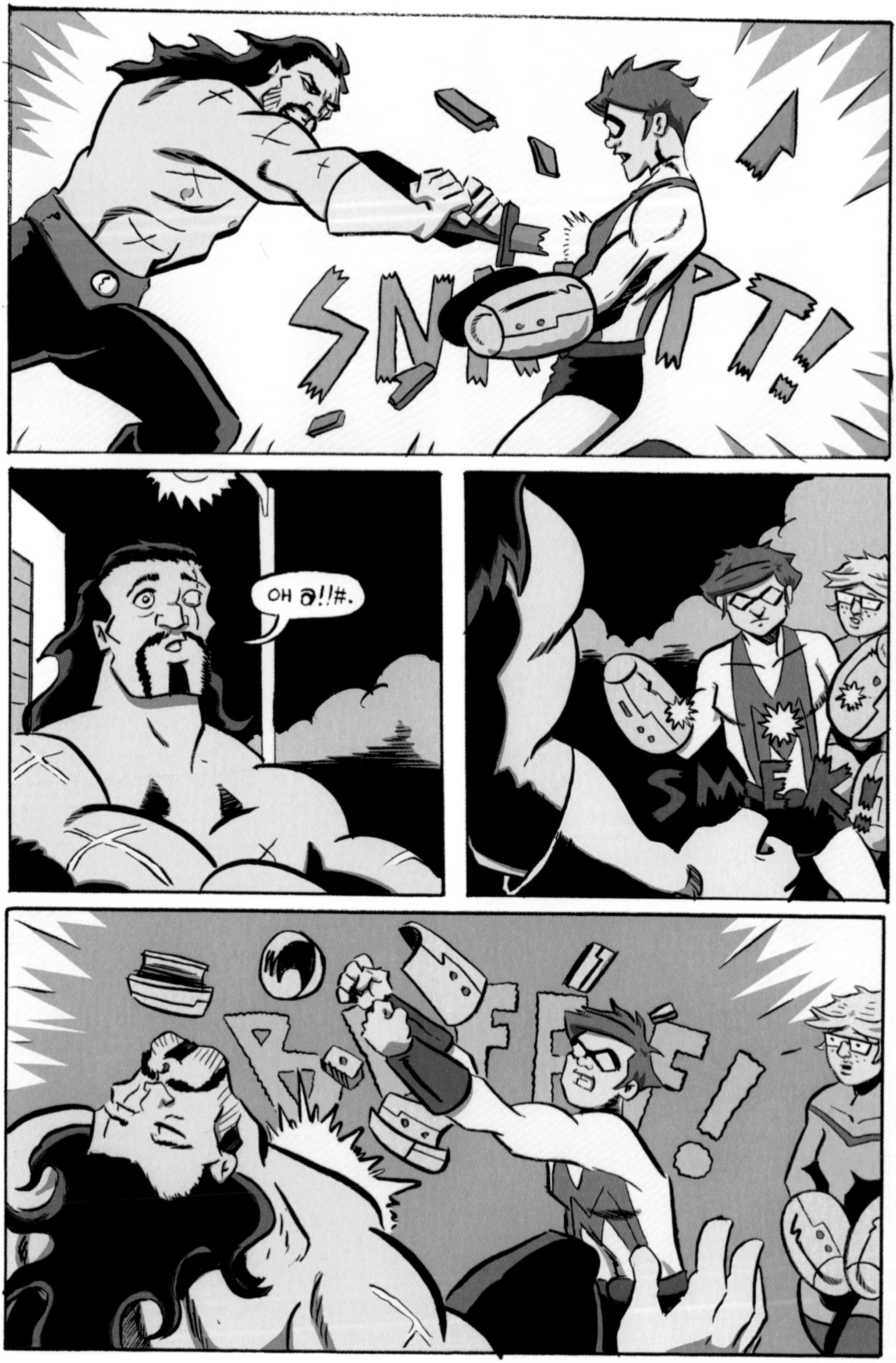
SNAPT!
OH @!!#.
SMEK
BIFF!

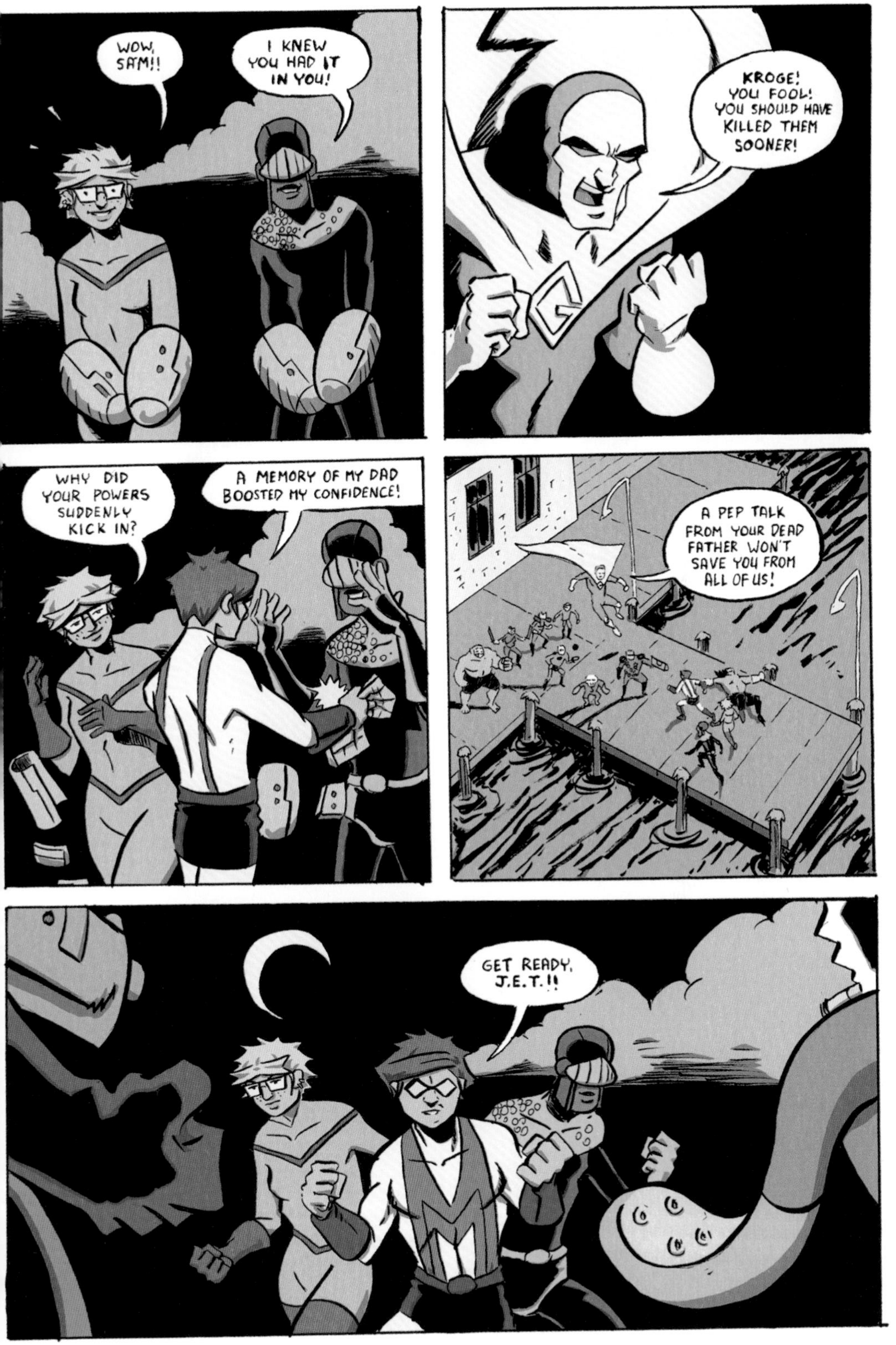
WOW, SAM!!
I KNEW YOU HAD IT IN YOU!
KROGE! YOU FOOL! YOU SHOULD HAVE KILLED THEM SOONER!
WHY DID YOUR POWERS SUDDENLY KICK IN?
A MEMORY OF MY DAD BOOSTED MY CONFIDENCE!
A PEP TALK FROM YOUR DEAD FATHER WON'T SAVE YOU FROM ALL OF US!
GET READY, J.E.T.!!

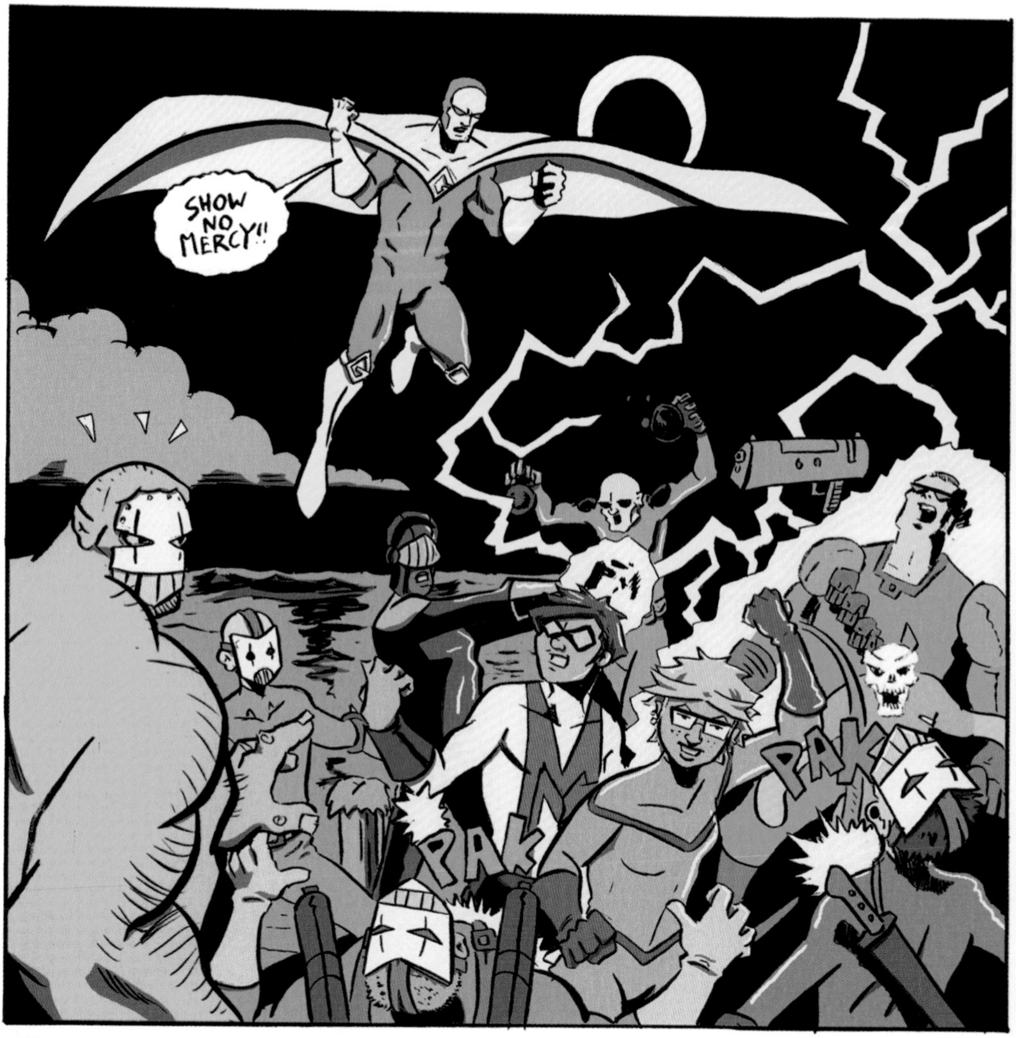
SHOW NO MERCY!!
PAK
PAK

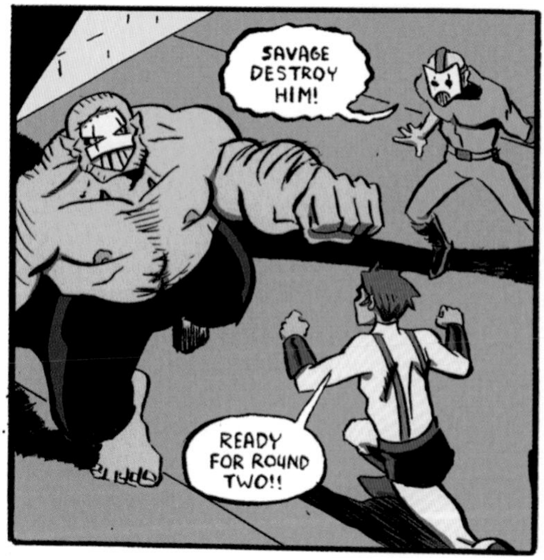
SAVAGE DESTROY HIM!
READY FOR ROUND TWO!!

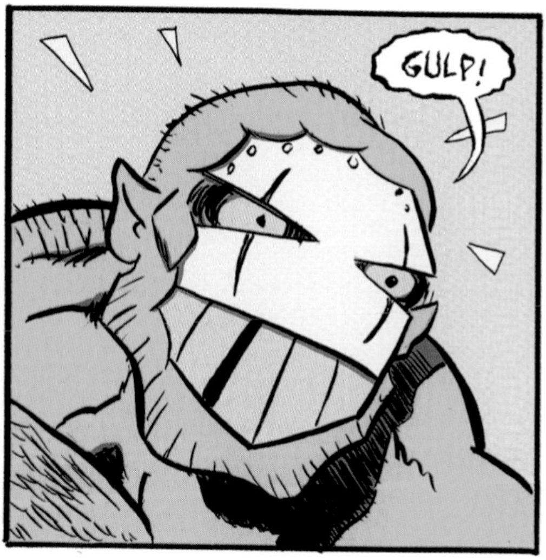
GULP!

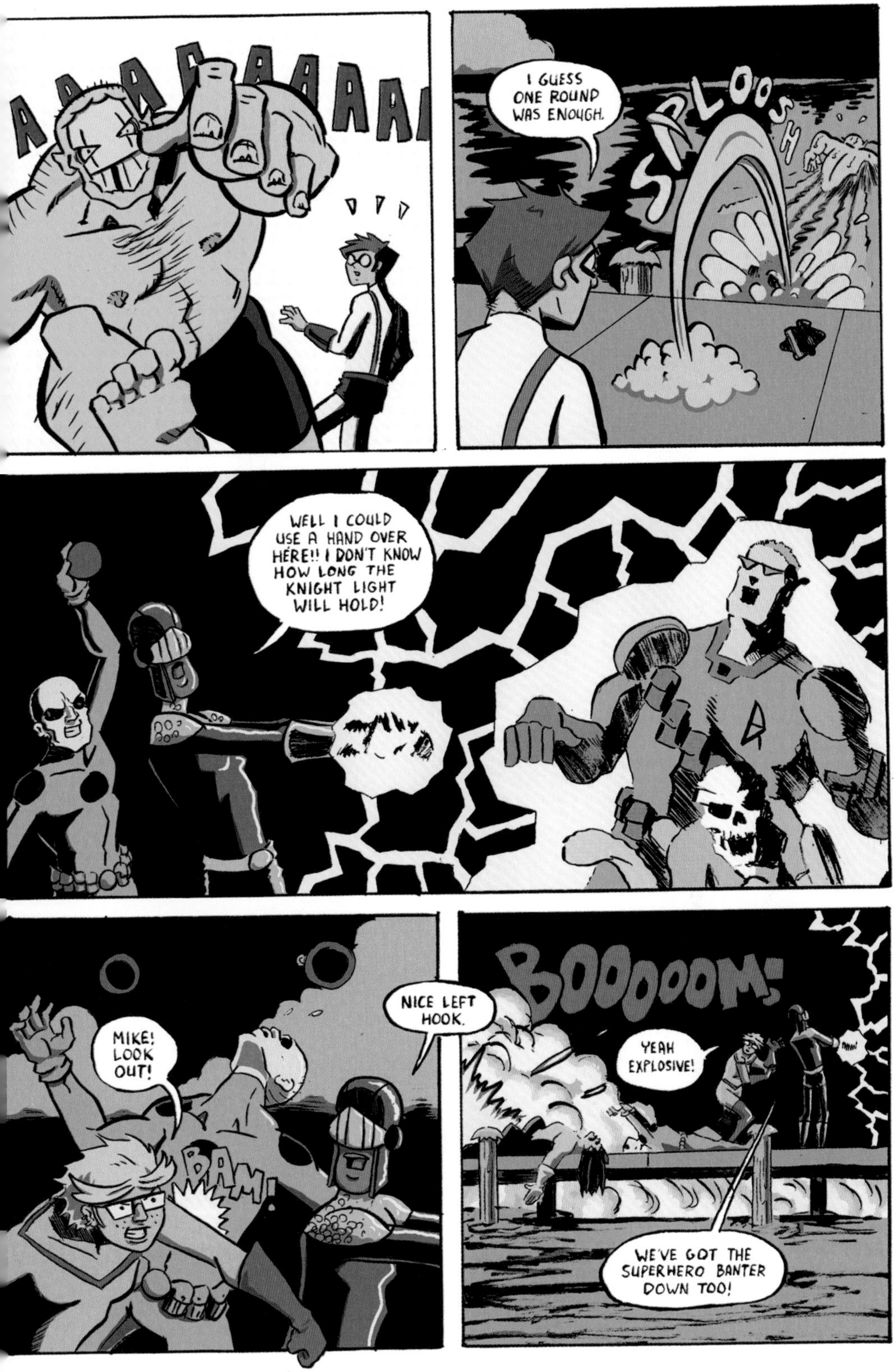
AAAAAAAAAA
I GUESS ONE ROUND WAS ENOUGH.
SPLOOSH
WELL I COULD USE A HAND OVER HERE!! I DON'T KNOW HOW LONG THE KNIGHT LIGHT WILL HOLD!
MIKE! LOOK OUT!
BAM!
NICE LEFT HOOK.
BOOOOOM!
YEAH EXPLOSIVE!
WE'VE GOT THE SUPERHERO BANTER DOWN TOO!

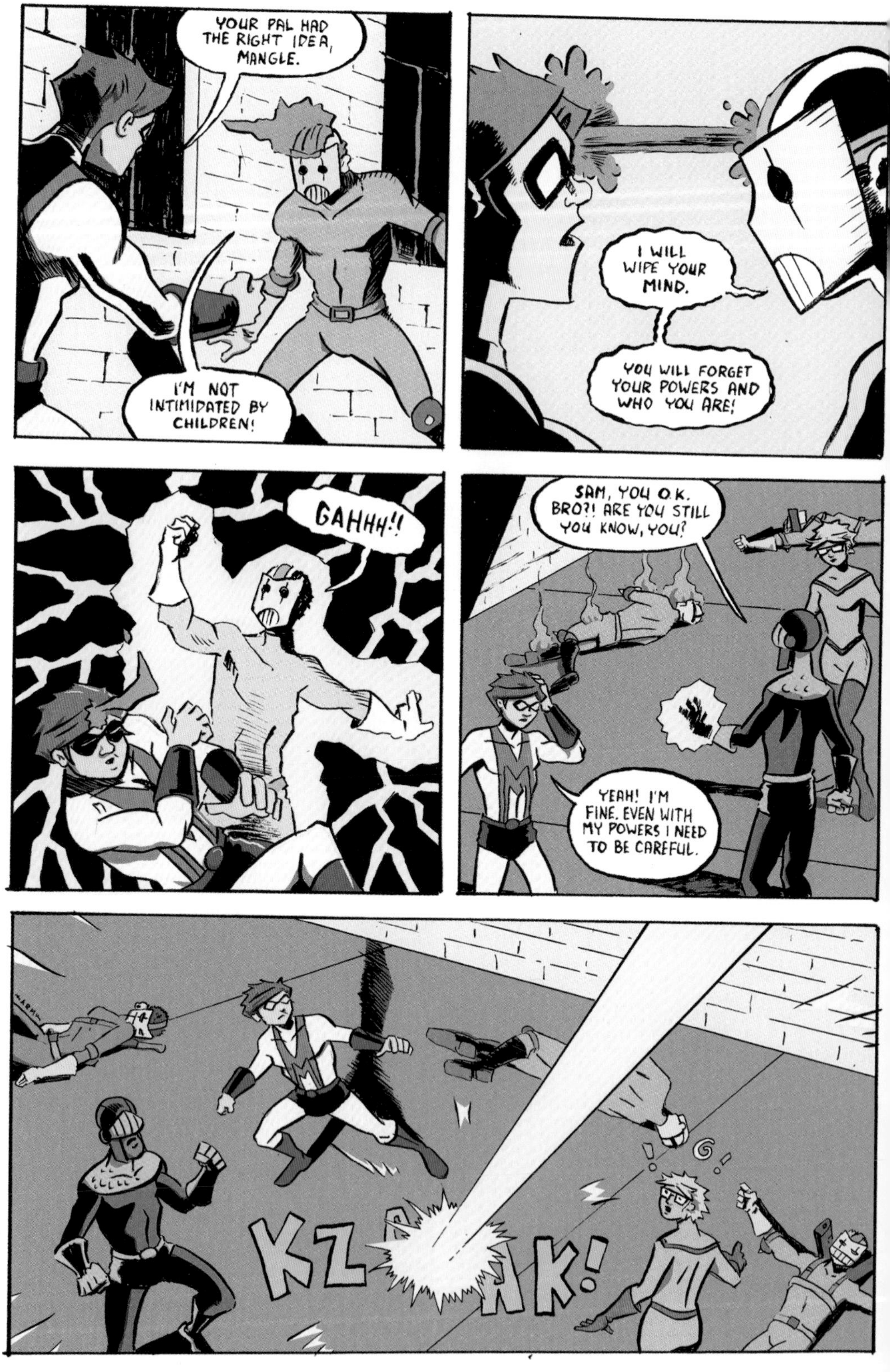
YOUR PAL HAD THE RIGHT IDEA, MANGLE.
I'M NOT INTIMIDATED BY CHILDREN!
I WILL WIPE YOUR MIND.
YOU WILL FORGET YOUR POWERS AND WHO YOU ARE!
GAHHH!!
SAM, YOU O.K. BRO?! ARE YOU STILL YOU KNOW, YOU?
YEAH! I'M FINE. EVEN WITH MY POWERS I NEED TO BE CAREFUL.
KZ
AK!

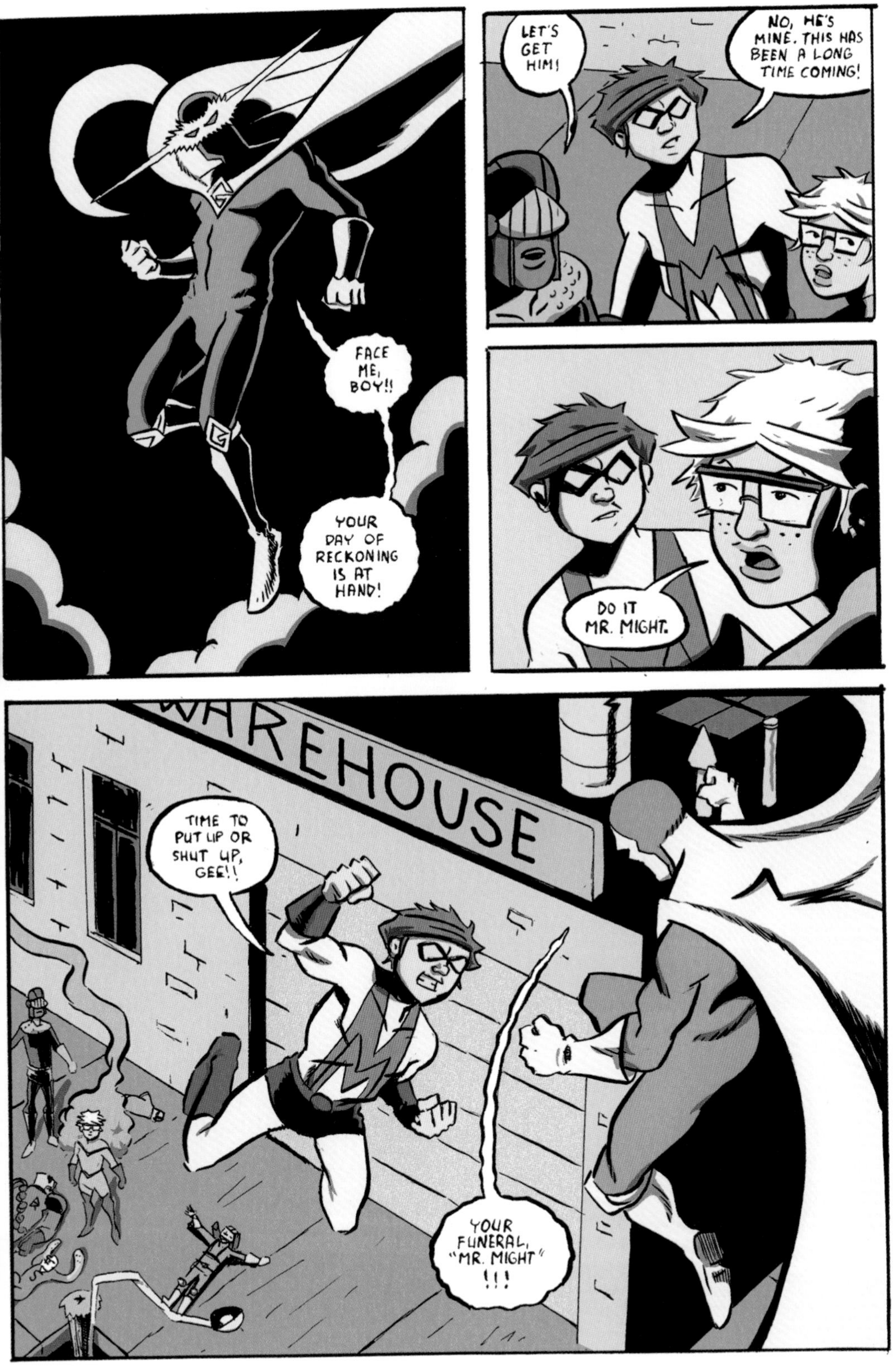
FACE ME, BOY!!
YOUR DAY OF RECKONING IS AT HAND!
LET'S GET HIM!
NO, HE'S MINE. THIS HAS BEEN A LONG TIME COMING!
DO IT MR. MIGHT.
WAREHOUSE
TIME TO PUT UP OR SHUT UP, GEE!!
YOUR FUNERAL, "MR. MIGHT" !!!

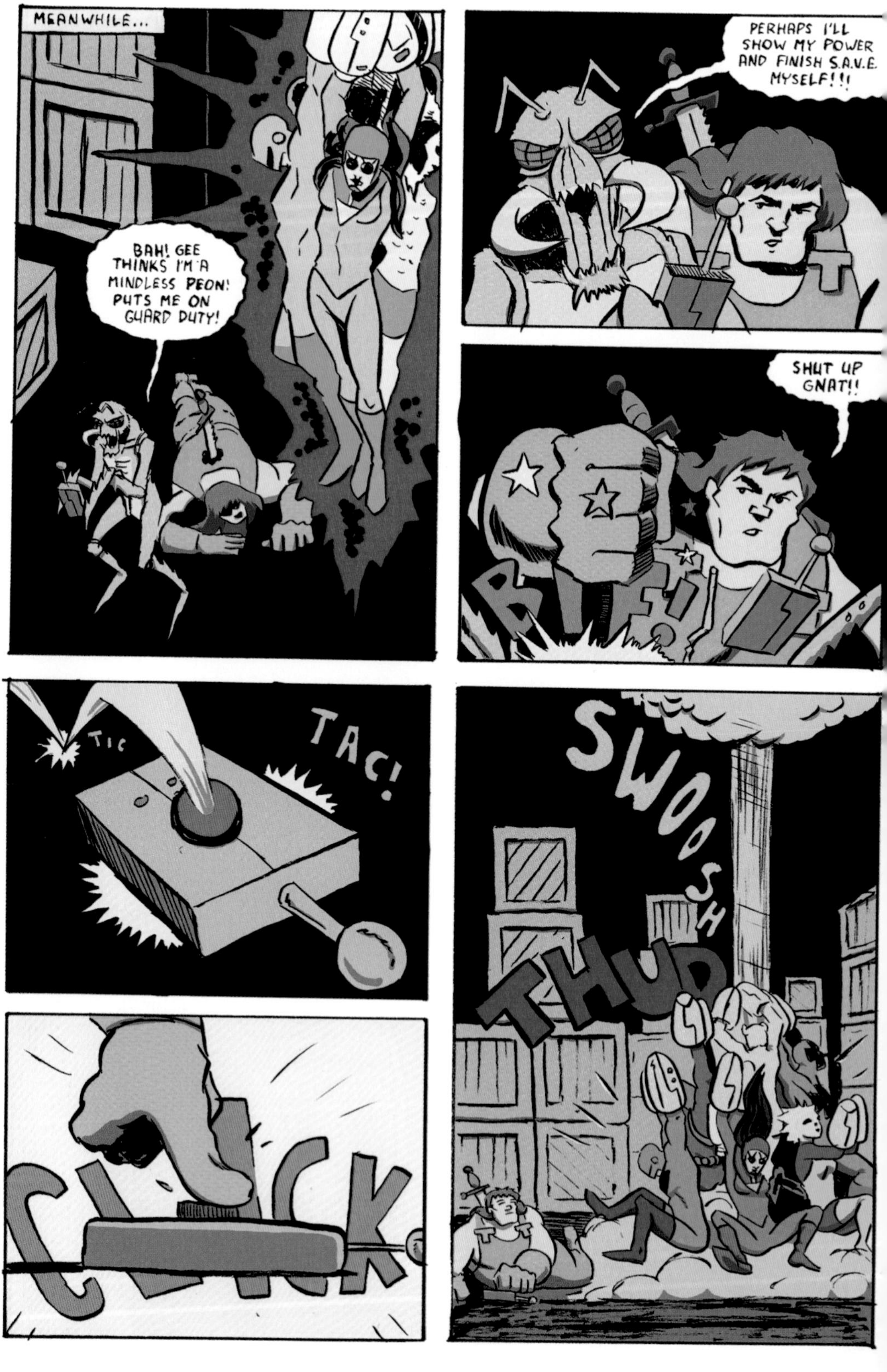
MEANWHILE...
BAH! GEE THINKS I'M A MINDLESS PEON! PUTS ME ON GUARD DUTY!
PERHAPS I'LL SHOW MY POWER AND FINISH S.A.V.E. MYSELF!!!
SHUT UP GNAT!!
TIC
TAC!
SWOOSH
THUD

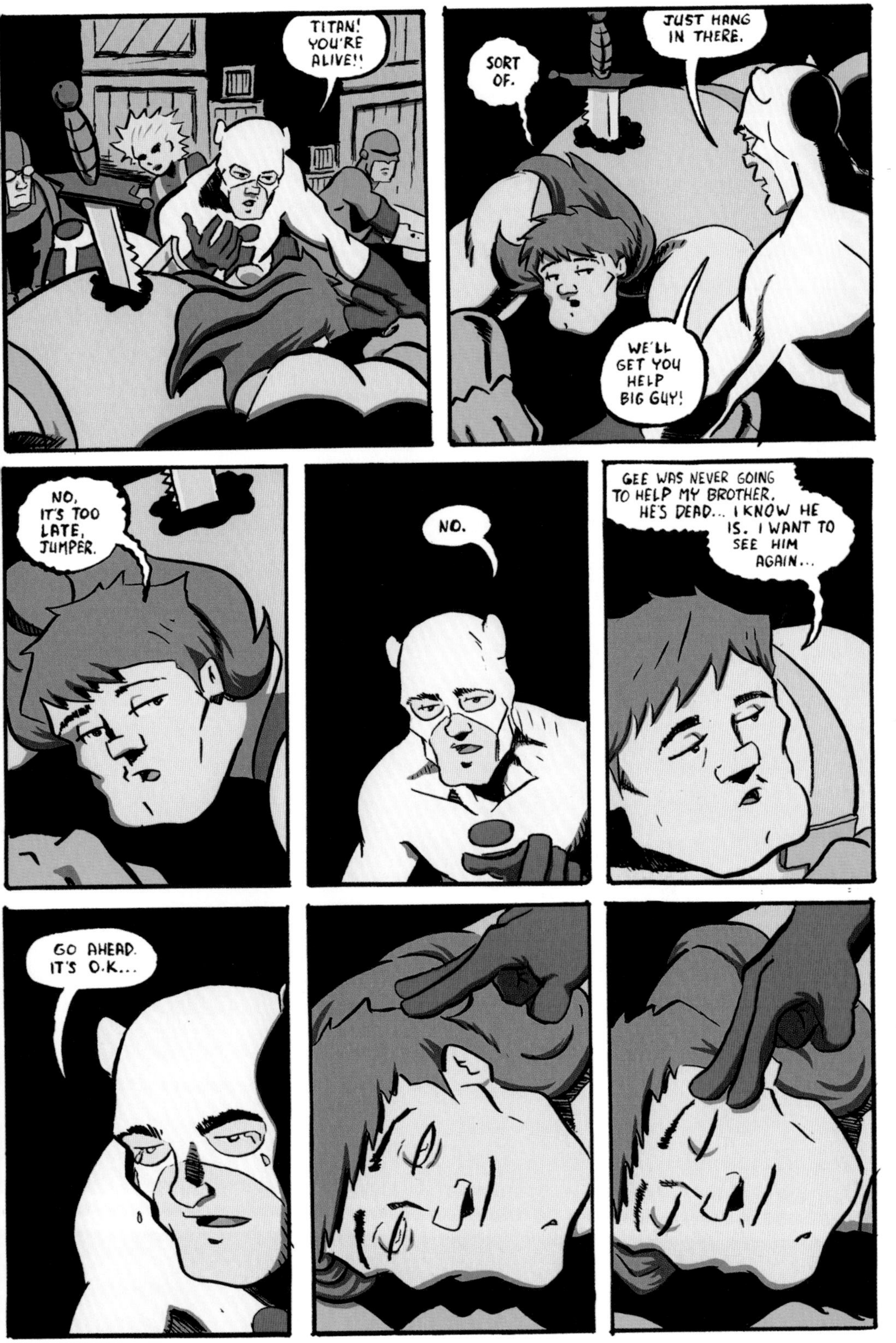
TITAN! YOU'RE ALIVE!!
SORT OF.
JUST HANG IN THERE.
WE'LL GET YOU HELP BIG GUY!
NO, IT'S TOO LATE, JUMPER.
NO.
GEE WAS NEVER GOING TO HELP MY BROTHER. HE'S DEAD... I KNOW HE IS. I WANT TO SEE HIM AGAIN...
GO AHEAD. IT'S O.K...

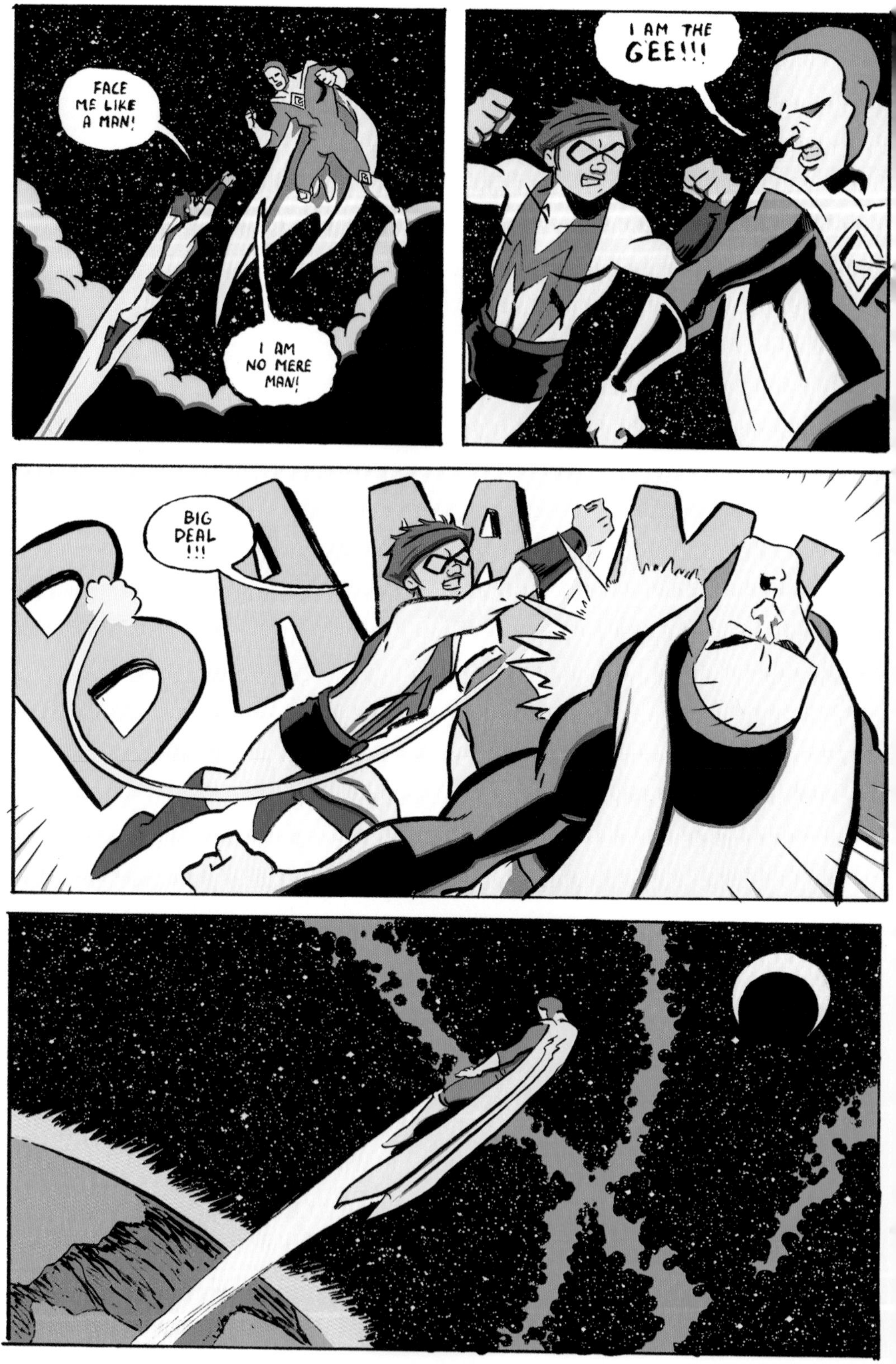
FACE ME LIKE A MAN!
I AM NO MERE MAN!
I AM THE GEE!!!
BIG DEAL!!!
BAM

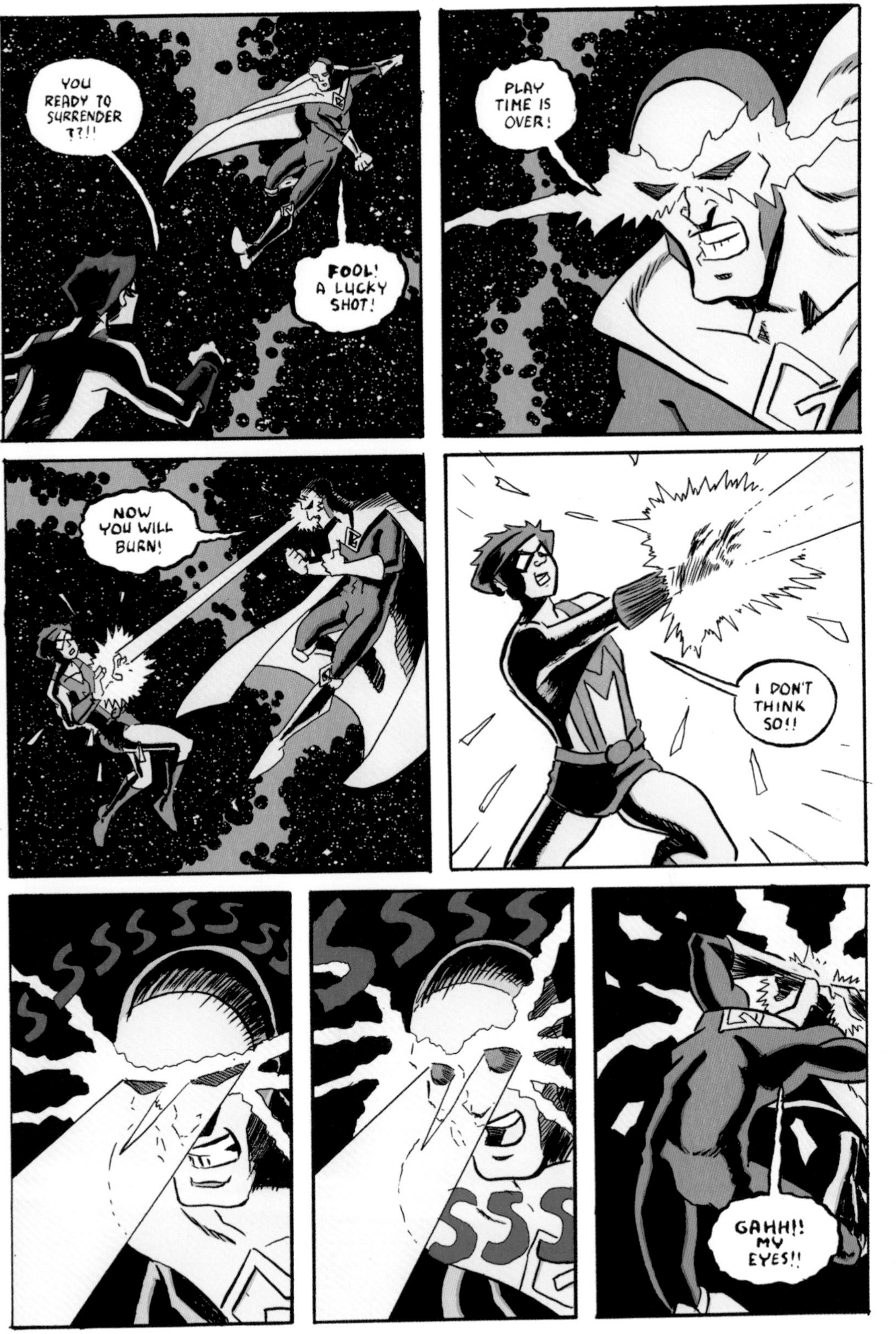
YOU READY TO SURRENDER ??!!
FOOL! A LUCKY SHOT!
PLAY TIME IS OVER!
NOW YOU WILL BURN!
I DON'T THINK SO!!
SSSSSSS
SSSSS
SSS
GAHH!! MY EYES!!

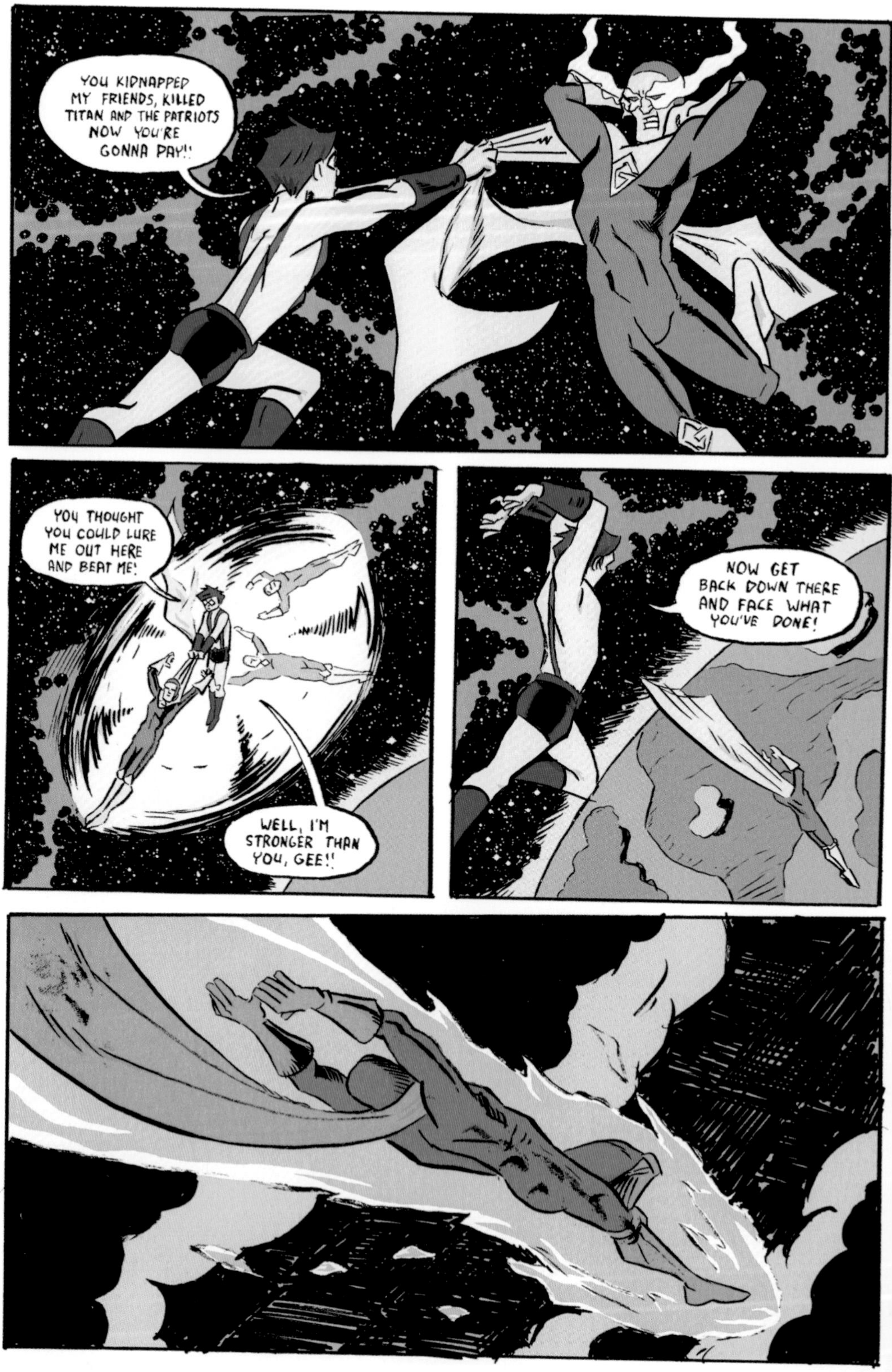
YOU KIDNAPPED MY FRIENDS, KILLED TITAN AND THE PATRIOTS NOW YOU'RE GONNA PAY!!
YOU THOUGHT YOU COULD LURE ME OUT HERE AND BEAT ME!
WELL, I'M STRONGER THAN YOU, GEE!!
NOW GET BACK DOWN THERE AND FACE WHAT YOU'VE DONE!

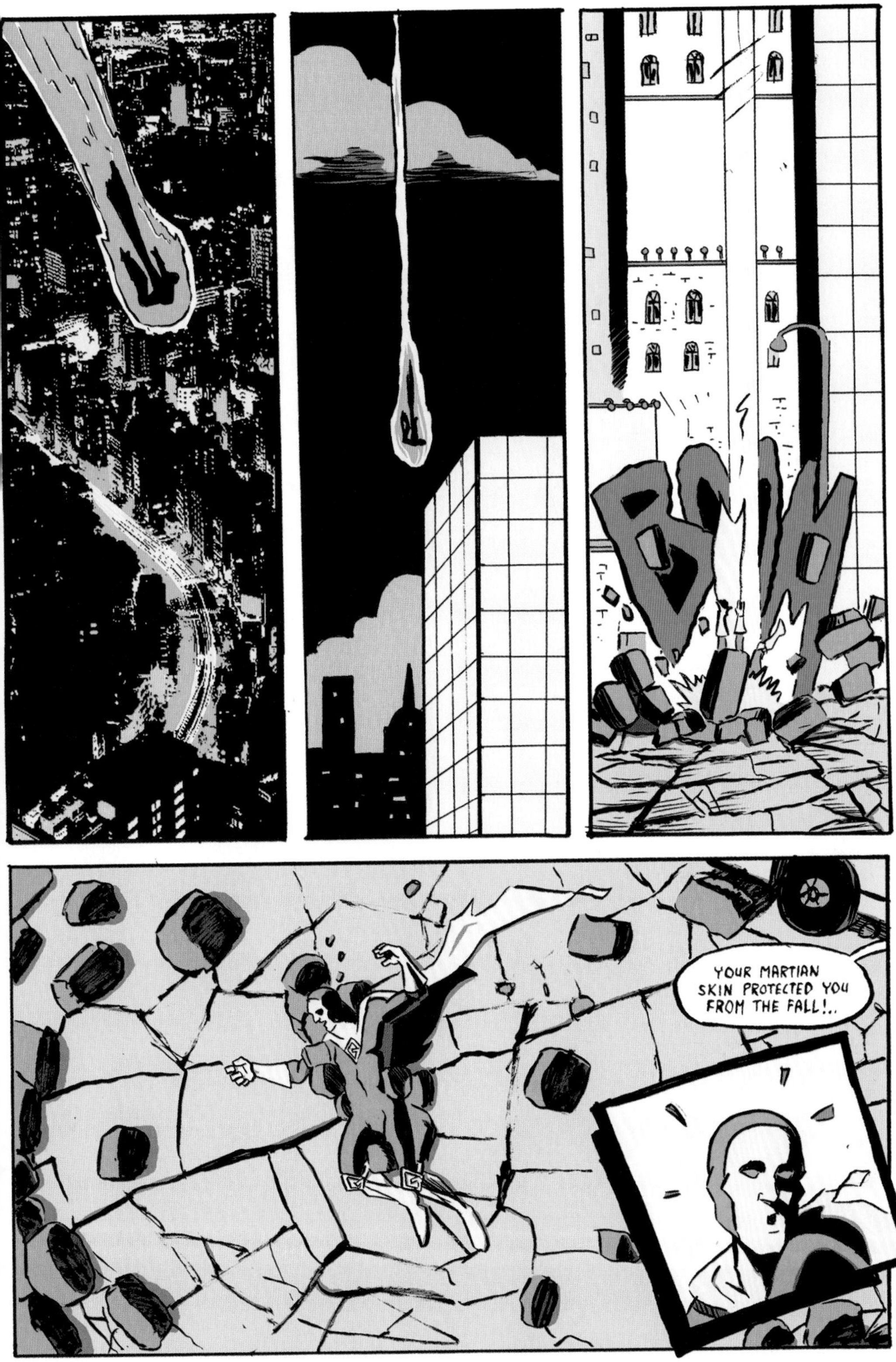
BOOM
YOUR MARTIAN SKIN PROTECTED YOU FROM THE FALL!..

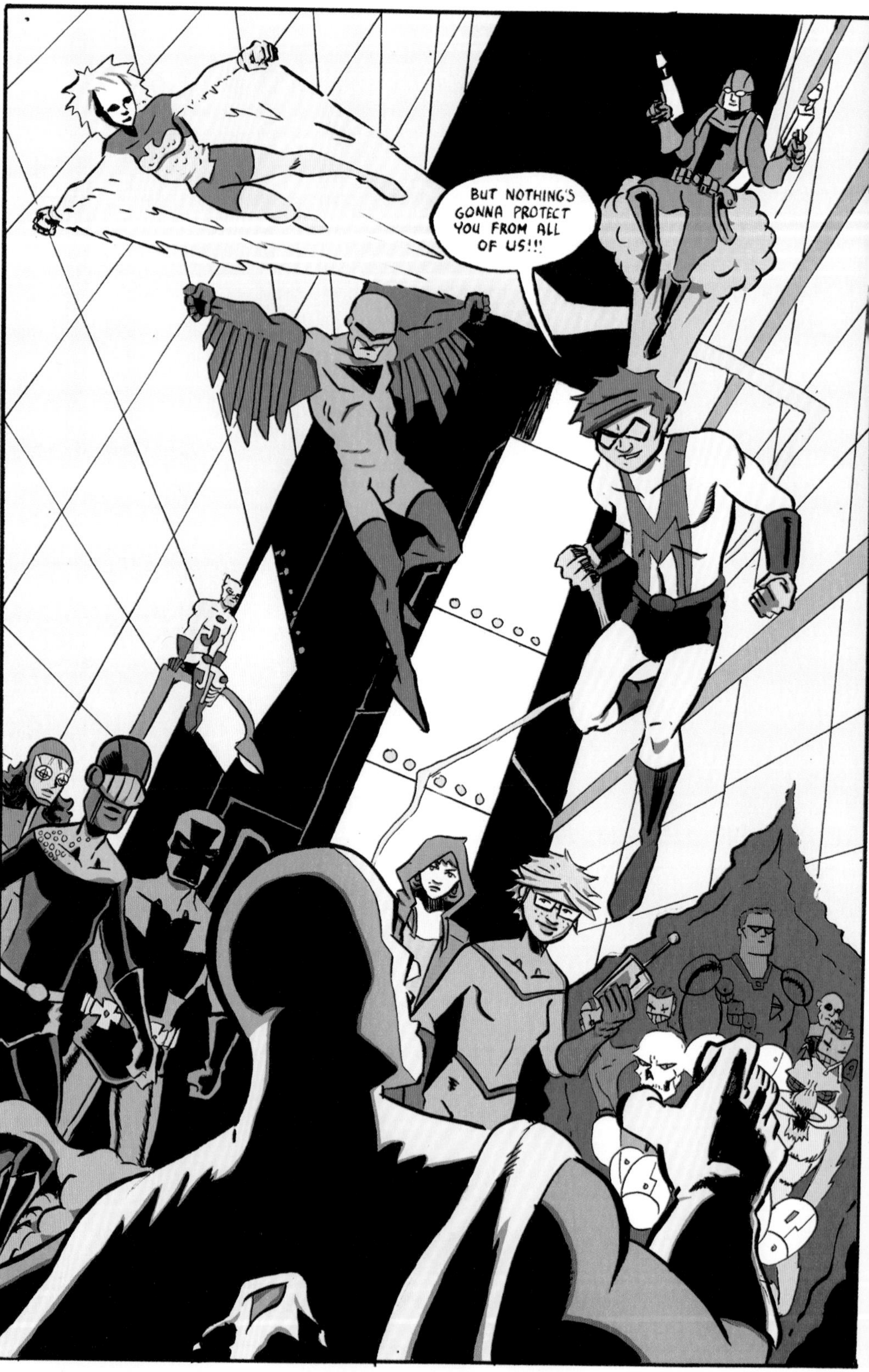
BUT NOTHING'S GONNA PROTECT YOU FROM ALL OF US!!!

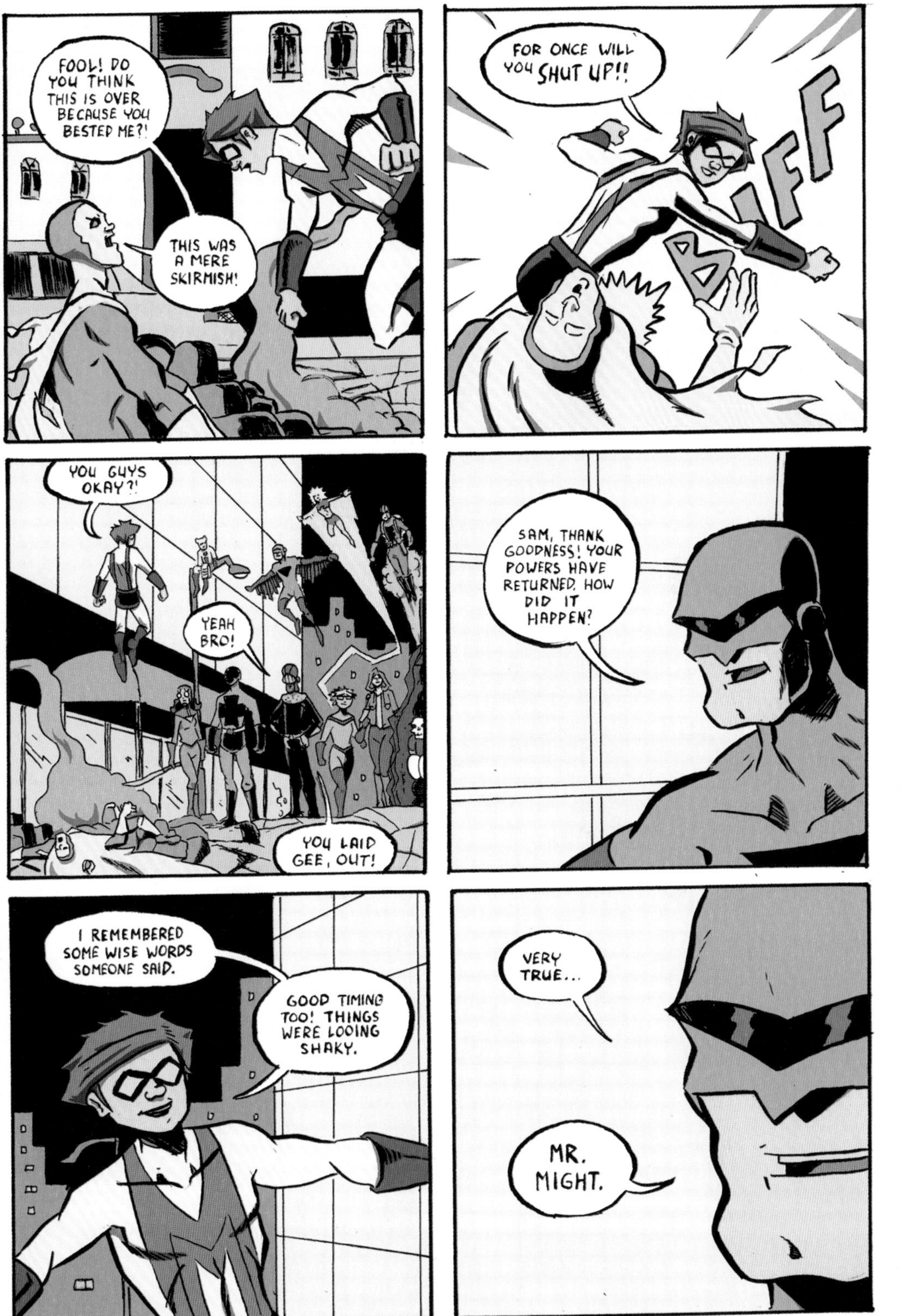
FOOL! DO YOU THINK THIS IS OVER BECAUSE YOU BESTED ME?!
THIS WAS A MERE SKIRMISH!
FOR ONCE WILL YOU SHUT UP!!
BIFF
YOU GUYS OKAY?!
YEAH BRO!
YOU LAID GEE, OUT!
SAM, THANK GOODNESS! YOUR POWERS HAVE RETURNED. HOW DID IT HAPPEN?
I REMEMBERED SOME WISE WORDS SOMEONE SAID.
GOOD TIMING TOO! THINGS WERE LOOING SHAKY.
VERY TRUE...
MR. MIGHT.

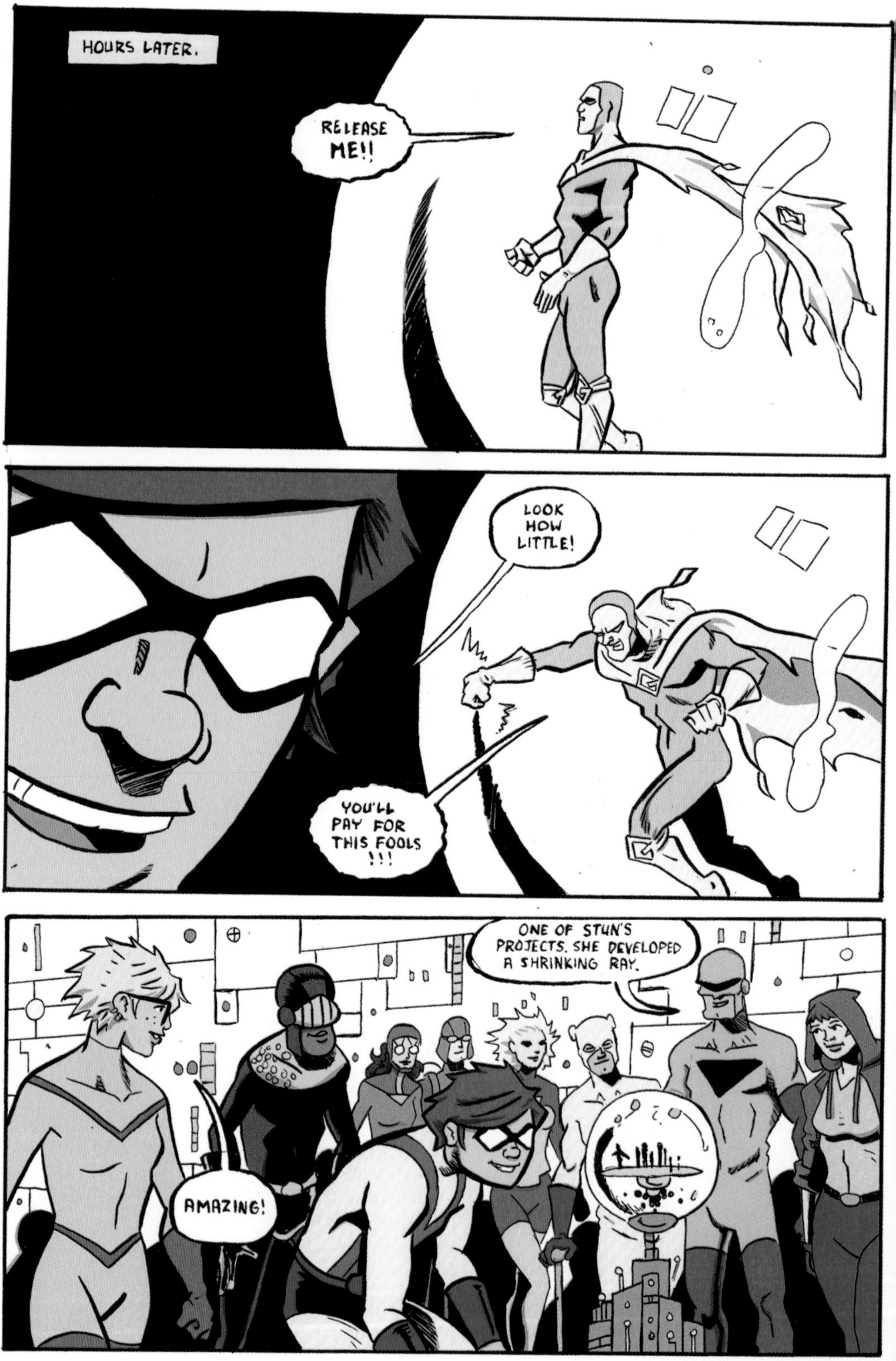
HOURS LATER.
RELEASE ME!!
LOOK HOW LITTLE!
YOU'LL PAY FOR THIS FOOLS !!!
ONE OF STUN'S PROJECTS. SHE DEVELOPED A SHRINKING RAY.
AMAZING!

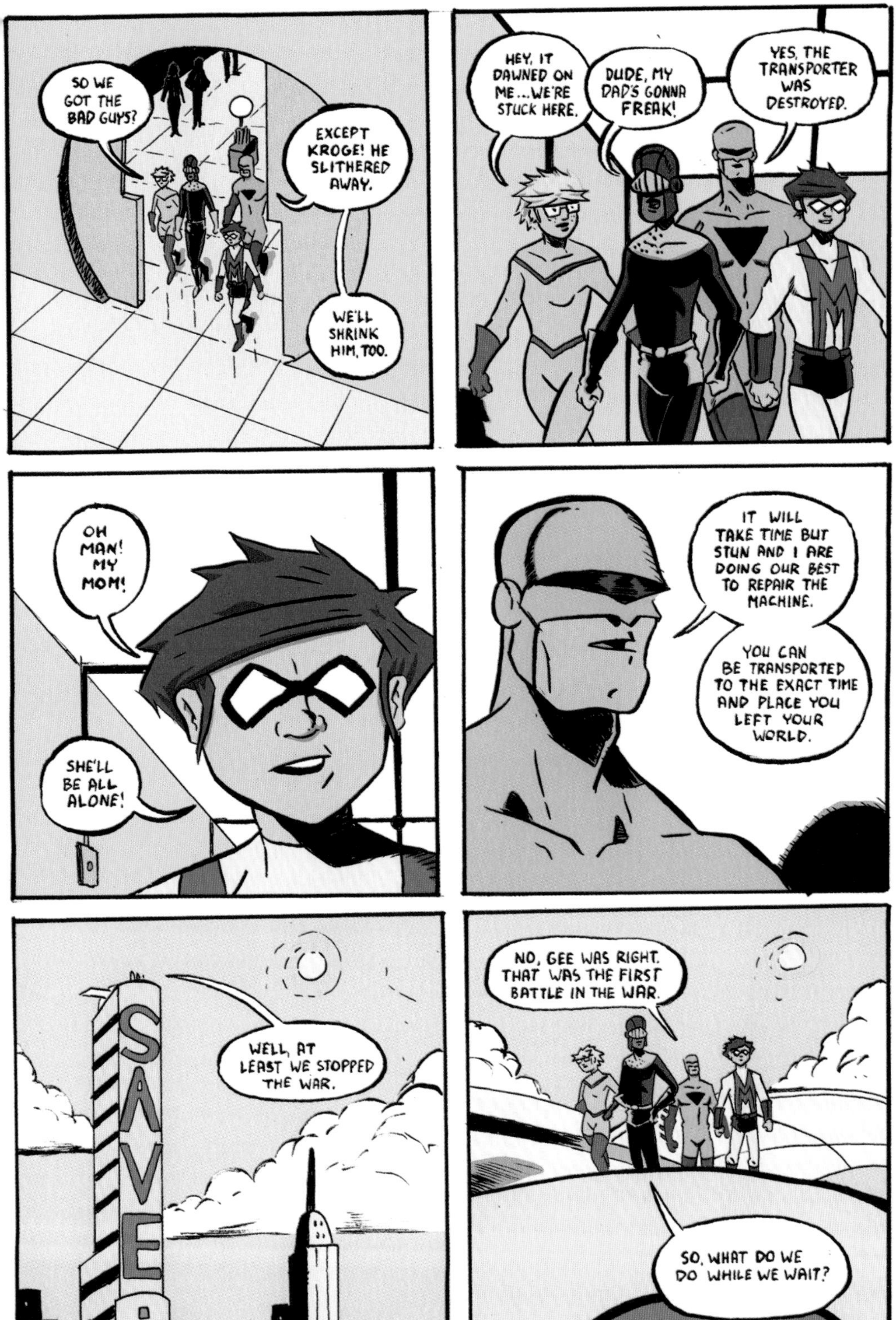
SO WE GOT THE BAD GUYS?
EXCEPT KROGE! HE SLITHERED AWAY.
WE'LL SHRINK HIM, TOO.
HEY, IT DAWNED ON ME...WE'RE STUCK HERE.
DUDE, MY DAD'S GONNA FREAK!
YES, THE TRANSPORTER WAS DESTROYED.
OH MAN! MY MOM!
SHE'LL BE ALL ALONE!
IT WILL TAKE TIME BUT STUN AND I ARE DOING OUR BEST TO REPAIR THE MACHINE.
YOU CAN BE TRANSPORTED TO THE EXACT TIME AND PLACE YOU LEFT YOUR WORLD.
SAVE
WELL, AT LEAST WE STOPPED THE WAR.
NO, GEE WAS RIGHT. THAT WAS THE FIRST BATTLE IN THE WAR.
SO, WHAT DO WE DO WHILE WE WAIT?

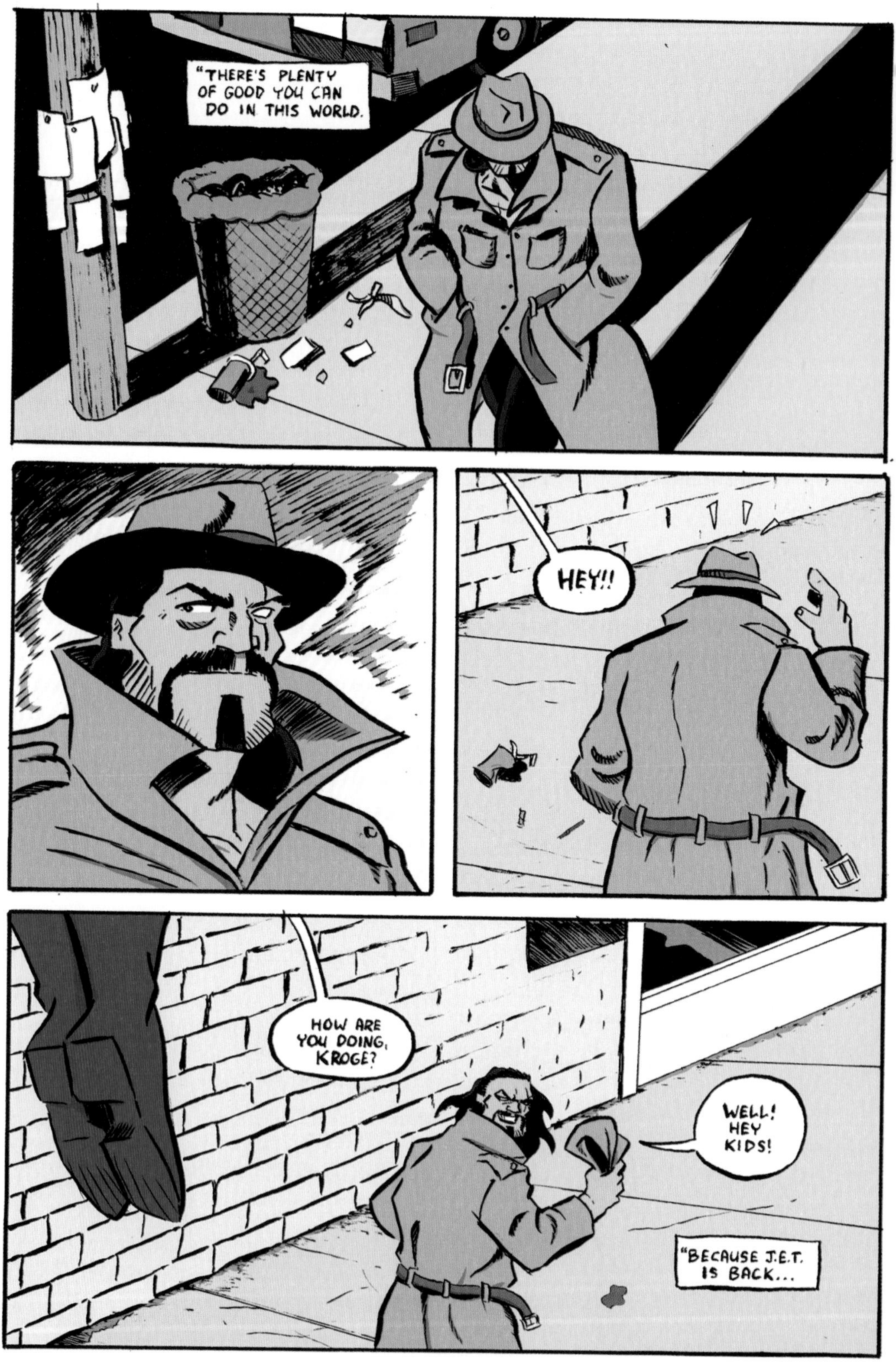
"THERE'S PLENTY OF GOOD YOU CAN DO IN THIS WORLD.
HEY!!
HOW ARE YOU DOING, KROGE?
WELL! HEY KIDS!
"BECAUSE J.E.T. IS BACK...

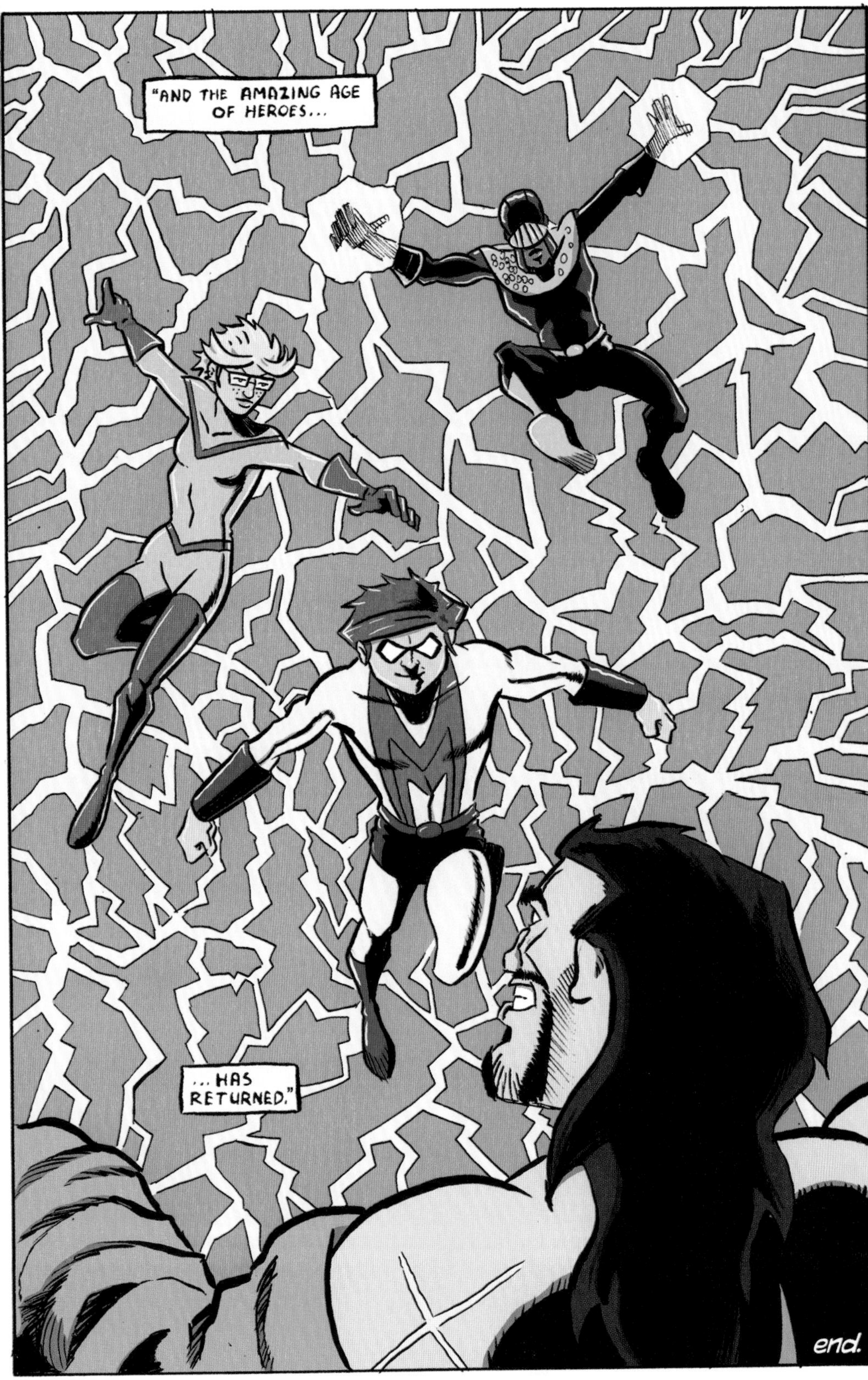
"AND THE AMAZING AGE OF HEROES...
...HAS RETURNED."
end.

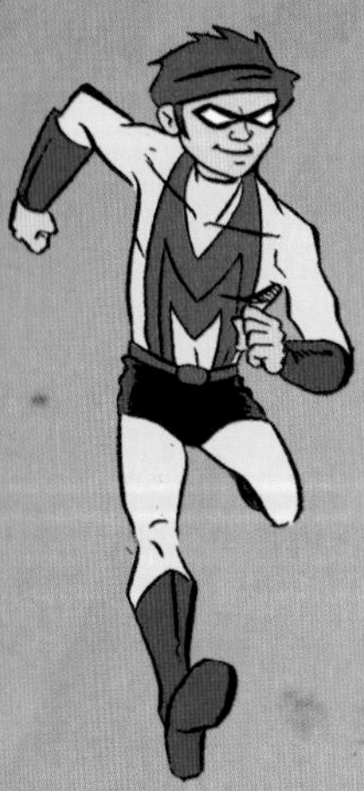

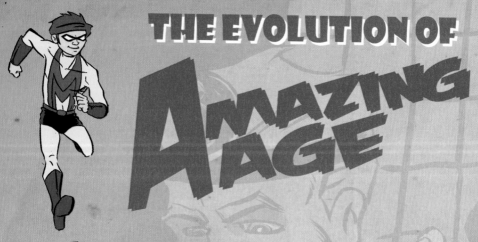

THE EVOLUTION OF AMAZING AGE

To say "Amazing Age" has come a long way is a huge understatement. What you are holding in your hands is truly a lifelong passion project. Like so many comic book fans, I started writing and drawing my own stories at a young age. Heavily influenced by the comics I purchased from the gas station spinner rack and even the Saturday morning cartoons I consumed, I spent countless hours constructing my own comic universe that became known as "Matthew Comics". My family and a few friends were my only readers, but I regularly cranked out a steady stream of solo and team books featuring my creations. A few dozen titles and nearly 200 characters were developed between the ages of 6 and 15, and I even "revived" a few of them during my high school years.

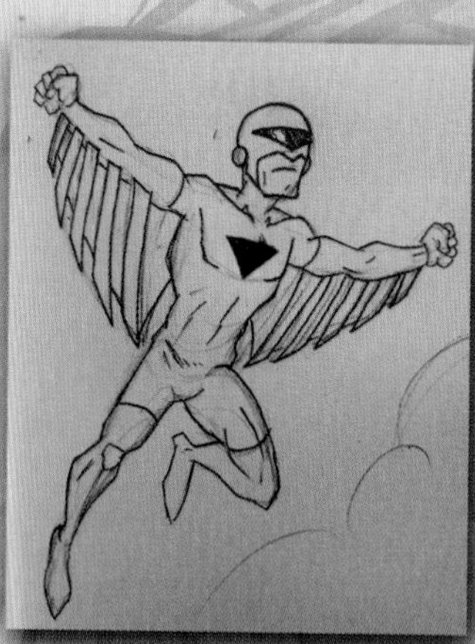

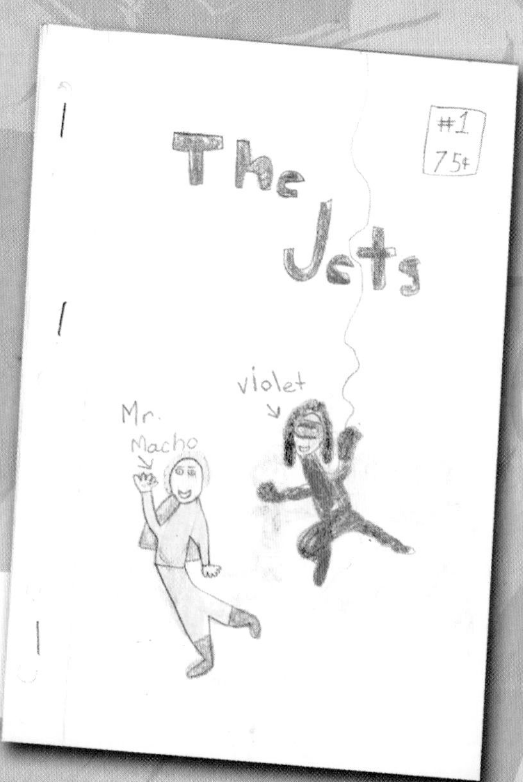
#1
75¢
The Jets
Mr. Macho
violet

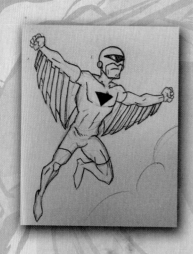

ABOVE: JEREMY MASSIE'S FIRST SKETCH OF BLADE HAWK (2014).

RIGHT: THE COVER TO "THE JETS" #1, VOL. 1 (1986)...THE FIRST MATTHEW COMIC!

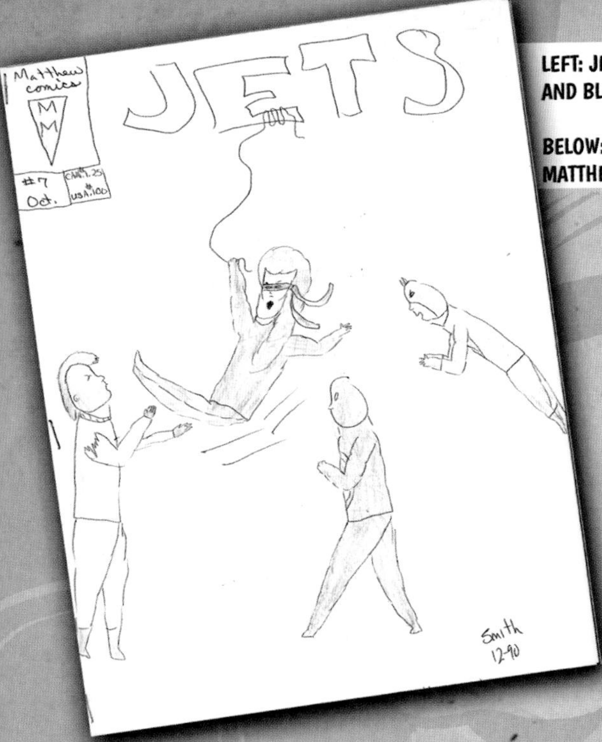
Matthew comics
MM
JETS
#7
Oct.
Smith
12-90

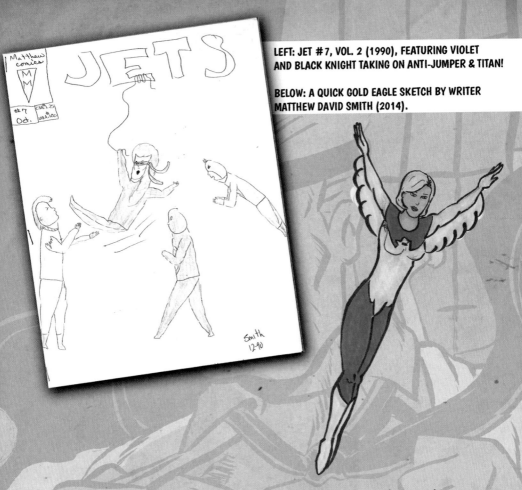

LEFT: JET #7, VOL. 2 (1990), FEATURING VIOLET AND BLACK KNIGHT TAKING ON ANTI-JUMPER & TITAN!

BELOW: A QUICK GOLD EAGLE SKETCH BY WRITER MATTHEW DAVID SMITH (2014).

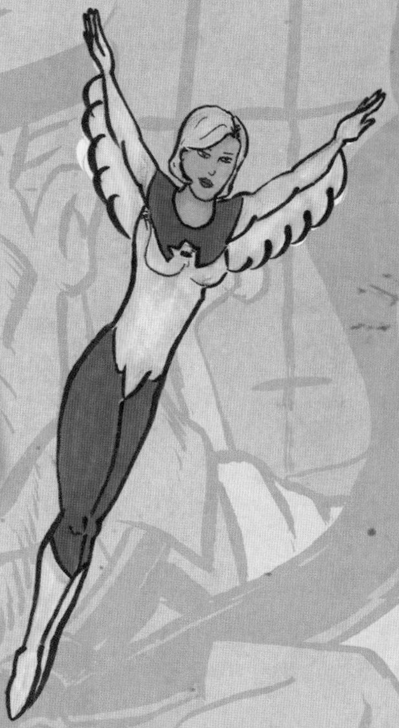

I always knew that I wasn't done with my heroes and villains, but I also wasn't quite sure how to bring them back! I wanted a unique way to introduce a new superhero book, but somehow maintain the integrity and back stories I had crafted all those years ago. Every bit of each character's history was important to me.

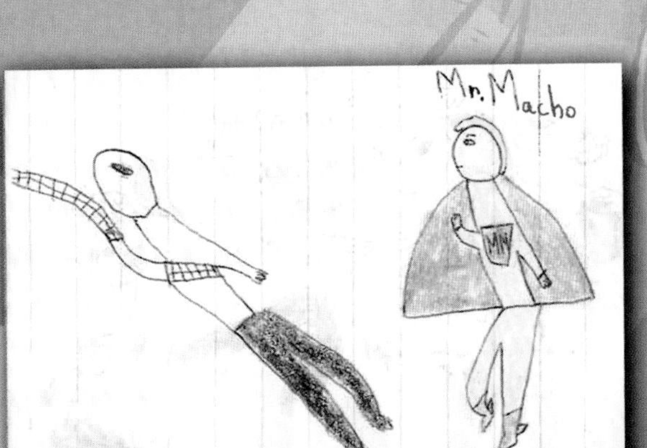
Mr. Macho
MM

RIGHT: A SHORT-LIVED COSTUME CHANGE FOR BLACK KNIGHT AS HE TEAMED UP WITH "MR. MACHO" (BEFORE HE WAS KNOWN AS MR. MIGHT) IN "WEB OF BLACK KNIGHT" #7 (1987).

RIGHT: "CROSS EYED & THE JETS" (1986) WAS A 3-ISSUE LIMITED SERIES, TAKING PLACE AFTER THE FIRST VOLUME OF JET ENDED. IT TEAMED UP MR. MIGHT AND VIOLET WITH THE HERO, CROSS EYED (WHO WOULD LATER GO BY CROSS).

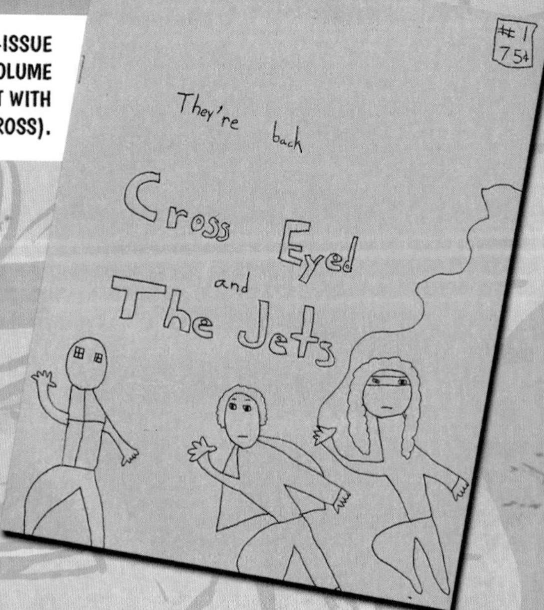
#1
75¢
They're back
Cross Eyed and The Jets

And that's how Amazing Age was born.

The "Matthew Comics" characters were revived in a way that was fresh, yet paid tribute to those stories contained in the stacks of stapled sketch pad paper that my older brother had held onto for the past 20+ years. And the most important thing... a book was born that could be enjoyed by comic fans, both young and old.

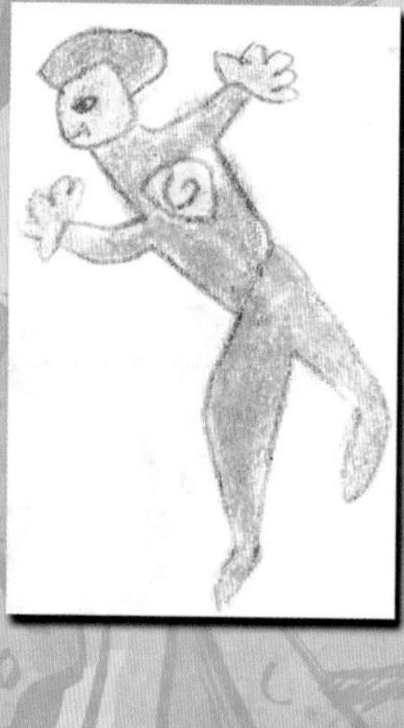

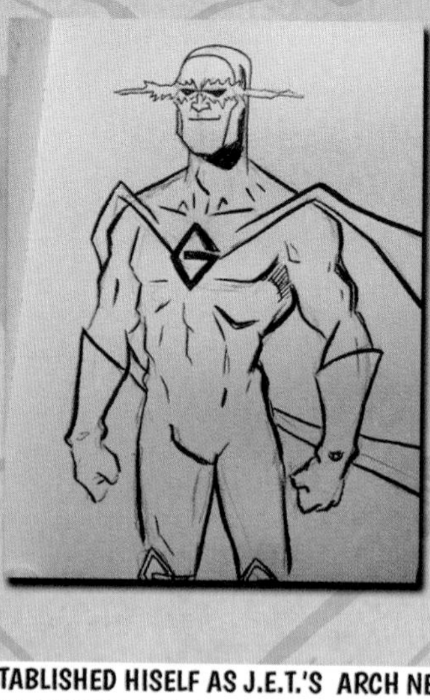

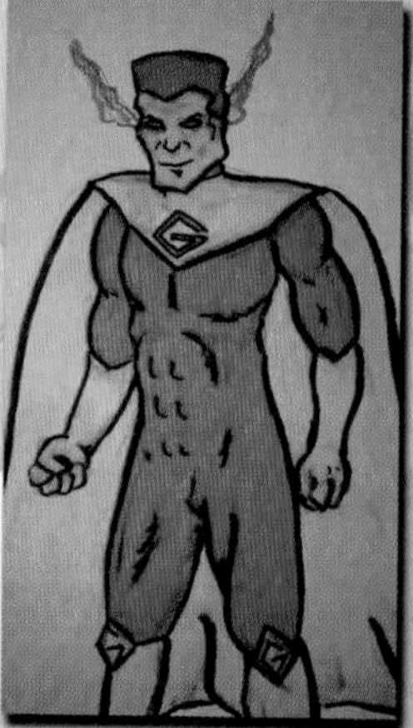

ABOVE: THE ALIEN KNOWN AS GEE ESTABLISHED HISELF AS J.E.T.'S ARCH NEMESIS IMMEDIATELY. HIS SUPER STRENGTH, FLIGHT, IMPOSING SIZE, AND DEADLY HEAT BLASTS HAVE MADE HIM A FORMIDABLE FOE TO EVERY HERO HE HAS ENCOUNTERED. SEEN HERE ARE GEE FROM "THE JETS" #2, VOL. 1 (1986), A SKETCH BY JEREMY MASSIE (2014), AND A CHARACTER DESIGN SKETCH BY MATTHEW DAVID SMITH (2014).

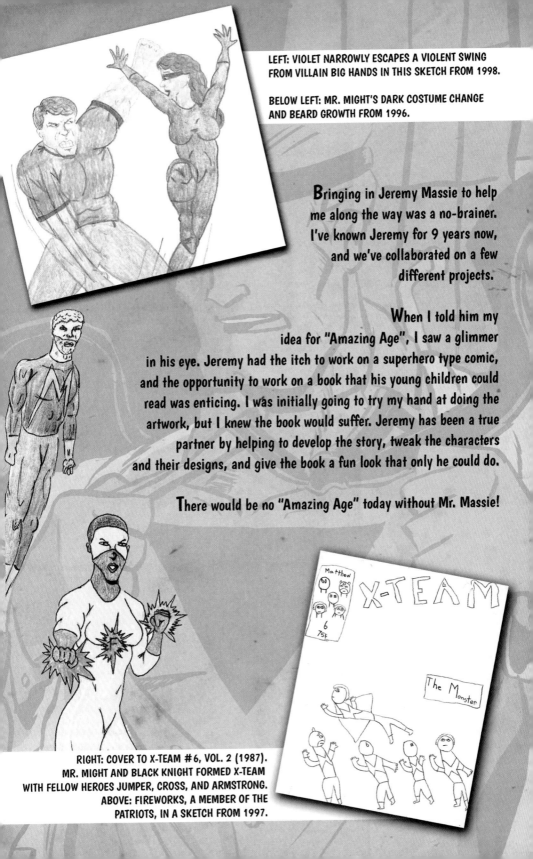

LEFT: VIOLET NARROWLY ESCAPES A VIOLENT SWING FROM VILLAIN BIG HANDS IN THIS SKETCH FROM 1998.

BELOW LEFT: MR. MIGHT'S DARK COSTUME CHANGE AND BEARD GROWTH FROM 1996.

Bringing in Jeremy Massie to help me along the way was a no-brainer. I've known Jeremy for 9 years now, and we've collaborated on a few different projects.

When I told him my idea for "Amazing Age", I saw a glimmer in his eye. Jeremy had the itch to work on a superhero type comic, and the opportunity to work on a book that his young children could read was enticing. I was initially going to try my hand at doing the artwork, but I knew the book would suffer. Jeremy has been a true partner by helping to develop the story, tweak the characters and their designs, and give the book a fun look that only he could do.

There would be no "Amazing Age" today without Mr. Massie!

RIGHT: COVER TO X-TEAM #6, VOL. 2 (1987). MR. MIGHT AND BLACK KNIGHT FORMED X-TEAM WITH FELLOW HEROES JUMPER, CROSS, AND ARMSTRONG. ABOVE: FIREWORKS, A MEMBER OF THE PATRIOTS, IN A SKETCH FROM 1997.

Matthew
X-TEAM
6
75¢
The Monster

RIGHT: BLACK KNIGHT STARRED IN A FEW DIFFERENT SOLO BOOKS AFTER J.E.T. INITIALLY DISBANDED. HIS FIRST SERIES WAS "WEB OF BLACK KNIGHT" (1987), AND ISSUE 4 GUEST-STARRED FORMER TEAMMATE VIOLET!

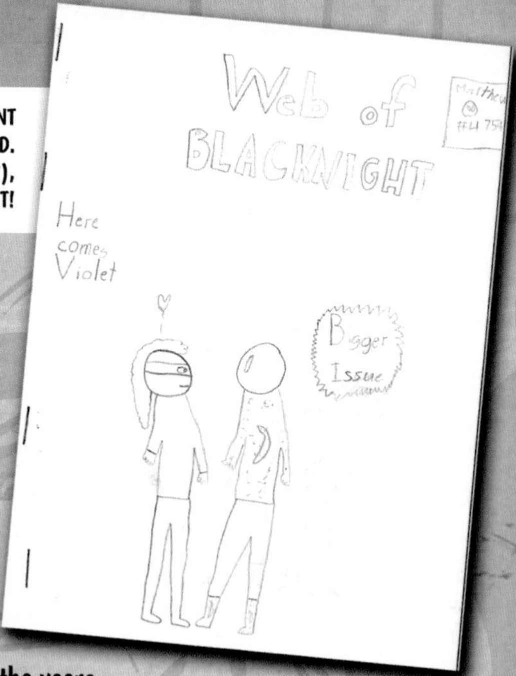
Web of
BLACKNIGHT
Here comes Violet
Bigger Issue

A book like this needed a standout colorist, and Christine Brunson was the first one to come to mine and Jeremy's minds.

I had worked with Christine a few times over the years. She colored a couple of covers for a self-published comic I did called "Simon Says", and I provided a pin-up for her own comic, "Undead Norm". I was impressed by the speed and quality of her coloring abilities. Jeremy and I were both glad to hear that Christine was just as excited about this project as we were!

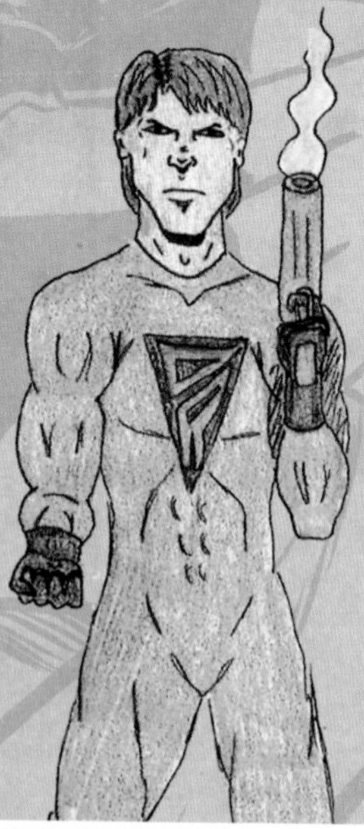

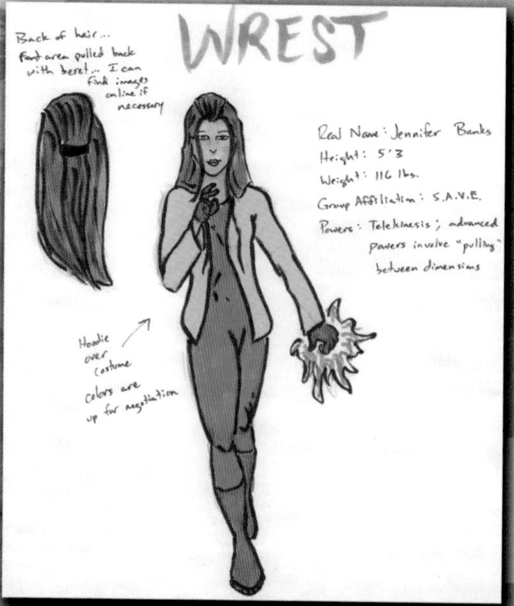
WREST
Back of hair... Front area pulled back with beret... I can find images online if necessary
Real Name: Jennifer Banks
Height: 5'3
Weight: 116 lbs.
Group Affiliation: S.A.V.E.
Powers: Telekinesis; advanced powers involve "pulling" between dimensions
Hoodie over costume
colors are up for negotiation

LEFT: CHARACTER DESIGN SHEET OF WREST BY WRITER MATTHEW DAVID SMITH (2014).

ABOVE: DEATH RAY SKETCH FROM 1998. HIS STATURE AND GUN SIZE INCREASED FOR AMAZING AGE!

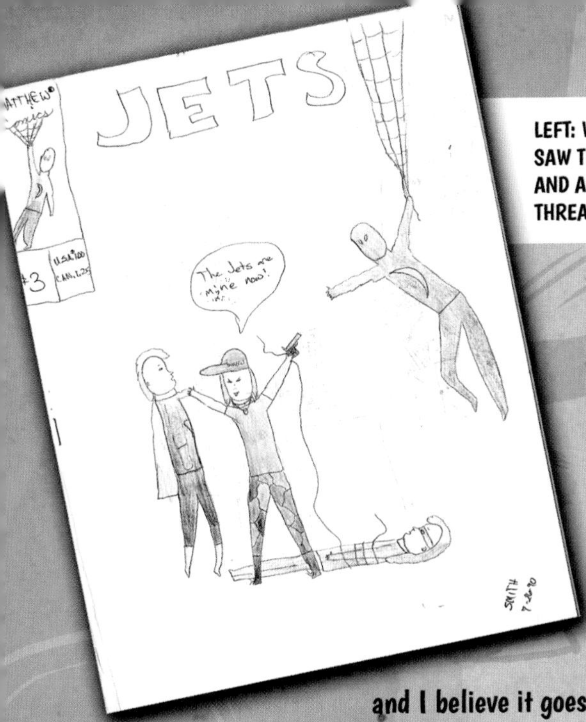
JETS
#3
The Jets are myne now!
SMITH 7-20-90

LEFT: WHILE THE SECOND VOLUME OF J.E.T. (1990) SAW THE RETURN OF CLASSIC VILLAINS LIKE GEE AND ANTI-JUMPER, THE TEAM ALSO FACED NEW THREATS LIKE THE DASTARDLY GENERAL DEATH!

Pardon my ramblings, but as I said, this book is important to me in many ways. And to be honest, this collected edition of the limited series wouldn't have been possible if the readers weren't there. We've been equally impressed and humbled by the responses to the book, and I believe it goes without saying that we have a lot more "Amazing Age" in store for you!

As an added bonus, these last few pages contain some conceptual sketches, pin-ups, and numerous peeks at those classic drawings from my youth. They are a reminder that, as cliche as it sounds, dreams can come true.

Til next time,
Matthew David Smith
March 2018

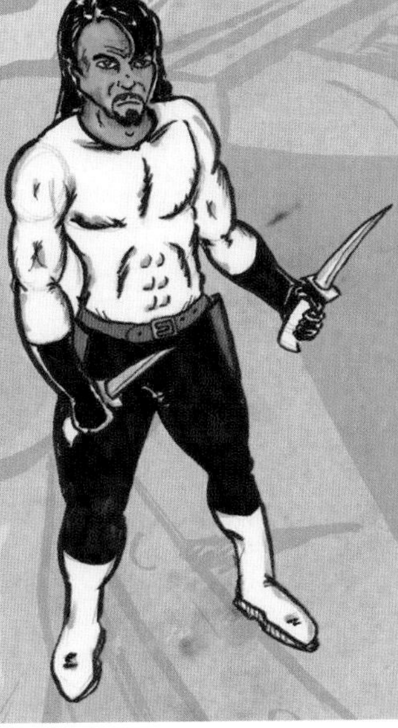

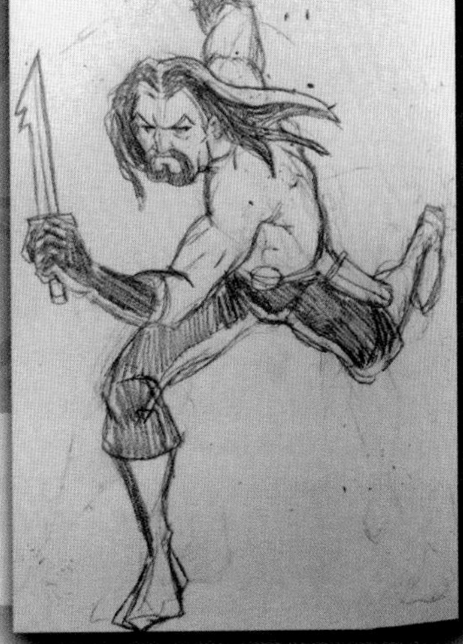

ABOVE: THE DEADLY AND MYSTERIOUS KROGE IN A CHARACTER SKETCH BY MATTHEW DAVID SMITH (2014).

RIGHT: JEREMY MASSIE'S FIRST CRACK AT DRAWING KROGE (2014).

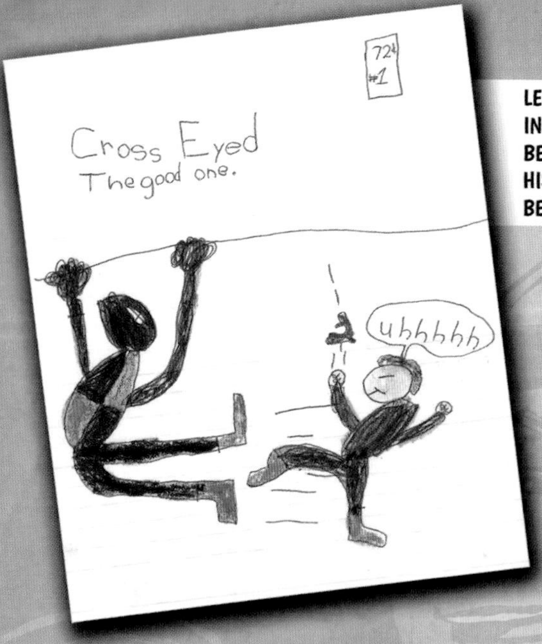
72¢
#1
Cross Eyed
The good one.
uhhhhh

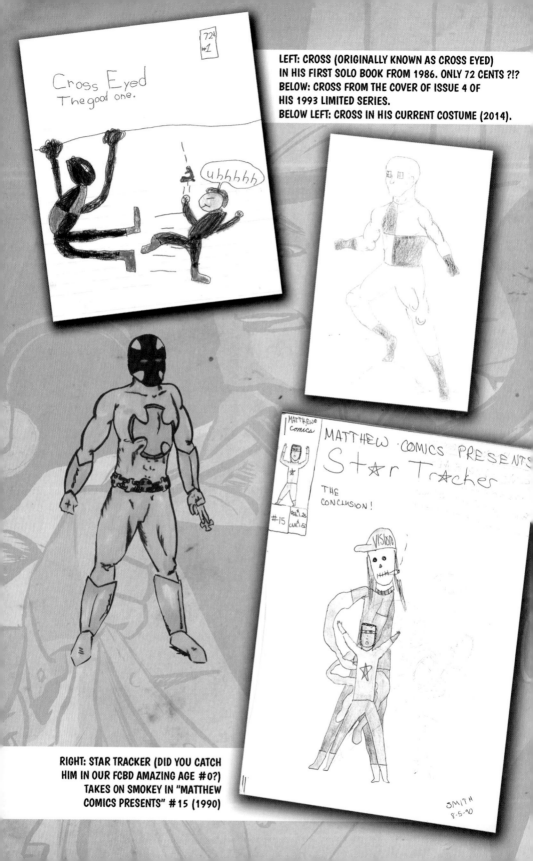

LEFT: CROSS (ORIGINALLY KNOWN AS CROSS EYED) IN HIS FIRST SOLO BOOK FROM 1986. ONLY 72 CENTS ?!?
BELOW: CROSS FROM THE COVER OF ISSUE 4 OF HIS 1993 LIMITED SERIES.
BELOW LEFT: CROSS IN HIS CURRENT COSTUME (2014).

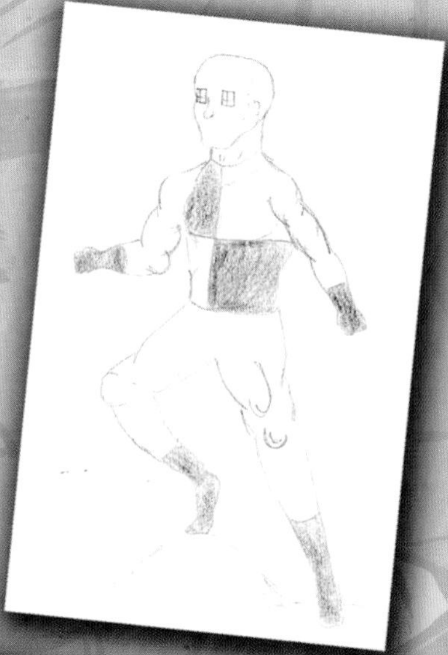

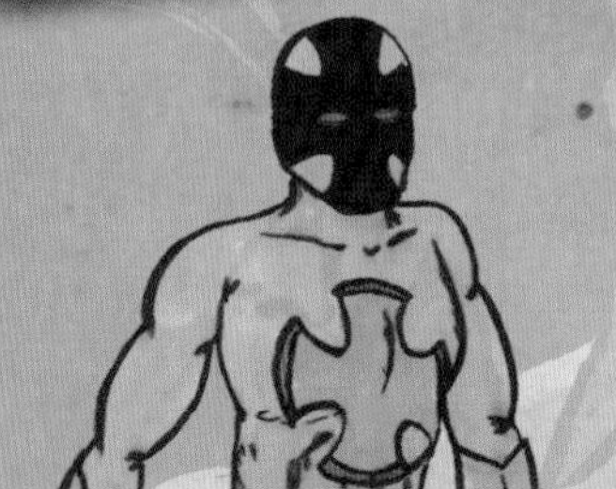

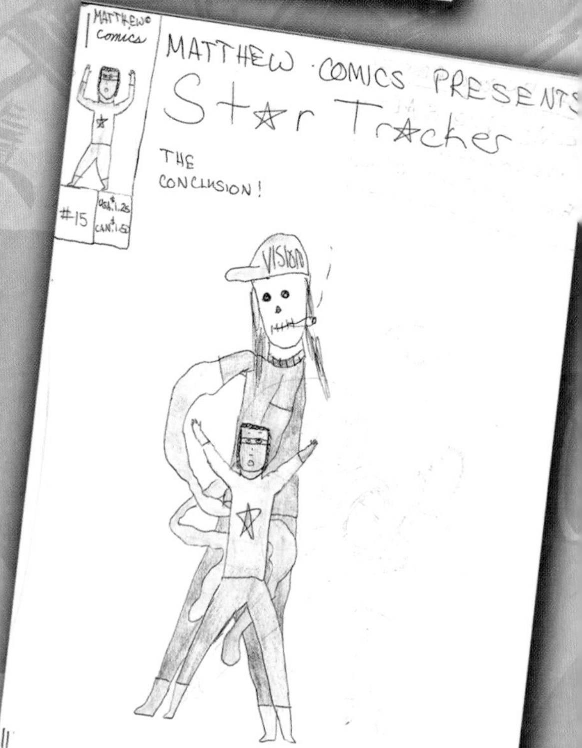
MATTHEW Comics
MATTHEW COMICS PRESENTS
Star Tracker
THE CONCLUSION!
#15
VISION
SMITH
8-5-90

RIGHT: STAR TRACKER (DID YOU CATCH HIM IN OUR FCBD AMAZING AGE #0?) TAKES ON SMOKEY IN "MATTHEW COMICS PRESENTS" #15 (1990)

RIGHT: JUMPER GUEST-STARS IN "THE AMAZING BLACK KNIGHT" #3 (1988)
BELOW: JEREMY MASSIE'S SON BEGAN DRAWING HIS OWN AMAZING AGE TALES, WHICH JEREMY HELPED COLOR AND LETTER (2017)!

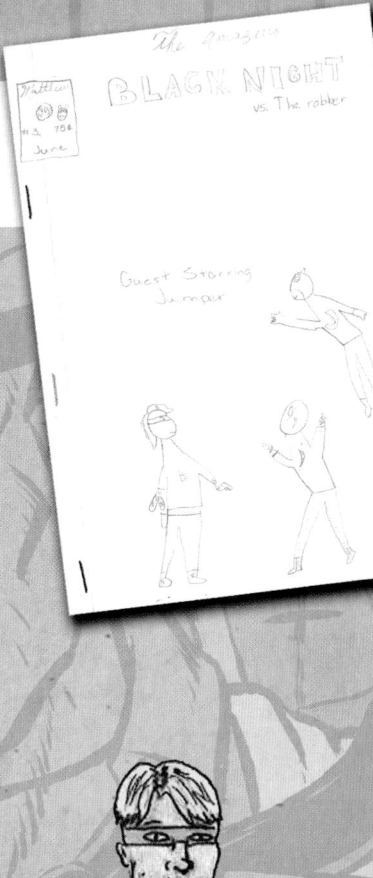
BLACK NIGHT
vs. The robber
Guest Starring
Jumper

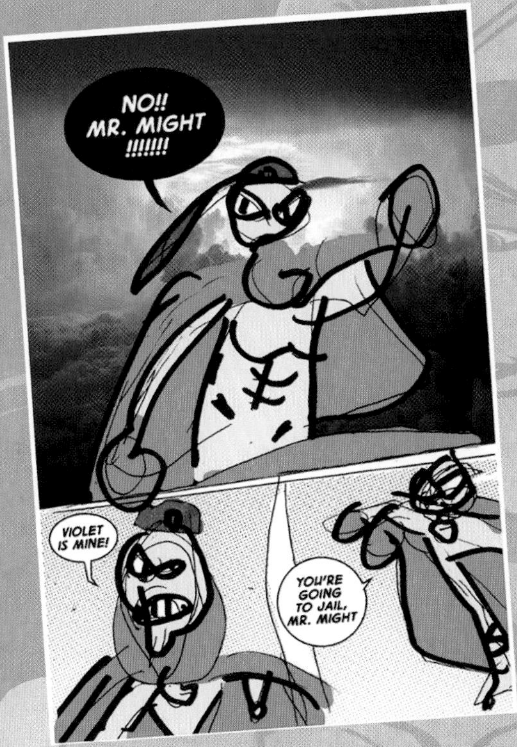
NO!! MR. MIGHT !!!!!!!
VIOLET IS MINE!
YOU'RE GOING TO JAIL, MR. MIGHT

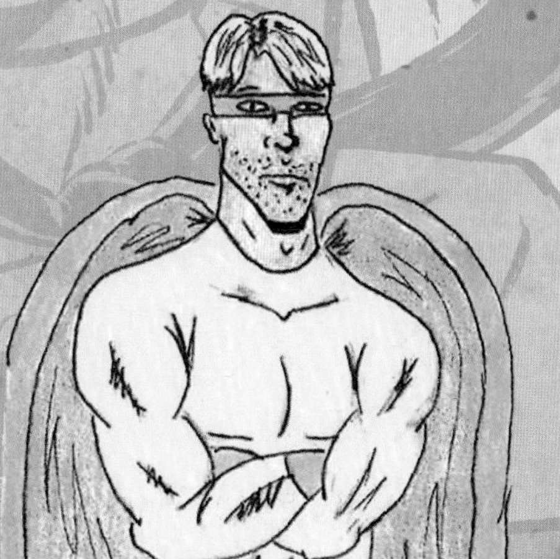

ABOVE: FLYER ORIGINALLY HAD A MUCH MORE CLASSIC LOOK. AS SEEN IN THIS 1998 SKETCH. THE AMAZING AGE REDISGN IS MORE ROCKETEER-INSPIRED, WHICH BETTER FITS THE CHARACTER'S POWER SET AND ATTITUDE.
LEFT: GEE CAPTURES THE TEAM IN J.E.T. #5 (1986)

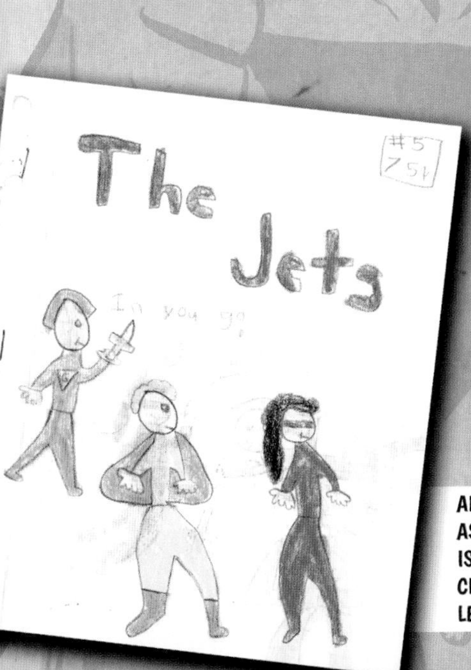
The Jets
#5

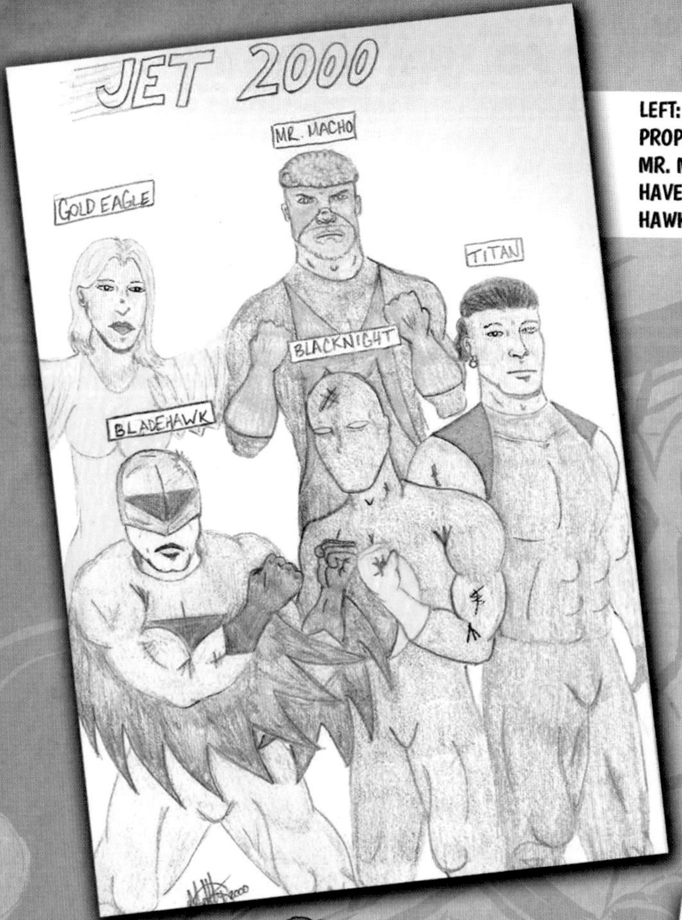
JET 2000
MR. MACHO
GOLD EAGLE
TITAN
BLACKNIGHT
BLADEHAWK

LEFT: A SKETCH BOOK DRAWING OF A PROPOSED J.E.T. RELAUNCH IN 2000. MR. MIGHT AND BLACK KNIGHT WOULD HAVE REFORMED THE TEAM WITH BLADE HAWK, GOLD EAGLE, AND TITAN.

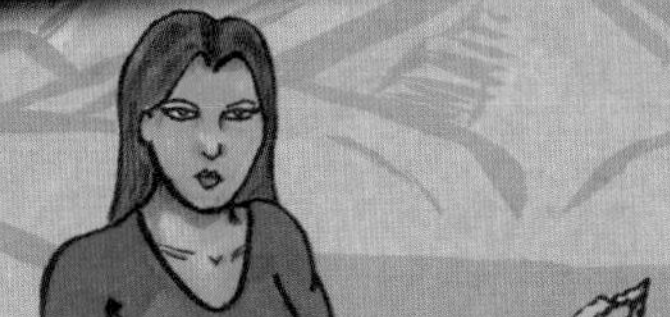

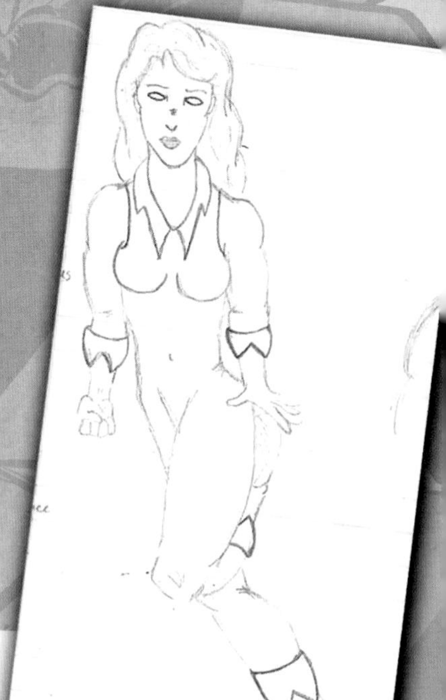

RIGHT: HAVING BEEN MISSING FOR YEARS AND POSSESSING A NEW COSMIC SET OF POWERS, AN AMNESIAC VIOLET WOULD HAVE BEEN SLOWLY RE-INTRODUCED IN "J.E.T. 2000".
ABOVE: CHARATER DESIGN SKETCH OF STUN BY MATTHEW DAVID SMITH (2014)

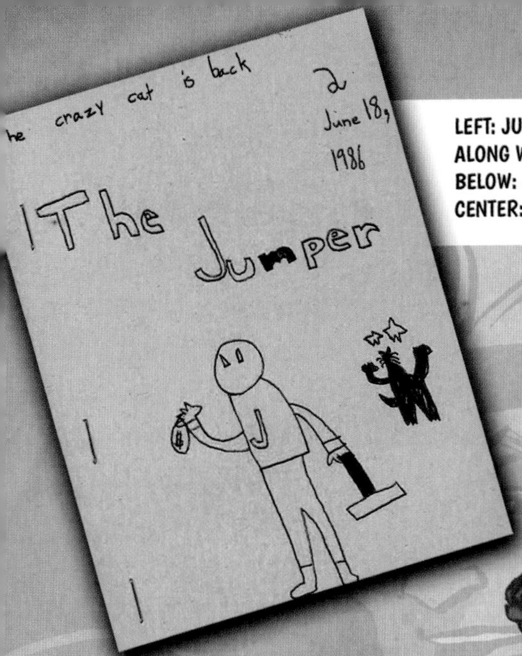
he crazy cat is back
2
June 18, 1986
The Jumper

LEFT: JUMPER FIRST APPEARED IN HIS SOLO COMIC FROM 1986, ALONG WITH HIS ARCH ENEMY, THE CRAZY CAT.
BELOW: JEREMY MASSIE'S SKETCH OF JUMPER (2014).
CENTER: MATTHEW DAVID SMITH'S JUMPER DESIGN (2014).

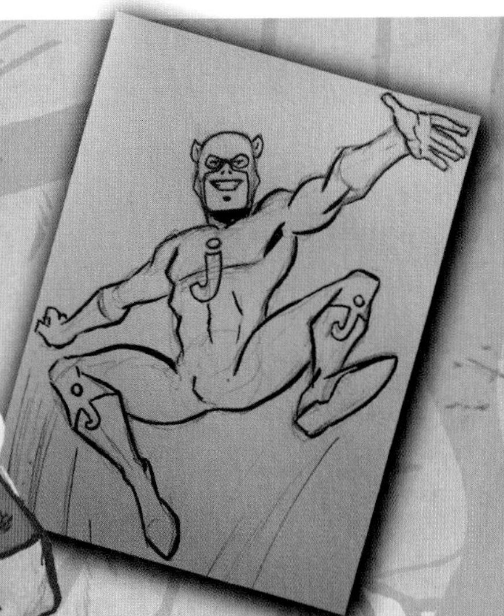

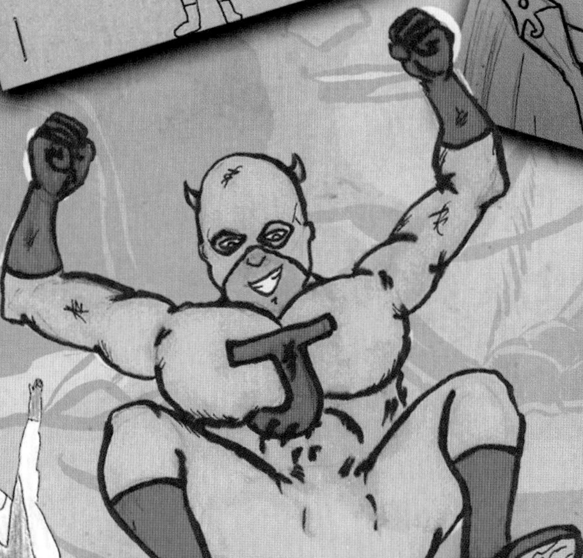

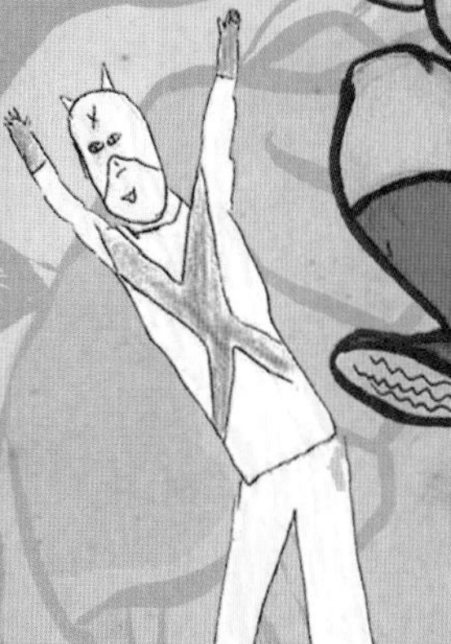

ABOVE: JUMPER'S SECOND COSTUME DESIGN HAS STUCK WITH HIM OVER THE YEARS, AS SEEN IN THIS 1990 DRAWING.
RIGHT: THE CHARACTER VERY BRIEFLY WENT BY THE NAME HIGH JUMP WHEN HE WAS A MEMBER OF X-TEAM (1987).

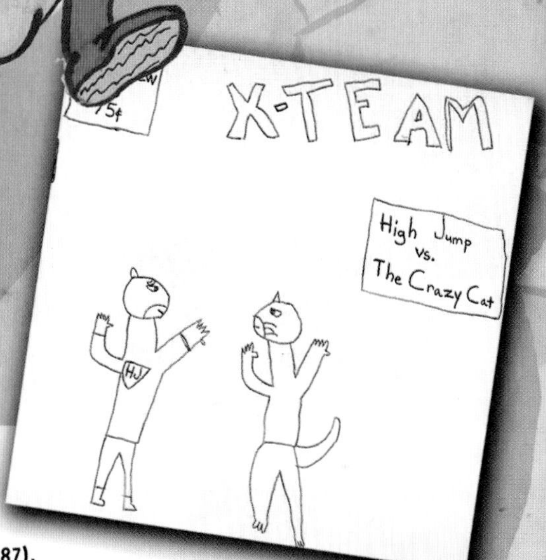
75¢
X-TEAM
High Jump vs. The Crazy Cat
HJ

THE AMAZING AGE UNIVERSE IS PACKED WITH CHARACTERS, MANY OF WHOM WE HAVEN'T SEEN YET! THE TIME WILL COME FOR HEROES LIKE THE BLACK SHADOW (RIGHT, IN A SKETCH BY JEREMY MASSIE FROM 2014) AND NINJA MASTER (BELOW, BY MATTHEW DAVID SMITH, 2014).

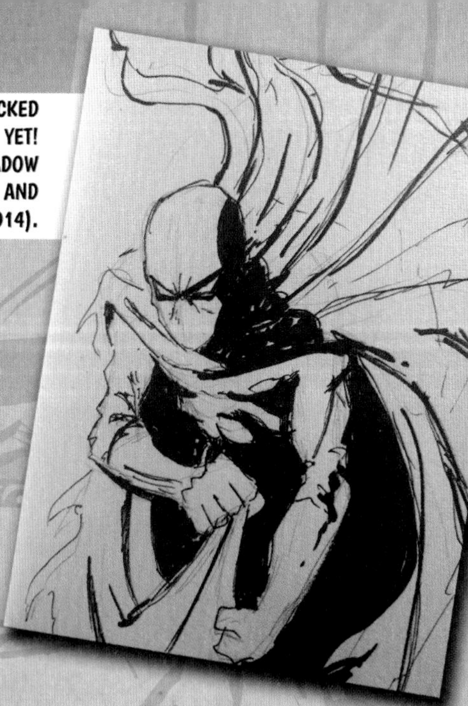

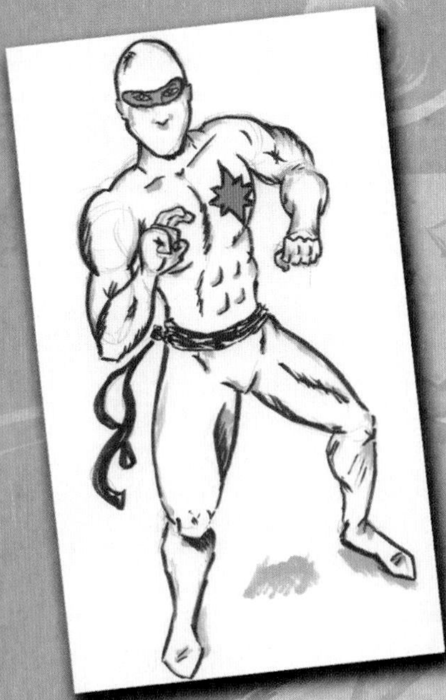

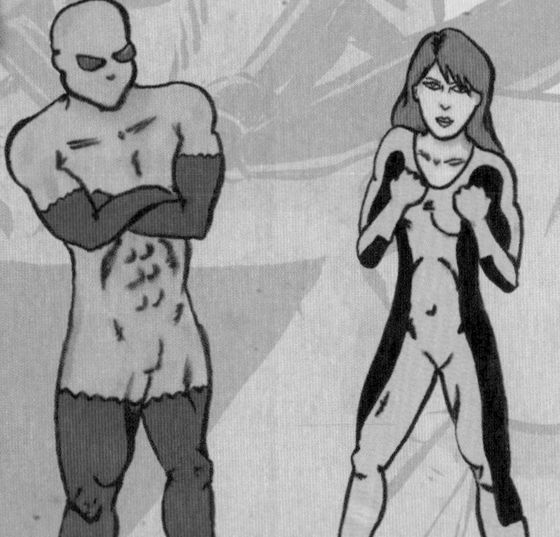

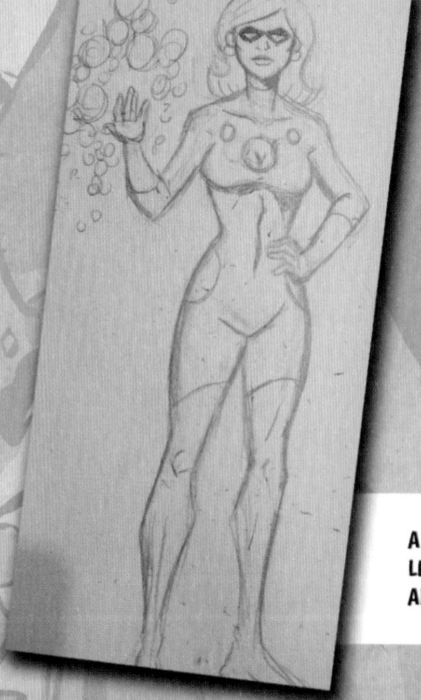

A FEW MORE GLIMPSES OF CHARACTERS TO COME!
LEFT: FULGENT BY JEREMY MASSIE, 2014.
ABOVE: BLACK ICE AND STRIPE BY MATTHEW DAVID SMITH, 2014.

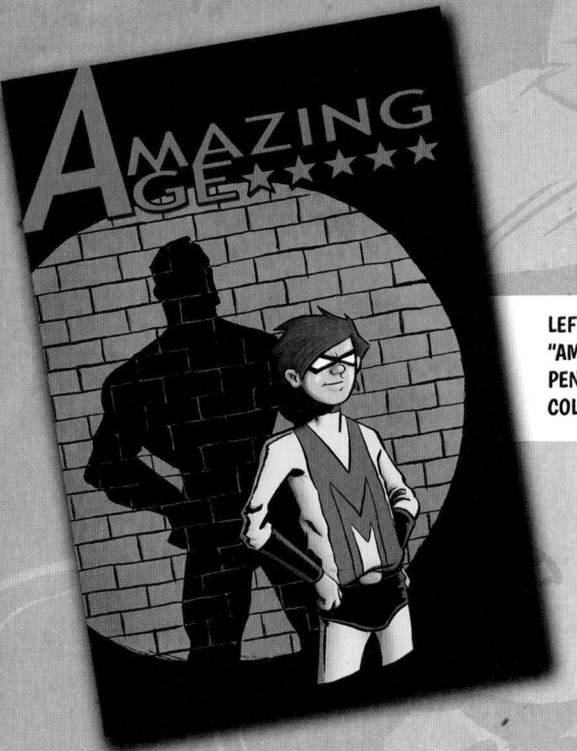
AMAZING
AGE

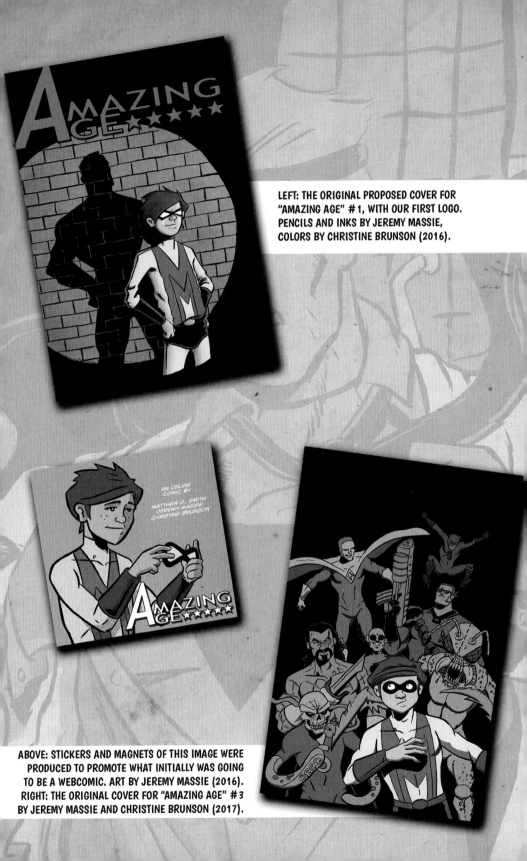

LEFT: THE ORIGINAL PROPOSED COVER FOR "AMAZING AGE" #1, WITH OUR FIRST LOGO. PENCILS AND INKS BY JEREMY MASSIE, COLORS BY CHRISTINE BRUNSON (2016).

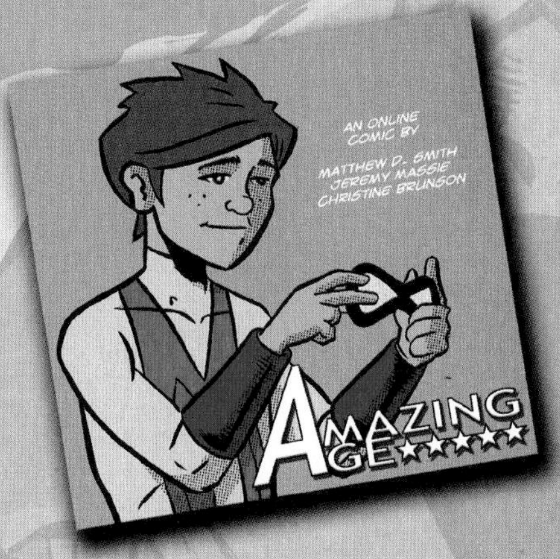
AN ONLINE
COMIC BY
MATTHEW D. SMITH
JEREMY MASSIE
CHRISTINE BRUNSON
AMAZING
AGE

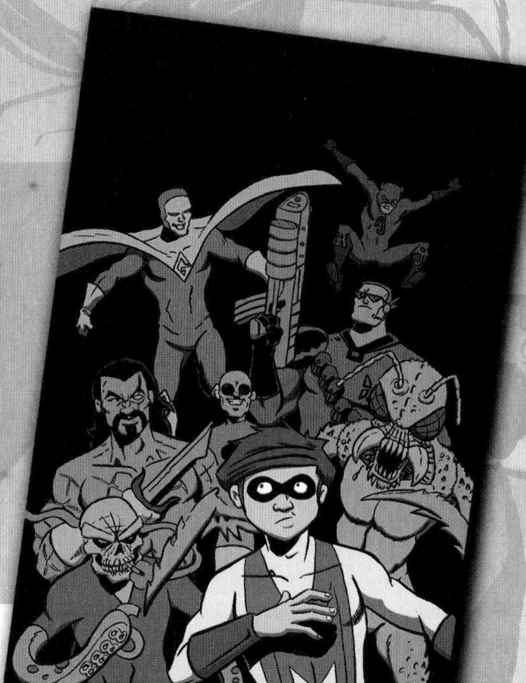

ABOVE: STICKERS AND MAGNETS OF THIS IMAGE WERE PRODUCED TO PROMOTE WHAT INITIALLY WAS GOING TO BE A WEBCOMIC. ART BY JEREMY MASSIE (2016). RIGHT: THE ORIGINAL COVER FOR "AMAZING AGE" #3 BY JEREMY MASSIE AND CHRISTINE BRUNSON (2017).

VIOLET, MR. MIGHT, AND BLACK KNIGHT
1986, 2001, 2018

WELCOME TO THE...

AMAZING AGE

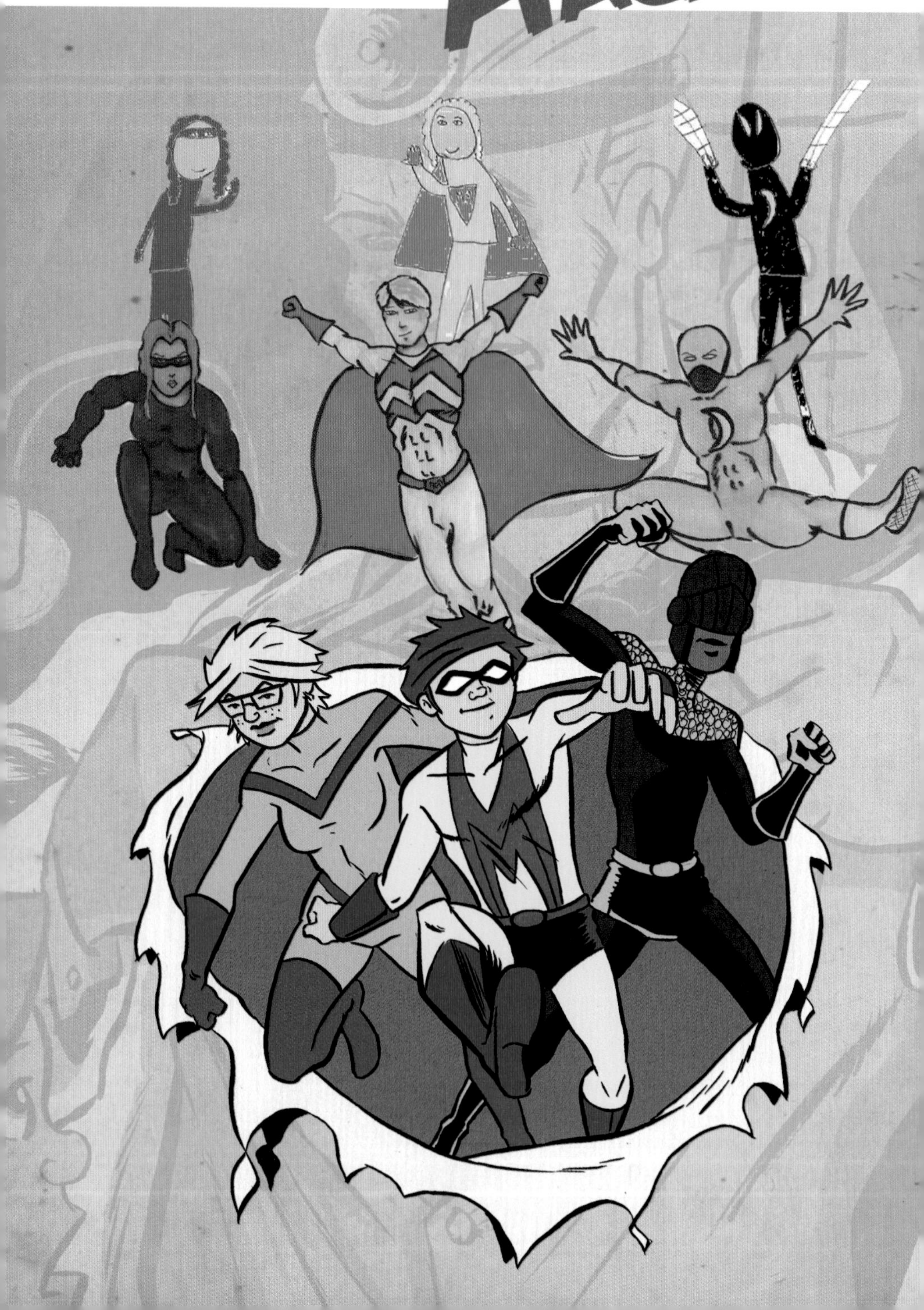